Mental Health Information for Teens

Second Edition

TEEN HEALTH SERIES

Second Edition

Mental Health Information for Teens

Health Tips about Mental Wellness and Mental Illness

Including Facts about Mental and Emotional Health, Depression and Other Mood Disorders, Anxiety Disorders, Behavior Disorders, Self-Injury, Psychosis, Schizophrenia, and More

Edited by Karen Bellenir

Omnigraphics

615 Griswold Street • Detroit, MI 48226

Bibliographic Note

Because this page cannot legibly accommodate all the copyright notices, the Bibliographic Note portion of the Preface constitutes an extension of the copyright notice.

Edited by Karen Bellenir

Teen Health Series

Karen Bellenir, *Managing Editor*
David A. Cooke, M.D., *Medical Consultant*
Elizabeth Barbour, *Permissions and Research Coordinator*
Cherry Stockdale, *Permissions Assistant*
Laura Pleva Nielsen, *Index Editor*
EdIndex, Services for Publishers, *Indexers*

* * *

Omnigraphics, Inc.

Matthew P. Barbour, *Senior Vice President*
Kay Gill, *Vice President—Directories*
Kevin Hayes, *Operations Manager*
David P. Bianco, *Marketing Director*

* * *

Peter E. Ruffner, *Publisher*

Frederick G. Ruffner, Jr., *Chairman*

Copyright © 2006 Omnigraphics, Inc.

ISBN 0-7808-0863-0

Library of Congress Cataloging-in-Publication Data

Mental health information for teens : health tips about mental wellness and mental illness : including facts about mental and emotional health, depression and other mood disorders, anxiety disorders, behavior disorders, self-injury, psychosis, schizophrenia, and more / edited by Karen Bellenir. -- 2nd ed.
    p. cm. -- (Teen health series)
  Summary: "Provides basic consumer health information for teens on mental health and mental illness. Includes index, resource information and recommendations for further reading"--Provided by publisher.
  Includes bibliographical references and index.
  ISBN 0-7808-0863-0 (hardcover : alk. paper) 1. Teenagers--Mental health. 2. Adolescent psychology. 3. Child mental health. I. Bellenir, Karen. II. Series.
  RJ499.M419 2006
  616.8900835--dc22
                                                        2006016689

Table of Contents

Part Three: Behavioral, Personality, And Psychotic Disorders

Part Four: Getting Help For Mental Illness

Part Five: Other Issues Related To Mental Wellness In Teens

Part Six: If You Need More Information

Preface

About This Book

According to the National Institute of Mental Health, half of all lifetime cases of mental illness begin by age 14. Anxiety disorders often begin in late childhood, and mood disorders often begin in late adolescence. Unfortunately, many young people experience a long delay between the onset of their symptoms and when they eventually seek treatment. This delay can be decades long. Without prompt treatment, however, sufferers can experience varying levels of disability, and illnesses can become more severe and more difficult to treat.

Mental Health Information For Teens, Second Edition provides updated information about mental and emotional health in teens. It describes mental wellness and offers tips for maintaining self-esteem, developing healthy relationships, managing anger, handling stress, and coping with other difficulties teens often face. It describes the symptoms and most common treatments used for depression and other mood disorders, phobias and other anxiety disorders, self-injury and other disorders related to behavior and personality, and psychotic disorders, such as schizophrenia. The book also addresses other issues that can impact mental wellness in teens, including learning disabilities, bullying, dating violence, child abuse, substance abuse, and suicide. Directories of resources for more information and suggestions for additional reading about mental wellness and mental illness are also included.

How To Use This Book

This book is divided into parts and chapters. Parts focus on broad areas of interest; chapters are devoted to single topics within a part.

Part One: Maintaining Mental Wellness describes the components of mental and emotional health, including having positive self-esteem, experiencing fulfilling relationships, adapting to change, and coping with adversity. Individual chapters address some of the specific concerns that teens often encounter, and the part concludes with a special chapter about parental substance abuse problems and mental illness.

Part Two: Mood and Anxiety Disorders addresses specific mental illnesses related to affect (mood) and chronic anxiety and fear. Beginning with depression—which strikes as many as one in eight teens—and concluding with fears and phobias, it describes common mental illnesses related to mood and anxiety, their symptoms, possible causes, and current treatments.

Part Three: Behavioral, Personality, and Psychotic Disorders focuses on mental illnesses that lead to behaviors that harm others, are self-injurious, impair interpersonal functioning, interfere with a person's ability to learn in school or function in a work environment, or involve a loss of touch with reality. Individual chapters describe the disorders, discuss their symptoms, and provide facts about available treatments.

Part Four: Getting Help For Mental Illness describes different types of mental health care providers and the services they offer. It explains "talk" therapies, medications commonly used to treat mental illnesses, and other kinds of treatments, including alternative therapies such as expressive therapies and culturally based healing arts.

Part Five: Other Issues Related To Mental Wellness In Teens discusses school-related and social concerns that may impact mental well being. Topics include learning disabilities, attention deficit hyperactivity disorder, bullying, abuse, addiction, and suicide.

Part Six: If You Need More Information includes directories of helplines and other resources for information about mental health as well as suggestions for additional reading.

Bibliographic Note

This volume contains documents and excerpts from publications issued by the following government agencies: Centers for Disease Control and Prevention; Health Resources and Services Administration; National Center for Complementary and Alternative Medicine; National Clearinghouse on Child Abuse and Neglect Information; National Drug Intelligence Center; National Institute of Diabetes and Digestive and Kidney Diseases; National Institute of Mental Health; National Institute of Neurological Disorders and Stroke; National Institute on Drug Abuse; National Institutes of Health; National Mental Health Information Center; National Women's Health Information Center; National Youth Violence Prevention Resource Center; Office on Women's Health; Substance Abuse and Mental Health Services Administration; U.S. Department of Health and Human Services; U.S. Department of Justice; and the U.S. Food and Drug Administration.

In addition, this volume contains copyrighted documents and articles produced by the following organizations: A.D.A.M., Inc.; American Association for Marriage and Family Therapy; American Psychiatric Association; American Psychological Association; Anxiety Disorders Association of America; Break the Cycle; Center for Healthy Aging; Center for the Advancement of Children's Mental Health at Columbia University; Cleveland Clinic Foundation; Go Ask Alice–Columbia University Health Education Program; Lippincott, Williams, and Wilkins; Love Is Not Abuse (Liz Claiborne, Inc.); Center for Women's Health at Massachusetts General Hospital; Mental Health Association of Westchester; Merck & Co., Inc.; Mood Disorders Society of Canada; NAMI: The Nation's Voice on Mental Illness; National Association for Children of Alcoholics; National Association of Social Workers; National Center for Learning Disabilities; Nemours Foundation; New York University Child Study Center; Raymond Crowe, M.D.; Royal College of Psychiatrists; Teen Health Centre; Texas A&M University; University of Illinois Counseling Center; and WomensLaw.org.

Full citation information is provided on the first page of each chapter. Every effort has been made to secure all necessary rights to reprint the copyrighted material. If any omissions have been made, please contact Omnigraphics to make corrections for future editions.

Acknowledgements

In addition to the organizations listed above, special thanks are due to Elizabeth Bellenir, editorial assistant, and Liz Barbour, permissions and research coordinator.

About The *Teen Health Series*

At the request of librarians serving today's young adults, the *Teen Health Series* was developed as a specially focused set of volumes within Omnigraphics' *Health Reference Series*. Each volume deals comprehensively with a topic selected according to the needs and interests of people in middle school and high school.

Teens seeking preventive guidance, information about disease warning signs, medical statistics, and risk factors for health problems will find answers to their questions in the *Teen Health Series*. The *Series*, however, is not intended to serve as a tool for diagnosing illness, in prescribing treatments, or as a substitute for the physician/patient relationship. All people concerned about medical symptoms or the possibility of disease are encouraged to seek professional care from an appropriate health care provider.

If there is a topic you would like to see addressed in a future volume of the *Teen Health Series*, please write to:

Editor
Teen Health Series
Omnigraphics, Inc.
615 Griswold Street
Detroit, MI 48226

Locating Information Within The *Teen Health Series*

The *Teen Health Series* contains a wealth of information about a wide variety of medical topics. As the *Series* continues to grow in size and scope, locating the precise information needed by a specific student may become more challenging. To address this concern, information about books within the *Teen Health Series* is included in *A Contents Guide to the Health Reference*

Series. The *Contents Guide* presents an extensive list of more than 12,000 diseases, treatments, and other topics of general interest compiled from the Tables of Contents and major index headings from the books of the *Teen Health Series* and *Health Reference Series.* To access *A Contents Guide to the Health Reference Series,* visit www.healthreferenceseries.com.

Our Advisory Board

We would like to thank the following advisory board members for providing guidance to the development of this *Series*:

Dr. Lynda Baker, Associate Professor of Library and Information Science, Wayne State University, Detroit, MI

Nancy Bulgarelli, William Beaumont Hospital Library, Royal Oak, MI

Karen Imarisio, Bloomfield Township Public Library, Bloomfield Township, MI

Karen Morgan, Mardigian Library, University of Michigan-Dearborn, Dearborn, MI

Rosemary Orlando, St. Clair Shores Public Library, St. Clair Shores, MI

Medical Consultant

Medical consultation services are provided to the *Teen Health Series* editors by David A. Cooke, M.D. Dr. Cooke is a graduate of Brandeis University, and he received his M.D. degree from the University of Michigan. He completed residency training at the University of Wisconsin Hospital and Clinics. He is board-certified in internal medicine. Dr. Cooke currently works as part of the University of Michigan Health System and practices in Ann Arbor, MI. In his free time, he enjoys writing, science fiction, and spending time with his family.

Part One

Maintaining Mental Wellness

Chapter 1

Mental And Emotional Health

What is mental or emotional health?

The U.S. Surgeon General's report defines mental health as "the successful performance of mental function, resulting in productive activities, fulfilling relationships with other people, and the ability to adapt to change and cope with adversity." Mental health generally refers to an individual's thoughts, feelings and actions, particularly when faced with life's challenges and stresses. Good mental health isn't just the absence of mental health problems. Although different cultures have differing expectations for health, many of the following characteristics are likely to be present in individuals with good mental health:

- a sense of well-being and contentment;

- a zest for living—the ability to enjoy life, to laugh and have fun;

- resiliency—being able to deal with life's stresses and bounce back from adversity;

- self-realization—participating in life to the fullest extent possible, through meaningful activities and positive relationships;

- flexibility—the ability to change, grow, and experience a range of feelings, as life's circumstances change;

- a sense of balance in one's life—between solitude and sociability, work and play, sleep and wakefulness, rest and exercise, etc.;

- a sense of well-roundedness—with attention to mind, body, spirit, creativity, intellectual development, health, etc.;

- the ability to care for oneself and for others;

- self-confidence and good self-esteem.

♣ **It's A Fact!!**

In Maslow's famous hierarchy, after basic physical survival needs are met, mental health concerns emerge.

Source: © 2006 Helpguide.org.

Why is mental health important?

Our minds are not separate entities from the rest of us. When we are distressed, our physical health is also affected, and our spirits flag. Many physical conditions are actually rooted in a state of mind, or in a history of stress that has never been balanced. Our personal relationships and work abilities are affected by both physical and mental health issues. Lives can even be endangered when people are stressed, depressed, anxious, or grief-stricken.

What is a mental health problem?

A mental health problem can be a short-term reaction to a stressor (such as a loss, painful event, illness, medication, etc.). If the situation does not abate or if the symptoms of distress are interfering with other aspects of life, assistance from a mental health professional may be needed. We do not generally avoid getting help for a physical problem (such as having a broken bone set by an orthopedist, or a cavity filled by a dentist). Yet some people believe it is shameful to seek help for an emotional health problem, or think that an emotional problem means you are "crazy." In many situations, the sooner help is sought, the less ongoing difficulty there will be with the problem.

Just as with medical conditions such as heart disease or diabetes, there are some mental health problems (such as major depression, schizophrenia, or bipolar disorder) that tend to run in families—either because of genetics or family interaction styles. The majority of people who experience mental health problems can overcome them or learn to live with them, especially if they seek help from a qualified source soon enough. Modern approaches to treatment can relieve symptoms and prevent long-term disabilities from mental health problems.

What events and experiences can increase the risk of mental health problems?

Mental health problems can be the outcome of many different kinds of experiences in a person's life, from early childhood to later life events. Some examples are as follows:

> ### ♣ It's A Fact!!
>
> Researchers supported by the National Institute of Mental Health (NIMH) have found that half of all lifetime cases of mental illness begin by age 14, and that despite effective treatments, there are long delays—sometimes decades—between first onset of symptoms and when people seek and receive treatment. The study also reveals that an untreated mental disorder can lead to a more severe, more difficult to treat illness, and to the development of co-occurring mental illnesses.
>
> Source: Excerpted from "Mental Illness Exacts Heavy Toll, Beginning in Youth," National Institutes of Health Press Release dated June 6, 2005.

- chaotic, unsafe, or dangerous environments (for example, living in a violent home, or living in a house with shedding asbestos, peeling lead paint, or toxic drinking water);

- early life serious losses or traumas (such as the death of a parent in childhood, or being abused or neglected);

- loss of social support (due to death of a loved one, divorce, moving away from friends and family, break up of a relationship, loss of a job, or loss of trust);

- unhealthy social conditions (such as poverty, homelessness, and community violence);

- experiences that undermine self-confidence (such as social or work related failures);

- learned helplessness and negative thought patterns (chronic or repeated stressful events leading to the belief of helplessness, reinforced by lack of control over the situation);

- chronic illness (such as heart disease, stroke, HIV, Parkinson's, cancer, or diabetes) that seriously restrict activity;

- side effects of medications (for example, blood pressure medications and numerous other drugs);

- hormonal changes (stage of life adjustments, such as the onset or end of menstruation that affect mood);

- substance abuse: alcohol and some drugs are known to have depressive effects, and the negative social and personal consequences of substance abuse can also be a contributing factor to depression (however, it is not clear which comes first—depression and attempts to control it with substances, or the use of substances that then cause depression);

- genetic causes: people with close family members who suffer from depression are more prone to depression (however, since no gene for depression has been found, this may be environmental rather than genetic);

- biochemical causes (an imbalance of neurotransmitters such as serotonin is known to affect the processing of thoughts and emotions).

♣ It's A Fact!!

Unlike most disabling physical diseases, mental illness begins very early in life. Half of all lifetime cases begin by age 14; three quarters have begun by age 24. Thus, mental disorders are really the chronic diseases of the young. For example, anxiety disorders often begin in late childhood, mood disorders in late adolescence, and substance abuse in the early 20's. Unlike heart disease or most cancers, young people with mental disorders suffer disability when they are in the prime of life, when they would normally be the most productive.

Source: Excerpted from "Mental Illness Exacts Heavy Toll, Beginning in Youth," National Institutes of Health Press Release dated June 6, 2005.

Self-Help For Improving Mental Health

Many minor mental health problems can be relieved by some common-sense measures. If you find yourself feeling "blue," "out of sorts," "stressed out," or "in a funk," you can take some steps such as the following to see if you feel better:

- Get enough rest.

- Eat a balanced diet.

- Avoid caffeine, alcohol, tobacco, or other drugs.

- Engage in physical activities.

- Do something that for you is fun or relaxing (go to a funny movie, take a walk on the beach, listen to music, read a good book, talk to a friend, etc.).

- Attend to your spiritual needs by meditating, praying, or appreciating a beautiful sunset.

- Make a list of the things that are troubling you; then fold it and put it away for the rest of the day.

- Prioritize your challenges and deal with the ones that are either most stressful or easiest to check off the list.

- Be sure to spend ample time with people whose company you enjoy, generally those who have an upbeat and positive attitude.

If you find you are continuing to feel depressed or anxious to the extent that these feelings are interfering with your work or personal life, consult a mental health specialist for assistance. The sooner you get help, the less negative outcomes you are likely to experience as a result.

Chapter 2

Self-Esteem

Deep inside of you is something called self-esteem. Self-esteem is the confidence or satisfaction you have in yourself. It is self-respect. Self-esteem is that voice inside of you that tells you that you are special and can achieve your goals. Self-esteem does come from the inside, but there are outside things that can affect your self-esteem, too. Here are some examples:

Your Peers

Everyone wants to have friends and feel part of a group. This is normal and part of growing up. It's good and healthy to have friends. But it's not healthy when it means giving into pressure just to fit in. Only you know what is best for you. Don't let your friends make decisions for you or tell you to do things that are unsafe, unhealthy, or unkind, and that you will later wish you hadn't done. Part of self-esteem is having the power to be yourself because you are such a special person.

Your Parents And Other Adults

Sometimes adults can get so busy that you may feel they don't even notice you exist. This is not how they really intend for you to feel. Sometimes

About This Chapter: This chapter includes excerpts from "Self-Esteem," BodyWise, U.S. Department of Health and Human Service (www.girlpower.gov), 2004; and "Mind-Emotion Commotion," produced by the National Women's Health Information Center (www.girlshealth.gov), August 2005.

✎ **What's It Mean?**

Self-esteem: Self-esteem describes the value and respect you have for yourself. If you have a healthy self-esteem, you feel good about yourself as a person and are proud of what you can do. However, it is normal to feel down sometimes.

Source: Excerpted from "Mind-Emotion Commotion," produced by the National Women's Health Information Center (www.girlshealth.gov), August 2005.

---

the pressures of being an adult make it hard for parents to take the time that they would like to spend listening to and helping you. Sometimes they are so used to working and being with adults that they forget that talking to young people is different from talking to adults.

When you start to feel that your parents are too busy, remember that the situation is temporary. In the meantime, talk to an older brother or sister, teacher, or another older person that you respect and trust. Ask your parents when a good time would be to talk and make a list of things you would like to talk about. Maybe you and your parents could choose a regular time to set aside just for you—a special time each day or week. Practice what you want to say to them and speak up.

Future Goals

What do you want to be when you grow up? What would you like to become really good at? What are some hobbies you would like to learn? If you put your mind to it, you can reach your goals. By setting goals for yourself and trying to meet them, you can feel great about yourself. Try a new sport, audition for the school play, or learn about careers in which you may be interested. Your self-esteem will improve when you have a goal to work toward. So go ahead, dream and plan, reach for the stars.

Positive Body Image

Think about all the things your body can do. Have you ever thought about just how amazing your body really is? Take a moment and appreciate all that your body does for you—running, dancing, breathing, laughing, thinking, smiling, etc. Every day your body carries you one step closer to your goals.

Bodies come in many different shapes, sizes, and colors. Your body type is uniquely yours, but your family genes may help to determine how it will be shaped. As you grow and develop, your body will begin to take on its genetically programmed shape. This basic shape can't be changed. It's all in your genes. Wear clothes that are comfortable and make you feel good about your body. Work with your body, not against it.

✤ It's A Fact!!
Feeling Beautiful

Everyone wants to be beautiful, but what is it about a person that really makes her beautiful? The truth is that it's not any one thing. Beauty is a combination of many qualities that give pleasure to the senses or mind. Your personality, sense of humor, and compassion for others are a large part of what makes you beautiful. The secret to being beautiful is feeling beautiful. It is more about inner qualities than physical appearance. You may not love all of your qualities, but if you see yourself as a strong person with many goals and talents, you will begin to feel more comfortable with yourself. Feel good about yourself and let your positive attitude shine.

Sometimes it can be a challenge to remember that beauty is about what's on the inside. Don't measure yourself against the media's unrealistic ideals and don't compare yourself to other girls either. You are a unique person. You'll never be someone else and no one else will ever be you. That's what makes our world so great. We live on a diverse planet and have many different gifts to share. Instead of trying to be like someone else, just try being you. Celebrate your differences. What is it that makes you special? Is it your great laugh? Your listening ear? Your sense of humor? Your athletic ability? Your concern for others? As you discover your own strengths you will begin to feel more comfortable with yourself. You will see that you are a beautiful person with the power to make your goals a reality.

Source: BodyWise, U.S. Department of Health and Human Service (www.girlpower.gov), 2004.

Some people are shaped like a spoon, their upper body is smaller than their lower body. Other people are shaped like an hourglass. This shape is curvy with a larger upper and lower body, but smaller waist. Another shape is a ruler. This shape is straight with not much difference between the upper and lower body. The lower body of someone who is funnel shaped is narrower than their upper body. No category is better or worse than any other, only different. Learn to like and respect your body the way it is built, and make the most of what you've got.

Do You Have Healthy Self-Esteem?

Find Out If You Have A Healthy Self-Esteem

If you have high or healthy self-esteem, you will agree with the following statements:

- I feel good about who I am.

- I am proud of what I can do, but I do not show off.

- I know there are some things that I am good at and some things I need to improve.

- I am responsible for the things I do and say, both good and bad.

- It is okay if I win or if I lose.

- Before I do something, I usually think "I can do it."

Does this sound like you? If some of the items in this checklist sound like you, that's good, you're on the right track. Remember to tell yourself every-day that you are a great person.

Do You Have Poor Self-Esteem?

Find Out If You Have Low Or Poor Self-Esteem

If you have low or poor self-esteem, you might agree with the following statements:

- I can't do anything right.

- I am ugly or dumb.

- I do not have any friends.

- I do not like to try new things.

- It really upsets me to make mistakes.

- I do not think I am as nice, pretty, or smart as the other girls in my class.

- I have a hard time making friends.

- I have a hard time making friends because I end up getting angry and fighting with people.

- It makes me uncomfortable when people say nice things about me.

- Sometimes I feel better if I say mean things to other people.

If many or all of these items sound like you, it will be helpful for you to work on raising your self-esteem.

What You Can Do To Boost Your Self-Esteem

Try these steps to boost your self-esteem.

- Tell yourself that it is okay not to be the best at everything.

- Help out by doing chores around the house and volunteering in your community.

- Do things that you enjoy, or learn about new things you would like to try.

- Understand that there will be times when you will feel disappointed in yourself and other people. No one is perfect.

- If you are angry, try talking it over with an adult you trust (parents/guardians, relatives or a school counselor).

- Think positively about yourself and the things you can do. Think: "I will try."

- If you still find that you are not feeling good about yourself, talk to your parents/guardian, a school counselor, or your doctor because you may be at risk for depression. (You can also ask the school nurse for help through tough times. Some schools offer counseling.) Learn more about depression and other health issues that can affect your mind.

✔ Quick Tip

What is self-esteem? Self-esteem is how you feel about yourself.

What does a person with good self-esteem look like? People with good self-esteem have self-confidence and self-worth. They also believe that they can accomplish goals and are able to focus on their strengths.

What does a person with low self-esteem look like? Individuals with low self-esteem tend to view themselves poorly and feel that others view them the same way. These people also may put themselves down a lot. For example, they may often say or feel, "I am so stupid," or, "Everyone hates me."

Tip 1: Look at all of your positive qualities: Sometimes we forget what our strengths are, but we all have them. If you think hard you can find and remember these qualities about yourself.

Tip 2: Take on a new challenge: Is there something you thought might be very difficult and were scared to try? Taking on a new challenge (even if you don't succeed) will help build your self-esteem.

Tip 3: Positive self-talk: Keep telling yourself, "I can do this," or, "I am smart." If you need to practice, try it in front of a mirror or with friends and family.

Tip 4: Keep a journal: Try writing down your positive qualities at least three times a week. If you start feeling bad about yourself, look at your journal as a reminder of your self worth.

Tip 5: Accept Defeat: Making mistakes is OK. Everyone makes mistakes; it does not mean you should feel bad about who you are. In fact, we learn and grow through making mistakes. You already succeeded by taking a chance.

Tip 6: Spend time with people who make you feel good: You will meet a lot of new people as you continue to grow. Some will see the best in you and make you feel good about yourself. Despite your best efforts, others will put you down and will leave you questioning yourself. It is important to spend time with people who make you feel good. Remember, people who put others down might not feel good about themselves.

Source: "Tips For Teens: Building Positive Self Esteem," © 2004 National Association of Social Workers. All rights reserved. Reprinted with permission.

Chapter 3

Getting Along With Friends, Siblings, Parents, And Teachers

Peer Relationships

Developing friendships is a healthy part of growing up. Relationships help you to know yourself better, to understand people, and enjoy the company of others. At this point in your life, your friends probably matter as much to you as your family. You care about what your friends say and do, what they think about you, and what they like and dislike. Their feelings and ideas are important to you.

What is a friend? Good friendships take time to develop, and you have to put forth some effort to make and keep friends. Friends should generally share a variety of interests and make your life more fun.

Listed below are some qualities that can be found between good friends:

- **Equality:** Both people contribute and consider one another equals.

- **Shared Responsibility:** Both people feel responsible for the friendship, and both invest their time and energy to make it work.

About This Chapter: This chapter includes "Peer Relationships," "Peer Pressure," "All about Brothers and Sisters," "How to Improve Your Relationship with Your Parents," and "Getting along with Teachers," reprinted with permission from the Teen Health Centre, Windsor, Ontario, http://www.teenhealthcentre.com. © 2004. All rights reserved.

- **Trust:** Good friendships are based on mutual honesty and trust.

- **Loyalty:** When you make mistakes, your good friends will forgive you and still like you. Real friends don't listen to gossip about you because they know and trust you.

- **Caring:** Real friends are interested in the details of your life (for example: your birthday or concerns or struggles that you are having.). They pay attention to your life and let you know that they care.

Peer Pressure

What is peer pressure?

Peer pressure is a type of force applied to get us to do something other people are doing. We all want to feel like we belong. We want to feel valued, cared about, appreciated and understood. With all of the competition over grades, athletics, having the right clothes, etc., teens can sometimes feel like an "outsider" among their peers.

If you feel left out of the "right" cliques, you may be tempted to find any clique just to belong somewhere.

> **✔ Quick Tip**
> **My friend is dealing with a lot of problems in her life right now. How can I help?**
>
> When a friend is suffering and asking for help, all you can do is show you care and lend some support. You are not responsible for solving that person's problems. Your friend will have to find her own solution. There are many ways to support a friend who is asking for your help:
>
> - Take the person and the problem seriously.
>
> - Be a good listener.
>
> - Don't give advice.
>
> - Share your own experiences.
>
> - Encourage your friend to talk to others, perhaps an adult or a professional.
>
> - Let your friend know you care.
>
> If your friend feels too overwhelmed by her problems, and threatens or even talks about suicide, take that friend seriously. Do not keep talk of suicide a secret—get help. Tell an adult (parent, teacher, counselor, etc.) immediately.

You don't have to choose between belonging to the "wrong" crowd or no crowd. Be patient. You will feel like you belong if you spend time with people whose values and behavior feel good to you, people who are doing things you enjoy and feel are right for you. This means making friends with those who will like you regardless of what you wear, where you came from, or what you look like.

There is a lot of talk about negative peer pressure. What about positive peer pressure? Can't friends be a good influence?

Although it seems more common to hear about peer pressure as the reason for many negative behaviors of adolescents, in reality peers play a very important part helping their friends. Peers can and do act as positive role models. For example peers often listen to, accept, and understand certain frustrations associated with being a teenager. Peers provide an opportunity for teens to feel capable and belong, and to have fun. If you do something positive (like volunteering or making a donation to charity) and encourage your friends to do the same, you are exerting "positive peer pressure."

How do I know if a peer group is not right for me?

If you find that you're changing in order to keep your friends, feel used, or are doing some things that you don't like (smoking, stealing, drug use) just to hold on to these friendships, then you need to find some new friends who share your values and common interests. It may be helpful for you to be aware of the traits you believe are found in peers that make good friends.

✔ Quick Tip

Some of my friends smoke and are asking me to try it too. Sometimes they really pressure me. How do I say "No" without offending them?

Your true friends won't insist you try. They'll respect your choice. You may want to rehearse your response with your parents, another adult, or another friend. Perhaps you might say you don't want to smoke as it is unhealthy, your boyfriend or girlfriend doesn't want to kiss an ashtray, or you're concerned your parents may find out. Smoking is a very dangerous, addicting, and expensive habit to start. Think very carefully about this one. Remember you cannot control your friend's behaviors, but you can continually make healthy personal choices that are right for you.

All About Brothers And Sisters

What do I do if my younger brother or sister follows me around everywhere and will not leave me alone?

First, it is important to realize that your younger brother or sister likely wants to be more like you and is, therefore, trying to copy your behavior and hang around with you and your friends. This is normal and is actually a complement to you, although it can be difficult to see it that way.

To deal with this, you can try to be a good role model for your younger brother or sister and let him or her know that you do not mind if he or she occasionally spends time with you or your friends, and you can try to schedule these times. Remember that you should try to be flattered by this and that you probably would act in a similar way if you were the younger sibling. Try to keep in mind as well that your younger brother or sister will gradually outgrow this behavior in time as he or she becomes more independent and thus this behavior is usually relatively short-lived. However, the more you complain and protest the more he or she will want to hang around because it annoys you so watch your reactions!

Why does my brother act as though he hates me?

It is important to keep in mind that even though your brother may act as though he hates you, chances are good that this is not true. He probably gets annoyed with your behavior but this does not mean that he hates you. Talk with your brother when you are both calm (that is, not when you are arguing) about your concerns. Maybe you are doing something that he finds annoying that you did not realize you were doing. I am sure he does something that annoys you as well. We can be annoyed by people and still care about them. When you are feeling down about your relationship, try to remember the good times and the things that your sibling admires about you. It is human nature to focus on the negative, but it is also important to look at the positive in order to see the complete picture. Also, try to remember that over time, sibling relationships tend to grow just as we do and that things will very likely improve between the two of you, even if it is gradual and in small steps.

How can I improve my relationship with my brother or sister?

It is perfectly normal to have rough spots and conflict in any relationship and your relationship with your brother or sister is no exception. All relationships, including sibling relationships, require some work, commitment, and effort, just as school and other activities require some work and effort. The important point is that you are family and will always likely share a very special bond and connection.

To improve your relationship, you can try to improve your communication with each other and be honest about your feelings, thoughts, and needs in a tactful manner. It is often good to let people in your life know how you feel about them because they often do not realize how you feel (they cannot read your mind). You can make an effort to spend more time with one another doing an activity you both enjoy, such as going to a movie, eating at a restaurant, or going swimming, biking, walking, etc. You may want to schedule one day every week or two or even join a club or class together. Spending quality time with each other is important to building and maintaining a good relationship.

Why do I fight with my brother and sister and what can I do about it?

All brothers and sisters have arguments and conflicts from time to time. It is common for people who live together or see each other frequently to have some arguments. Arguments may start from a misunderstanding or from personality traits or behaviors that annoy the other person. Another big factor is the past arguments. Many times one person is hurt by something another said, but rather than talk to them about it they just get into more arguments because they are hurt and angry.

If a conflict does arise, the best thing to do is agree ahead of time to leave the situation and come back when you are calm and talk about it (and really listen to what each other is saying), rather than argue or physically fight. Arguments rarely solve the conflict, because no one is listening, and will not help to reduce the likelihood of problems in the future. If you feel that the conflict is getting out of hand, an impartial person, preferably an adult such as a parent, teacher, minister, or a counselor, could get involved to help resolve it.

How To Improve Your Relationship With Your Parents

During adolescence, teens and parents may often argue about a number of issues. Usually this conflict is the result of a teen developing his or her own identity. This means that teens begin to have opinions, thoughts, and values about life.

Parents often have a hard time adjusting to this change. There is usually a big difference between when teens see themselves as adult and when their parents do. Remember that your parents are responsible for you, but most of all they want to protect you from getting hurt or getting into trouble.

In order to decrease the amount of conflict and arguing, it is important that both teens and their parents learn how to better communicate and compromise. One of the biggest problems with arguments is that no one listens to the other person. Within this section we have listed examples of typical stressful situations between teens and parents and some suggestions of how to compromise. It is usually a safe bet that no one wants to argue but many people just don't know how to stop. Here are some suggestions.

☞ Remember!!

Almost all conflicts can be solved. It is best to try to stay calm when one does arise and not to overreact but rather to try to appreciate the other person's point of view and be as understanding as possible. A good rule (which is often forgotten) is to try to treat other people as you yourself would like to be treated.

Wanting A Later Curfew

This is a very common and on-going request by teens, especially as they grow older. In order to have this wish even considered, teens must first prove that they are responsible enough to handle this added privilege. This may be done in several ways:

• Come home on time (or even early) for your current curfew.

• Complete any household chores by the agreed upon dates and times.

- Keep up good grades.

- Treat your parents with "respect" (no "mouthing back" or aggressive behavior).

Another way to earn a later curfew is to ensure that your parents trust you. This can be accomplished by being truthful about where you spend your time and with whom. If your parents believe that you are able to balance all the different areas of your life and be responsible and truthful, they will often consider a later curfew. Keep in mind that they do not care how late Joey's or Sandra's curfew is—so leave that out of your discussion.

Also, try to remember to be reasonable. You might start out by asking for a 15-minute extension and come up with some repercussions if you are late. Being willing to volunteer ideas for "fair" punishments and sticking to them is another way to show that you are maturing. Remember that in any case you will have to earn it, and keep in mind that there will still be limits placed upon your curfew according to your age and what your parents consider appropriate. Your parents may not be willing to consider a later curfew right now, perhaps they may consider extending it at your next birthday or just for special occasions (again provided you are truthful and responsible).

Chores

Parents often complain about having to repeatedly remind their teens to complete their chores. As a result, parents become quite frustrated which leads to an increase in conflict between teens and their parents. Teens feel that their parents are nagging, and parents see their teens as irresponsible. A major problem with nagging is that it does tend to make the teen less motivated to complete the task because they are annoyed. Another major problem is that parents tend to want the chore done on their schedule rather than the teen's schedule (that is, do it now, not at the end of that TV show).

One compromise is for parents and teens to write out a list of weekly chores together (or a specific chore for a specific day). No one likes chores, but maybe you don't mind doing laundry so much but you hate to dust or take out the garbage. If you can choose some that are your responsibility and assign both a day and/or time that they need to be completed you may feel more control. Also, it means that your parents don't have to nag you about it all the time.

You and your parents also need to decide on an appropriate consequence if the chore is not completed, and you need to stick to the consequence if you do not complete the chore. Doing chores involves being responsible, and parents should not be constantly reminding their teens of the list. Ask your parents to let you show that you can be responsible—but then actually be responsible about it, you might be surprised at how it can change things around your house.

Getting Along With Teachers

I don't think my teacher likes me. It seems he picks on me all the time. How do I handle this situation?

First, we need to look at why he might be picking on you. Think about your own behavior. Let's look at situations where a teacher might need to deal with students on unpleasant issues: is your homework complete; do you behave in class; are you on time? Secondly, are there other students who notice that you are being singled out, or are other students being "picked on" as well? Third, do you notice the teacher commenting consistently on the same problem area such as speaking out of turn?

Teachers are human too, and they do make mistakes but some of the common reasons for "picking on" students might include:

- Knowing that they can do better.

- Knowing that they have not done their homework and that not having the answer is embarrassing. They hope that embarrassment will motivate students to do their homework the next time and thus learn more. Not that nice, but it does work!

- Teachers feel that the student is disrupting the learning experience of others' in the classroom.

If you are having difficulty figuring out the reason for this teacher's behavior towards you, meeting with him is a good first step. Telling him how you feel when he singles you out or reprimands you and ask why. The teacher may justify his approach to give you a clearer understanding or at least it will let him know how you feel. If this does not settle the matter talk to your parents. If necessary a meeting with the principal can be arranged.

You have a right to a positive learning experience and if you feel that you are being treated unfairly, please speak to an adult about your concerns.

Chapter 4

Healthy Relationships

As a teen, you will have relationships with a lot of people. These relationships will includes friendships and dating relationships. Most of the time, these relationships are fun and healthy, and they make us feel good about ourselves. Sometimes, though, these relationships can be unhealthy. Unhealthy relationships can cause someone to get hurt physically or emotionally. The questions and answers below will help you understand how to spot and unhealthy relationship and how to change a bad situation.

What is a healthy relationship?

In healthy relationships, you and your friend or the person you are dating feel good about each other and yourselves. You do activities together, like going to movies or out with other friends, and you talk to one another honestly about how you feel. These relationships can last a few weeks, a few months, or even years.

In healthy relationships, there is respect and honesty between both people. This means that you listen to each other's thoughts and opinions and accept each other's right to say no or to change your mind without giving each other a hard time. You should be able to let the other person know how you are feeling. You might disagree or argue sometimes, but in healthy relationships you should be able to talk things out to reach a solution.

About This Chapter: Excerpted from "Safety: How to Be Safety Savvy," National Women's Health Information Center (www.4girls.gov), August 2005.

What are the signs that I am in an abusive or unhealthy relationship?

There are many signs that you could be in an abusive or unhealthy relationship. Take a look at this list of "warning signs" and see if any of these describe your relationship:

Your friend or the person you are going out with:

• gets angry when you talk or hang out with other friends or people of the opposite sex.

• bosses you around.

• often gets in fights with other people or loses his or her temper.

♣ It's A Fact!!
Test Your Relationship

Does your friend or person you are dating tell you the truth about things?

Truth is part of a healthy and safe relationship. You should be able to trust your friend or dating partner and believe what he or she tells you.

Does your friend or person you are dating make all the decisions in your relationship?

In a healthy and safe relationship, both people share in making decisions— it should never be one person's way all the time.

Has your friend or person you are dating ever told you that you couldn't wear something that you wanted to wear?

In a healthy and safe relationship, the way you dress, what you think, or how you act should not be controlled by a friend or dating partner.

Does the person you are dating pressure you to have sex?

In a healthy and safe relationship you should never be pressured for sex. Your friend or dating partner should always respect your values and your boundaries.

- pressures you to have sex or to do something sexual that you don't want to do.

- uses drugs and alcohol, and tries to pressure you into doing the same thing.

- swears at you or uses mean language.

- blames you for his or her problems, or tells you that it is your fault that he or she hurt you.

- insults or tries to embarrass you in front of other people.

- has physically hurt you.

- makes you feel scared of their reactions to things.

- always wants to know where you are going and who you are with.

Does your friend or person you are dating lose his/her temper a lot and always blame you for things?

In a healthy and safe relationship, each person takes responsibility for his or her feelings and actions. You should never have to worry about getting yelled at by your friend or dating partner, and you shouldn't be blamed for everything that goes wrong in his or her life.

Does your friend or person you are dating prevent you from spending time with your friends and family?

Your friend or dating partner should understand that you need time with other friends and with your family.

Has your friend or person you are dating ever pushed, grabbed, or touched you in a way that hurts?

Your friend or dating partner should never threaten you.

Does your friend or the person you are dating do things to make you feel afraid?

In a healthy and safe relationship both people feel safe with one another. You should never feel afraid of your friend or dating partner.

Source: National Women's Health Information Center (www.4girls.gov), August 2005.

These are just a few of the signs that you may be in an unhealthy or abusive relationship. Sometimes there are only one or two "warning signs" and sometimes there are many. If any of these signs are a part of your relationship, you should speak to a trusted adult such as a parent/guardian, teacher, doctor, nurse, or counselor right away.

My friend gets mad if I hang out with other people, what should I do?

Be honest and stick to your decision. Tell your friend you like spending time with him or her but that you also want to spend time with other friends and family. Whether you are in a close friendship or a dating relationship, it is important for both of you to stay involved with the activities and interests you enjoyed before you became close. In a healthy relationship, you both need time to hang out with other friends as well as time for yourselves.

What are unhealthy relationships?

In an unhealthy relationship, you usually feel the exact opposite of how you feel when you're in a "healthy relationship." You and your friend do not usually feel good about each other and yourselves. Not all unhealthy relationships are abusive but sometimes they can include verbal, physical, emotional, or sexual abuse. This can involve both people being violent or abusive toward each other or can involve only one person doing this to the other. Many times, a relationship is not unhealthy in the very beginning, but becomes so over time.

What is abuse?

Some people think that their relationship isn't abusive unless there is physical fighting. There are other types of abuse, though. Below is a list of different types of abuse:

- Physical abuse is when a person touches your body in an unwanted or violent way. This may include: hitting, kicking, pulling hair, pushing, biting, choking, or using a weapon or other item to hurt you.

- Verbal/emotional abuse is when a person says something or does something that makes you afraid or feel bad about yourself. This may include: yelling, name-calling, saying mean things about your family and friends, embarrassing you on purpose, telling you what to do, or threatening to hurt you or hurt themselves. Pressuring you to use drugs or alcohol is also abuse, as is keeping you from spending time with your friends and family.

- Sexual abuse is any sexual contact that you do not want. You may have said "no" or may be unable to say no because the abuser has threatened you or stopped you from getting out of the situation. This may include forcing you to have sex or unwanted touching or kissing.

♣ **It's A Fact!!**

True Or False?

One in 10 teens experience physical violence in their relationships.

The correct answer is "True." Physical violence is a sign of an unhealthy relationship. Domestic violence can be a problem for teens as well as adults.

If your boyfriend calls to check up on you all of the time, and demands to know where you are and who you are with, it just means that he really likes you.

The correct answer is "False." If someone calls to check up on you all the time, it is a sign that he/she is trying to control you. Control is a form of emotional abuse. A friend should not demand to know where you are or who you are with at all times.

When you start dating someone new, it is a good idea to go out with a group of friends to a public place for the first time.

The correct answer is "True." When you start dating someone new, you will be safer in a public place with other trusted friends until you get to know the person better. You will be less likely to be in an uncomfortable or dangerous situation. Let your parents know where you are going and who you will be with.

Source: Excerpted from "How to Stay Safe in a Relationship," National Women's Health Information Center (www.4girls.gov), August 2005.

Why are some people violent?

There are many reasons why a person could be violent or abusive to someone in any relationship. For example, a person who has grown up in a violent family may have learned that violence, like hitting or verbal control, was the way to solve a problem. They may be violent because they feel bad about themselves and think they will feel better if they make someone else feel worse. Others may get pressured by their friends to prove how strong they are. Sometimes people have trouble controlling their anger. Yet, violence never solves problems.

Drugs and alcohol can also play a part in abusive behavior. There are some people who lose control and act abusively after they have been drinking or taking drugs. But this is no excuse! Just because someone is under the influence of drugs and alcohol or has a bad temper does not mean that their abusive behavior is okay. No matter why a person is violent physically, verbally/emotionally, or sexually, it is important for you to know that it is not your fault. You are not the reason for the violence. Violence is never okay.

Why do some people stay in unhealthy or violent relationships?

Sometimes it may be hard to get out of an abusive relationship, because violent relationships often go in cycles. After a person is violent, he or she may apologize and promise never to hurt you again. They may even say that they will work on the relationship, and it may be a while before that person acts violently again. These ups and downs can make it hard to leave a relationship.

It's also hard to leave someone you care about. You may be scared or ashamed to admit that you are in an abusive relationship, or you may be simply scared to be alone without that person. You may be afraid that no one will believe you, or that your friend or partner will hurt you more if you tell someone. Whatever the reasons, leaving an unhealthy relationship is hard but it is something you should do.

✔ Quick Tip

The National Sexual Assault Hotline (800-656-HOPE) is available 24 hours a day. The call is free and confidential.

Chapter 5

Dealing With Anger In A Healthy Way

Introduction

Anger is a normal human emotion. It can be caused by anything from a friend's annoying behavior to worries about personal problems or memories of a troubling life event.

When handled in a positive way, anger can help people stand up for themselves and fight injustices. On the other hand, anger can lead to violence and injury when not addressed positively. This chapter is meant to help teens understand and control anger.

What is anger?

Anger is an emotional state that can range from mild irritation to intense fury and rage. Feelings of anger actually produce physical changes in the body such as increased heart rate, blood pressure, and adrenaline.

When does anger become a problem?

Laws, social norms, and just plain common sense tell us not to lash out physically or verbally every time something irritates us. Otherwise, we could hurt ourselves and others.

About This Chapter: "Anger Management," National Youth Violence Prevention Resource Center (www.safeyouth.org), October 2005.

What are some ways to deal with anger?

Some people choose to ignore or bottle up anger, but this approach may actually cause more harm because the root problem is never addressed. Instead, try to manage anger so it can become a more positive emotion.

Here are some ideas:

Relax: Breathe deeply from your diaphragm (your belly, not your chest) and slowly repeat a calming word or phrase like "take it easy." Think of relaxing experiences, such as sitting on a beach or walking through a forest.

♣ It's A Fact!!

Emotions such as stress, sadness or fear may cause someone to feel angry. Tell a parent, teacher, or other trusted adult if you feel:

- Irritable, grumpy, or in a bad mood more often than not;

- Angry for days at a time;

- Like you want to hurt yourself or someone else.

These feelings could be signs of depression.

Source: NYVP Resource Center, 2005.

Think positively: Remind yourself that the world is not out to get you, but rather you're just experiencing some of the rough spots of daily life.

Problem-solve: Identify the specific problem that is causing the anger and approach it head-on—even if the problem does not have a quick solution.

Communicate with others: Angry people tend to jump to conclusions. Slow down and think carefully about what you want to say. Listen carefully to what the other person is saying. At times, criticism may actually be useful to you.

Manage stress: Make sure to set aside personal time to deal with the daily stresses of school, activities, and family. Ideas include the following:

- Listening to music

- Writing in a journal

- Exercising

- Meditating

- Talking about your feelings with someone you trust

Change the scene: Maybe a change of environment would help reduce angry feelings. For example, if your friends are angry frequently and/or make you angry, consider making some new ones who may contribute more to your self-confidence and well-being.

✔ Quick Tip

Here is a simple way to remember how to deal with anger:

Avoid don't let your anger or other angry people control you.

Never use your body or voice to hurt others

Get away from the situation so your feelings don't overwhelm you.

Evaluate your choices. Think before your react.

Responsibility: Remember, you are responsible for your choices.
No one can make you angry, you allow yourself to become angry.
And you can choose not to get angry too.

Source: "BAM! Guide to Getting Along," Centers for Disease Control and Prevention (www.bam.gov), 2003.

Chapter 6

Learning To Handle Stress

Got Butterflies? Find Out Why

What is short-term stress?

Have you ever started a new school, argued with your best friend, or moved? Do you have to deal with the ups and downs of daily life—like homework or your parents' expectations? Then you already know about stress. In fact, everyone experiences stress. Your body is pre-wired to deal with it—whether it is expected or not. This response is known as the stress response, or fight or flight.

The fight or flight response is as old as the hills. In fact, when people used to have to fight off wild animals to survive, fight or flight is what helped them do it. Today, different things cause stress (when was the last time you had to fend off a grizzly bear?), but we still go through fight or flight. It prepares us for quick action—which is why the feeling goes away once whatever was stressing you out passes. It can also happen when something major happens—like if you change schools or have a death in your family.

About This Chapter: This chapter includes "Got Butterflies? Find Out Why" and "Feelin' Frazzled," both are BAM! (Body and Mind) publications produced by the Centers for Disease Control and Prevention, 2003.

Everyone has weird feelings when they are stressed. Fight or flight can cause things like sweaty palms or a dry mouth when you are nervous, or knots in your stomach after an argument with someone. This is totally normal and means that your body is working exactly like it should. There are lots of signs of stress—common types are physical (butterflies in your stomach), emotional (feeling sad or worried), behavioral (you don't feel like doing things), and mental (you can't concentrate). Most physical signs of stress usually don't last that long and can help you perform better, if you manage them right.

So, when you feel stress, what happens to make your body do the things it does? According to the experts, three glands "go into gear" and work together to help you cope with change or a stressful situation. Two are in your brain and are called the hypothalamus (hipe-o-thal-a-mus) and the pituitary (pi-to-i-tary) gland. The third, the adrenal (a-dree-nal) glands, are on top of your kidneys. The hypothalamus signals your pituitary gland that it is time to tell your adrenal glands to release the stress hormones called epinephrine (ep-in-efrin), norepinephrine (nor-ep-in-efrin), and cortisol (cor-ti-sol). These chemicals increase your heart rate and breathing and provide a burst of energy—which is useful if you're trying to run away from a bear. These chemicals can also control body temperature (which can make you feel hot or cold), keep you from getting hungry, and make you less sensitive to pain. Because everyone is different, everyone will have different signs. Not to worry—everyone experiences these physical signs of stress sometimes. The good news is that, once things return to normal, your body will turn off the stress response. After some rest and relaxation, you'll be good as new.

> ### ♣ It's A Fact!!
> ### Is stress always
> ### a bad thing?
>
> No. A little bit of stress can work in a positive way. For instance, during a sports competition, stress might push you to perform better. Also, without the stress of deadlines, you might not be able to finish schoolwork or get to where you need to be on time.
>
> Source: Excerpted from "Handling Stress," National Women's Health Information Center (www.girls health.gov), August 2005.

What is long-term stress?

But what happens when life continues to throw curves at you and if you have one stressful event after another? Your stress response may not be able to stop itself from running overtime, and you may not have a chance to rest, restore, and recuperate. This can add up and, suddenly, the signs of overload hit you—turning short-term stressors into long-term stress. This means that you may have even more physical signs of stress. Things like a headache, eating too much or not at all, tossing and turning all night, or feeling down and angry all the time, are all signs of long-term stress. These signs start when you just can't deal with any more.

Long-term stress can affect your health and how you feel about yourself, so it is important to learn to deal with it. No one is completely free of stress and different people respond to it in lots of different ways. The most important thing to learn about long-term stress is how to spot it. You can do that by listening to your body signals and learning healthy ways to handle it.

Cold Hands, Dry Mouth, Pounding Heart

You're about to take a big test or star in the school play and you've got cold hands, a mouth as dry as the desert, and your heart is pounding.

Cold Hands: Because you're nervous and under pressure to perform, your body has kicked the stress response into high gear. The stress hormones are shooting through your bloodstream and moving your blood away from your skin. This can give your heart and muscles more strength—which you would really need if you were trying to run away. Because your blood is going to the places that really need it (like your heart, lungs, and liver), your hands can be left feeling like ice.

Dry Mouth: Once that stress response is running full force, your body sends your blood to only those parts that are truly necessary for you to survive. Lots of the fluid in your body goes to really important places (like your organs) and can leave you with a mouth as dry as the desert. Because your blood is busy with your organs and not your muscles, your throat (which is made of muscle) can tighten, making it hard to swallow.

Pounding Heart: When you're starring in the school play, your body wants to give you what you need to succeed—which goes back to the fight or flight response. Your heart will start pounding to help you out. In fact, it is one of the first signs of the stress response. It happens because the release of stress hormones can speed up the flow of your blood by 300–400 percent. Your heart has to beat much faster to move all of that blood to your organs and your muscles. This provides a burst of energy that can help you get through backstage jitters and the first few minutes of your play.

Everyone experiences stress. If you have any of these signs of stress, it means that your body is dong its job.

Butterflies, Knots

It's your first day back at school, or maybe you're starting a new school, and you've got butterflies in your stomach.

Stomachaches, or a queasy feeling, happen all the time in stressful situations like this, and it's no wonder. Once the stress response kicks into high gear, one of the stress hormones (cortisol) shuts the stomach down and won't let food digest. It can also put your digestive tract into high speed, making you feel nauseated.

Can't Concentrate?

You have so much to do, but you just can't seem to concentrate.

Got too much to do? You know how it goes—you have tons of homework to do right now, you've got a game this afternoon, your little brother is annoying you, and your mom is insisting that you clean your room—but you just can't seem to focus on any one thing. You feel like you have no energy to finish all that you've got to do. This is because the stress hormones fill up your short-term memory with the immediate demands of dealing with stress. They also signal your brain to store the memory of the stressful event in your long-term memory so you know how to respond the next time something stressful happens. All of this means you are more likely to forget something, feel like you can't concentrate, snap at your family, be mean to a friend, or feel tongue-tied.

Headache

It's been a long, tense day and you feel like you've got a rubber band squeezing around your head that just won't stop.

Headaches are one of the most common signs of long-term stress. They can feel dull and achy—just like a rubber band tightening around your head. Although it is unclear what exactly causes these headaches, tight head and neck muscles are generally thought to be to blame. The chemical messengers in your brain get really busy and tell your blood vessels to get really small. This means that less blood is getting to your head—and that can cause a headache. Your eyes, forehead, or the top of your head will be the first places you feel the pain.

Sleeplessness

You're exhausted but when you try to sleep, you lie awake for hours.

During the day, the levels of hormones that give you energy (epinephrine and norepinephrine) and those that help you stay happy (called dopamine) stay consistent. Towards the end of a normal day, these hormones begin to decrease and the hormone that helps you sleep (called serotonin) kicks into high gear. If you've been trapped in a stress cycle, your body continues to produce those stress hormones from the adrenal glands. They "rev" up your body and block out the serotonin, making it hard to sleep even if you feel tired.

Change In Appetite

You've just had a fight with your best friend and eating is the only thing that makes you feel better or, maybe you feel like you could never eat again.

While you might become ravenous after a stressful event, your best friend might be grossed out by the thought of food. It just depends on how your body reacts to stress. If you get hungry, you may crave comfort foods (like candy bars, soda, or ice cream) because they increase the levels of a feel-good hormone called serotonin in the body—meaning that you will be in a better mood. Keep in mind that your body is just responding to the stress you are feeling and that your appetite will go back to normal.

On the other hand, your best friend might lose her appetite because the stress hormones make it difficult for her to eat. If you can't eat when you're stressed, try something small—like peanut butter on toast or a piece of fruit.

Overwhelmed?

You are starting to feel overwhelmed by it all and you don't know if you can handle it.

Everyone has different ideas of what you should be doing and it feels like you have so many different roles to play—good student, kid, brother, sister, and friend—that things can sometimes seem out of control. It can make you tired just thinking about all you have to do. If you're feeling overwhelmed, you may notice that you can't sleep—which makes you tired and cranky. Then, you realize that you don't feel like doing the things you like to do and you feel a little bit sad or anxious. You may begin to feel achy and tired all over. These are signs of being stressed out. Your stress response system is having a hard time turning off. Don't panic—your body is just trying to tell you something. Take the time to figure out what is stressing you out and try to lessen the load you're carrying.

> ✔ **Quick Tip**
> **I heard deep breathing could help my stress. How do I do it?**
>
> Deep breathing is a good way to relax. Try it a couple of times every day. Here's how to do it.
>
> - Lie down or sit in a chair.
>
> - Rest your hands on your stomach.
>
> - Slowly count to four and inhale through your nose. Feel your stomach rise. Hold it for a second.
>
> - Slowly count to four while you exhale through your mouth. To control how fast you exhale, purse your lips like you're going to whistle. Your stomach will slowly fall.
>
> - Repeat five to ten times.
>
> Source: Excerpted from "Stress and Your Health," National Women's Health Information Center (www.4woman.gov), August 2004.

Anger

Things are crazy right now and you just don't have any patience with anyone. You feel angry at someone at the drop of a hat.

Anger is another common response to stress. Often, people who have been locked into a stress cycle feel helpless and overwhelmed. Once this happens, they can get angry much more quickly and they lash out at anyone that gets in their way. In fact, everyone at one point or another gets angry because they are stressed out.

Feelin' Frazzled?

Finding yourself in a hectic situation, whether it's forgetting your homework or missing your ride home, can really stress you out. Are you looking for a safety net for those days that seem to get worse by the second? Could you really use some advice on how to de-stress both your body and your mind? Knowing how to deal can be half the battle. Check out these ten tips to keep you cool, calm, and collected.

Put Your Body In Motion

Moving from the chair to the couch while watching TV is not being physically active. Physical activity is one of the most important ways to keep stress away by clearing your head and lifting your spirits. Physical activity also increases endorphin levels—the natural "feel-good" chemicals in the body which leave you with a naturally happy feeling.

Whether you like full-fledged games of football, tennis, or roller hockey, or you prefer walks with family and friends, it's important to get up, get out, and get moving.

Fuel Up

Start your day off with a full tank—eating breakfast will give you the energy you need to tackle the day. Eating regular meals (this means no skipping dinner) and taking time to enjoy them (nope, eating in the car on the way to practice doesn't count) will make you feel better too.

Make sure to fuel up with fruits, vegetables, proteins (peanut butter, a chicken sandwich, or a tuna salad) and grains (wheat bread, pasta, or some crackers)—these will give you the power you need to make it through those hectic days.

Don't be fooled by the jolt of energy you get from sodas and sugary snacks—this only lasts a short time, and once it wears off, you may feel sluggish and more tired than usual. For that extra boost of energy to sail through history notes, math class, and after school activities, grab a banana, some string cheese, or a granola bar for some power-packed energy.

LOL

Some say that laughter is the best medicine—well, in many cases, it is. Did you know that it takes 15 facial muscles to laugh? Lots of laughing can make you feel good—and, that good feeling can stay with you even after the laughter stops. So, head off stress with regular doses of laughter by watching a funny movie or cartoons, reading a joke book (you may even learn some new jokes), or even make up your own riddles, laughter can make you feel like a new person.

Everyone has those days when they do something really silly or stupid—instead of getting upset with yourself, laugh out loud. No one's perfect. Life should be about having fun. So, lighten up.

Have Fun With Friends

Being with people you like is always a good way to ditch your stress. Get a group together to go to the movies, shoot some hoops, or play a board game—or just hang out and talk. Friends can help you work through your problems and let you see the brighter side of things.

Spill To Someone You Trust

Instead of keeping your feelings bottled up inside, talk to someone you trust or respect about what's bothering you. It could be a friend, a parent, someone in your family, or a teacher. Talking out your problems and seeing them from a different view might help you figure out ways to deal with them. Just remember, you don't have to go it alone.

✔ Quick Tip

How can you deal with the stress of a disaster, or a violent or tragic event?

Whether or not you were directly affected by a disaster or violent event, it is normal to feel nervous about your own safety and wonder how you would react in an emergency. People react in different ways to trauma or scary events. Some become cranky or depressed, others lose sleep or have nightmares, and some people put the event out of their minds.

Here are some things you can do to handle this special kind of stress:

- You may think it feels better to pretend the event did not happen, but it is best to be honest about how you are feeling. Ignoring or hiding your feelings can be worse for your health in the long run. It is okay to feel scared and uncertain.

- Try to remember that, while you might feel like a changed person and everything seems off balance right now, your life will calm down and you will find a new normal groove.

- Talk to a teacher, your parents, or a counselor about your sadness, anger, and other emotions. It can be tough to get started, but it is important to confide in someone you trust with your thoughts and feelings.

- It is common to want to strike back at people who have caused you or those you love great pain. This feeling is normal, but it is important to understand that it is useless to respond with more violence. Nothing good can come from using hateful words or actions.

- While you will always remember and feel changed by the event, the feelings will become less painful over time. In learning to cope with tragedy, you will become stronger and better at handling stressful situations. You may also find yourself appreciating life and the people you love even more.

Source: Excerpted from "Handling Stress," National Women's Health Information Center (www.girlshealth.gov), August 2005.

Take Time To Chill

Pick a comfy spot to sit and read, daydream, or even take a snooze. Listen to your favorite music. Work on a relaxing project like putting together a puzzle or making jewelry.

Stress can sometimes make you feel like a tight rubber band—stretched to the limit. If this happens, take a few deep breaths to help yourself unwind. If you're in the middle of an impossible homework problem, take a break. Finding time to relax after (and sometimes during) a hectic day or week can make all the difference.

Catch Some ZZZZZ...

Fatigue is a best friend to stress. When you don't get enough sleep, it's hard to deal—you may feel tired, cranky, or you may have trouble thinking clearly. When you're overtired, a problem may seem much bigger than it actually is. You may have a hard time doing a school assignment that usually seems easy, you don't do your best in sports or any physical activity, or you may have an argument with your friends over something really stupid.

Sleep is a big deal. Getting the right amount of sleep is especially important for kids your age. Because your body (and mind) is changing and developing, it requires more sleep to re-charge for the next day. So don't resist, hit the hay.

Keep A Journal

If you're having one of those crazy days when nothing goes right, it's a good idea to write things down in a journal to get it off of your chest—like how you feel, what's going on in your life, and things you'd like to accomplish. You could even write down what you do when you're faced with a stressful situation, and then look back and think about how you handled it later. So, find a quiet spot, grab a notebook and pen, and start writing.

Get It Together

Too much to do but not enough time? Forgot your homework? Feeling overwhelmed or discombobulated? Being unprepared for school, practice, or other activities can make for a very stressful day.

Remember!!

You're not alone—everyone has stresses in their lives, it's up to you to choose how to deal with them.

Source: CDC, 2003.

Getting everything done can be a challenge, but all you have to do is plan a little and get organized.

Lend A Hand

Get involved in an activity that helps others. It's almost impossible to feel stressed out when you're helping someone else. It's also a great way to find out about yourself and the special qualities you never knew you had. Signing up for a service project is a good idea, but helping others is as easy as saying hello, holding a door, or volunteering to keep a neighbor's pet. If you want to get involved in a more organized volunteer program, try working at a local recreation center, or helping with an after school program. The feeling you will get from helping others is greater than you can imagine.

Most importantly, don't sweat the small stuff. Try to pick a few really important things and let the rest slide—getting worked up over every little thing will only increase your stress. So, toughen up and don't let stressful situations get to you.

Chapter 7

Dealing With Divorce

For many people, the divorce of their parents marks a turning point in their lives, whether the divorce happened many years ago or is taking place right now. About half the marriages in the United States today end in divorce, so children of divorce are certainly not alone. It may seem hard, but it is possible to cope with divorce—and have a happy family life in spite of some changes divorce may bring. After all, couples divorce one another, not their kids.

Why Are My Parents Divorcing?

There are many reasons why parents divorce. They may include serious problems like alcoholism or abuse, but often couples divorce because they can no longer live together in harmony. One parent may have changed in some ways, and the other could not adapt. Some couples may have simply drifted apart over time. Others find that they no longer love each other as they once did.

It's common for teens to think that their parents' divorce is somehow their fault, but nothing could be further from the truth. Some teens may wonder if they could have helped to prevent the split. Others may wish

About This Chapter: This information was provided by TeensHealth, one of the largest resources online for medically reviewed health information written for parents, kids, and teens. For more articles like this one, visit www.TeensHealth.org, or www.KidsHealth.org. © 2004 The Nemours Center for Children's Health Media, a division of The Nemours Foundation.

they had prevented arguments by cooperating more within the family; but separation and divorce are a result of a couple's problems with each other, not with their kids. The decisions adults make about divorce are their own.

If your parents are divorcing, you may experience a variety of feelings, and your emotions may change frequently, too. You may feel angry, upset, or sad. You might feel protective of one parent or blame one for the situation. You may feel abandoned, afraid, worried, or guilty. You may also feel relieved. These feelings are normal and talking about them with a trusted friend or adult can help.

How Will Divorce Change My Life?

There's no doubt that your parents' divorce will affect your daily life. Depending on your particular situation, you may have to adjust to many changes. These could include things like moving and changing schools, spending time with both parents separately, and dealing with some parents' unpleasant feelings toward one another.

♣ **It's A Fact!!**
Some teens have to travel between parents, and that may pose problems both socially and practically. There may be some hassles, but with time you can create a new routine that works.

Issues of money may change for your parents, too. A parent who didn't work during the marriage may need to find a job to pay for rent or a mortgage. There are expenses associated with divorce, from lawyers' fees to the cost of moving to a new place to live. Your family may not be able to afford all the things you were used to before the divorce.

Your parents may go to court to determine custody arrangements. You may end up living with one parent most of the time and visiting the other, or your parents may split their time with you evenly. Often, it takes a while for custody arrangements to be finalized. This can give people time to adapt to these big changes and for families to figure out together what works best.

What Parents And Teens Can Do To Make Divorce Easier

Keep the peace: Dealing with divorce is easiest when parents get along. Teens find it especially hard when their parents fight and argue or act with bitterness toward each other. You can't do much to influence how your parents behave during a divorce, but you can ask them to do their best to call a truce to any bickering or unkind things they might be saying about each other. No matter what problems a couple may have faced, as parents they need to handle visiting arrangements peacefully to minimize the stress their kids may feel.

Be fair: Most teens say it's important that parents don't try to get them to "take sides." You need to feel free to relate to one parent without the other parent acting jealous, hurt, or mad. It's unfair for anyone to feel that relating to one parent is being disloyal to the other or that the burden of one parent's happiness is on your shoulders.

When parents find it hard to let go of bitterness or anger, or if they are depressed about the changes brought on by divorce, they can find help from a counselor or therapist who specializes in working with people who are dealing with divorce. This can help parents to get past the pain divorce may have created, to find personal happiness, and to lift any burdens from their kids.

Keep in touch: Going back and forth between two homes can be tough, especially if parents live far apart. It can be a good idea to keep in touch with a parent you see less often because of distance. Even a quick e-mail just to say "I'm thinking of you" helps ease the feelings of missing each other. Making an effort to stay in touch when you're apart can keep both of you up to date on everyday activities and ideas.

Work it out: You may want both parents to come to special events, like games, meets, plays, or recitals, but one parent may find it difficult to attend if the other is present. It helps if parents can figure out a way to make this work, especially because a teen may need to feel the support and presence of both parents even more during divorce. You might be able to come up with an idea for a compromise or solution to this problem and suggest it to both parents.

Talk about the future: Lots of teens whose parents divorce worry that their own plans for the future could be affected. Some are concerned that the costs of divorce (like legal fees and expenses of two households) might mean there will be less money for college or other things.

Pick a good time to tell your parents about your concerns—when there's enough time to sit down with one or both parents to discuss how the divorce will affect you. Don't worry about putting added stress on your parents. It's better to bring your concerns into the open than to keep them to yourself and let worries or resentment build. There are solutions for most problems and counselors who can help teens and their parents find those solutions.

> **☞ Remember!!**
>
> Most teens learn—sometimes to their surprise—that they can make it through this difficult situation successfully. Giving it time, letting others support you along the way, and keeping an eye on the good things in your life can make all the difference.

Live your life: Sometimes during a divorce, parents may be so caught up in their own changes it can feel like your own life is on hold. In addition to staying focused on your own plans and dreams, make sure you participate in as many of your normal activities as possible. When things are changing at home, it can really help to keep some things, such as school activities and friends, the same. Take care of yourself, too, by eating right and getting regular exercise—two great stress busters.

Let others support you: Talk about your feelings and reactions to the divorce with someone you trust. If you're feeling down or upset, let your friends and family members support you. These feelings usually pass. If they don't, and if you're feeling depressed or stressed out, or if it's hard to concentrate on your normal activities, let a counselor or therapist help you. There are therapists who specialize in working with teens who are dealing with divorce. Your parents, school counselor, or a doctor or other health professional can help you find one. Also, many communities and schools have support groups for kids and teens whose parents have divorced. It can really help to talk with other people your age who are going through similar experiences.

Bringing Out The Positive

There will be ups and downs in the process, but teens can cope successfully with their parents' divorce and the changes it brings. You may even discover some unexpected positives. Many teens find their parents are actually happier after the divorce or they may develop new and better ways of relating to both parents when they have separate time with each one.

Some teens become more compassionate and kind when a younger brother or sister needs their support and care. Siblings who are closer in age may form tighter bonds, learning to count on each other more because they're facing the challenges of their parents' divorce together. Coping well with divorce also can bring out strength and maturity in teens. They may become more responsible, independent, and thoughtful. Some become better problem solvers, better listeners, or better friends.

Chapter 8

Working Through Grief

If someone close to you has died, you may be feeling many different emotions. You may be sad, worried, or scared. You might be shocked, unprepared, or confused. You might be feeling angry, cheated, relieved, guilty, exhausted, or just plain empty. Your emotions might be stronger or deeper than usual or mixed together in ways you've never experienced before.

You might also notice that your loss is affecting what you're thinking about and how you behave. If you're grieving, you might be having trouble concentrating, sleeping, eating, or feeling interested in the things you usually enjoy. You might be trying to act like you feel OK (even if you don't) because you want to be strong for someone else; and you may wonder if you will ever get over losing someone who means so much to you.

All of these emotions can be natural reactions to the death of someone close. They're part of the process of grieving.

About This Chapter: This information was provided by TeensHealth, one of the largest resources online for medically reviewed health information written for parents, kids, and teens. For more articles like this one, visit www.TeensHealth.org, or www.KidsHealth.org. © 2004 The Nemours Center for Children's Health Media, a division of The Nemours Foundation.

What Is Grief?

Grief is the emotion people feel when they experience a loss. There are many different types of loss, and not all of them are related to death. A person can also grieve over the breakup of an intimate relationship or after a parent moves away from home.

Grief is a natural reaction to the loss of someone important to you. Grief is also the name for the healing process that a person goes through after someone close has died. The grieving process takes time, and the healing usually happens gradually.

Although everyone experiences grief when they lose someone, grieving affects people in different ways. How it affects you partly depends on your situation and relationship with the person who died.

The circumstances under which a person dies can influence grief feelings. For example, if someone has been sick for a long time or is very old, you may have expected that person's death. Although it doesn't necessarily make it any easier to accept (and the feelings of grief will still be there), some people find that knowing someone is going to die gives them time to prepare; and if a loved one suffered a lot before dying, a person might even feel a sense of relief when the death occurs. If the person who has died is very young, though, you may feel a sense of how terribly unfair it seems.

Losing someone suddenly can be extremely traumatic, though, no matter how old that person is. Maybe someone you know died unexpectedly—as a result of violence or a car accident, for example. It can take a long time to overcome a sudden loss because you may feel caught off guard by the event and the intense feelings that are associated with it.

If you've lost someone in your immediate family, such as a parent, brother, or sister, you may feel cheated out of time you wanted to have with that person. It can also feel hard to express your own grief when other family members are grieving, too. Some people may hold back their own grief or avoid talking about the person who died because they worry that it may make a parent or other family member sad.

♣ It's A Fact!!

Losing someone because he or she committed suicide can be especially difficult to deal with. People who lose friends or family members to suicide may feel intense despair and sadness because they feel unable to understand what could have led to such an extreme action. They may even feel angry at the person—a completely normal emotion. Or they could feel guilty and wonder if there was something they might have done to prevent the suicide. Sometimes, after a traumatic loss, a person can become depressed and may need extra help to heal.

Grief can cause some people to feel guilty for no reason. Depending on the circumstances, some people might wonder if something they did—or didn't do—caused the person's death. Others might think if only they had been better people that their loved ones might not have died. These things aren't true, of course—but sometimes feelings and ideas like this are just a way of trying to make sense of something that's difficult to understand.

All of these feelings and reactions are OK—but what can people do to get through them? How long does grief last? Will things ever get back to normal? And how will you go on without the person who has died?

Coping With Grief

The grieving process is very personal and individual—each person goes through his or her grief differently. Some people reach out for support from others and find comfort in good memories. Others become very busy to take their minds off the loss. Some people become depressed and withdraw from their peers or go out of the way to avoid the places or situations that remind them of the person who has died. Just as people feel grief in many different ways, they handle it differently, too.

For some people, it may help to talk about the loss with others. Some do this naturally and easily with friends and family, others talk to a professional therapist. Some people may not feel like talking about it much at all because it's hard to find the words to express such deep and personal emotion or they wonder whether talking will make them feel the hurt more. This is fine, as long you find other ways to deal with your pain.

A few people may act out their sorrow by engaging in dangerous or self-destructive activities. Doing things like drinking, drugs, or cutting yourself to escape from the reality of a loss may seem to numb the pain, but the feeling is only temporary. The person isn't really dealing with the pain, only masking it, which makes all those feelings build up inside and only prolongs the grief.

What To Expect

✔ **Quick Tip**

If your pain just seems to get worse, or if you feel like hurting yourself, or have suicidal thoughts, tell someone you trust about how you feel.

It may feel impossible to recover after losing someone you love, but grief does get gradually better and become less intense as time goes by. To help get you through the pain, it can help to know some of the things you might expect during the grieving process.

The first few days after someone dies can be intense, with people expressing strong emotions, perhaps crying and comforting each other, and gathering to express their support and condolences to the ones most affected by the loss.

Family and friends often participate in rituals that may be part of their religious, cultural, community, or family traditions—such as memorial services, wakes, or funerals. These activities can help people get through the first days after a death and honor the person who died. People might spend time together talking and sharing memories about the person who died. This may continue for days or weeks following the loss as friends and family bring food, send cards, or stop by to visit.

Many times, people show their emotions during this time, but sometimes a person can be so surprised or overwhelmed by the death that he or she doesn't show any emotion right away—even though the loss is very hard. For example, Joey's friends expected he'd be really upset at his mom's funeral, so they were surprised that he was smiling and talking with people as if nothing had happened. When they asked him about it, Joey said that seeing his friends at the funeral cheered him up because it reminded him that some things would still be the same. Joey was able to cry and talk about how he felt when he was alone with his dad after the funeral.

Sometimes, when the rituals associated with grieving end, people might feel like they should be "over it" because everything seems to have gone back to normal. When people who are grieving first go back to their normal activities, it might be hard to put their hearts into everyday things. Many people go back to doing regular things after a few days or a week, but although they may not talk about their loss as much, the grieving process continues.

It's natural to continue to have feelings and questions for a while after someone dies. It's also natural to begin to feel somewhat better. A lot depends on how your loss affects your life. It's OK to feel grief for days, weeks, or even longer, depending on how close you were to the person who died.

No matter how you choose to grieve, there's no one right way to do it. The grieving process is a gradual one that lasts longer for some people than others. There may be times when you worry that you'll never enjoy life the same way again, but this is a natural reaction after a loss.

Caring For Yourself

The loss of someone close to you can be stressful. It can help you to cope if you take care of yourself in certain small but important ways. Here are some that might help:

- **Remember that grief is a normal emotion:** Know that you can (and will) heal from your grief.

- **Participate in rituals:** Memorial services, funerals, and other traditions help people get through the first few days and honor the person who died.

- **Be with others:** Even informal gatherings of family and friends bring a sense of support and help people not to feel so isolated in the first days and weeks of their grief.

- **Talk about it when you can:** Some people find it helpful to tell the story of their loss or talk about their feelings. Sometimes a person doesn't feel like talking, and that's OK, too. No one should feel pressured to talk.

- **Express yourself:** Even if you don't feel like talking, find ways to express your emotions and thoughts. Start writing in a journal about the memories you have of the person you lost and how you're feeling since the loss. Or write a song, poem, or tribute about the person who died. You can do this privately or share it with others.

- **Exercise:** Exercise can help your mood. It may be hard to get motivated, so modify your usual routine if you need to.

- **Eat right:** You may feel like skipping meals or you may not feel hungry—but your body still needs nutritious foods.

- **Join a support group:** If you think you may be interested in attending a support group, ask an adult or school counselor about how to become involved. The thing to remember is that you don't have to be alone with your feelings or your pain.

- **Let your emotions be expressed and released:** Don't stop yourself from having a good cry if you feel one coming on. Don't worry if listening to particular songs or doing other activities is painful because it brings back memories of the person that you lost; this is common. After a while, it becomes less painful.

- **Create a memorial or tribute:** Plant a tree or garden, or memorialize the person in some fitting way, such as running in a charity run or walk (a breast cancer race, for example) in honor of the lost loved one.

🖝 Remember!!

Going forward and healing from grief doesn't mean forgetting about the person you lost. Getting back to enjoying your life doesn't mean you no longer miss the person; and how long it takes until you start to feel better isn't a measure of how much you loved the person. With time, the loving support of family and friends, and your own positive actions, you can find ways to cope with even the deepest loss.

Getting Help For Intense Grief

If your grief isn't letting up for a while after the death of your loved one, you may want to reach out for help. If grief has turned into depression, it's very important to tell someone. How do you know if your grief has been going on too long? Here are some signs:

- You've been grieving for four months or more and you aren't feeling any better.

- You feel depressed.

- Your grief is so intense that you feel you can't go on with your normal activities.

- Your grief is affecting your ability to concentrate, sleep, eat, or socialize as you normally do.

- You feel you can't go on living after the loss or you think about suicide, dying, or hurting yourself.

It's natural for loss to cause people to think about death to some degree, but if a loss has caused you to think about suicide or hurting yourself in some way, or if you feel that you can't go on living after your loss, it's important that you tell someone right away.

Counseling with a professional therapist can help because it allows you to talk about your loss and express strong feelings. Many counselors specialize in working with teens who are struggling with loss and depression. If you'd like to talk to a therapist and you're not sure where to begin, ask an adult or school counselor. Your doctor may also be able to recommend someone.

Will I Ever Get Over This?

Well-meaning friends and family might tell a grieving person they need to "move on" after a loss. Unfortunately, that type of advice can sometimes make people hesitate to talk about their loss, or make people think they're grieving wrong or too long, or that they're not normal. Every person takes his or her own time to heal after a loss. The way someone grieves a particular loss and the time it takes is very individual.

It's important for grieving people to not drop out of life, though. If you don't like the idea of moving on, maybe the idea of "keeping on" seems like a better fit. Sometimes it helps to remind yourself to just keep on doing the best you can for now. If you feel sad, let yourself have your feelings and try not to run away from your emotions; but also keep on doing things you normally would such as being with friends, caring for your pet, working out, or doing your schoolwork.

Chapter 9

If Your Parent Has A Substance Abuse Problem Or Mental Illness

If Your Mom Or Dad Drinks Too Much Or Uses Drugs

Millions of youth like yourself worry about their parents drinking too much or using drugs. It's a big problem that happens in every kind of family, whether rich or poor, single parent, or traditional or blended family, and families that attend places of worship.

When you parents have been drinking, do they:

• embarrass you?

• blame you for things you didn't do?

• break promises?

• drive under the influence?

• behave in confusing and unpredictable ways?

About This Chapter: This chapter includes text from "It Feels So Bad... It Doesn't Have To," © 2005, and "Questions and Answers About Addiction," © 2006; both reprinted with permission by the National Association for Children of Alcoholics (www.nacoa.org). The chapter concludes with "When Your Parent Has a Mental Illness," http://www.couns.uiuc.edu/brochures/parents.htm, © 1995 University of Illinois at Urbana-Champaign Counseling Center. Reprinted with permission. Despite the age of this document, the suggestions it offers are still pertinent.

Your parent could be misusing or be addicted to alcohol or drugs. Addiction to alcohol or drugs is a disease. People with this disease often do things that are confusing and hurtful. They need help to stop the alcohol or drug use. Sometimes that help is through an alcohol or drug abuse program; sometimes it is through Alcoholics Anonymous or other self-help groups, which often meet in churches and synagogues. These groups have helped millions of moms and dads recover, regain their health, and begin to heal their families. Caring adults are available to help your mom or dad get the treatment and recovery support they need.

✔ Quick Tip
What should you do if it is your friend's mom or dad who drinks too much?

Don't walk away, and don't pretend you don't see it.

Things you can say that might help:

• It's not your fault that your parent drinks or uses drugs.

• You're not alone—lots of kids come from families where this is a problem.

• There are people who can help.

Things you can do:

• Tell your pastor or youth minister that you are worried about your friend.

• Be a good friend—include your friend in your activities and your family's fun.

• Encourage your friend to talk to a trusting adult.

Source: © 2005; reprinted with permission by the National Association for Children of Alcoholics.

Things You Should Know

Lots of teens live in families with alcohol abuse or alcoholism—one in four. Many also live with parental drug abuse. You are not alone.

Addiction to alcohol or drugs affects all members of the family, even if only one person has this disease. This is why it is called a "family disease."

Nothing you have done has ever caused anyone else to drink too much or use drugs. It's not your fault. You need and deserve help for your self.

You didn't CAUSE it.

You can't CURE it.

You can't CONTROL it.

BUT

You can take better care of yourself by communicating your feelings, making healthy choices, and celebrating yourself.

People with alcohol or drug addiction in their families are at greater risk of getting this disease when they choose to drink or use drugs. You can never get this disease if you don't drink or use drugs.

It is important for you to concentrate on finding help and support for yourself.

Take Care Of Yourself

If you feel bad because your mom or dad is drinking too much or using drugs, there are steps you can take to make things better for yourself even though you cannot stop your parent from drinking or using:

Talk to a caring adult: There are many adults who will listen and help you deal with problems at home, even when it seems no one has noticed. Sometimes they are not sure if you want or need support and are waiting for you to say something first. Often a teacher, a counselor at school, a youth minister, a coach, doctor, nurse, friend's parent, grandparent, aunt, or uncle is knowledgeable and anxious to help.

Families with alcohol or drug problems often try to keep it a secret: It is important to find caring adults who can help you. Taking to them really helps, and it is not being disloyal to your family if you seek help for yourself.

If you don't get the help you need from the first person you approach, it is important to reach out to another adult you can trust.

Get involved in youth programs: Join in activities offered through your church or synagogue, your school's extracurricular programs, or your community recreational departments. Here you can hang out with other young people, use your special talents and strengths, and learn now skills while making friends and having fun.

♣ It's A Fact!!

Alateen is a group for teens who are affected by someone else's alcohol or drug use. It holds meetings, like a club, where young people share tips on how to make their lives easier when a family member drinks too much or uses drugs.

The meetings are sponsored by Al-Anon. You can find the location of meetings near you by looking in the phone book under Al-Anon or Alateen, or ask a youth minister, your school counselor, your doctor or another adult you trust to help you get to a meeting near you. You can also find out about Alateen at www.alateen.org or by calling toll-free at 1-888-425-2666.

Source: © 2005; reprinted with permission by the National Association for Children of Alcoholics.

Join A Support Group

Many schools have assistance programs that offer support groups for students who are living with alcohol or drug abuse in their families. These programs help with problem solving, and they give you the opportunity to meet other young people who are struggling with the same problems at home that you might face. They can help you see how others are able to have a good life in spite of what is happening at home.

Questions And Answers About Addiction

What is alcoholism?

Alcoholism is a disease. People who have the disease have lost control over their drinking and are not able to stop without help. They also lose control over how they act when they are drunk.

How does alcoholism start?

Doctors don't know all the reasons why people become alcoholics. Some start out drinking a little bit and end up hooked on alcohol. A person might drink to forget problems or to calm nerves, but then they end up needing alcohol to feel normal. Once a person loses control over drinking, he or she needs help to stop drinking.

If the alcoholic is sick why doesn't he or she just go to the hospital?

At first, the alcoholic is not aware that he or she is ill. Even when the alcoholic becomes aware that something is wrong, he or she may not believe that alcohol is the problem. An alcoholic might keep blaming things on other people, or might blame their job, or the house, or whatever. But, really, it's the alcohol that's the biggest problem.

Is there an "average" alcoholic?

No. There is no such person as the average alcoholic. Alcoholics can be young, old, rich, poor, male, or female.

What is the cure for alcoholism?

There is no cure for alcoholism except stopping the disease process by stopping the drinking. People with alcoholism who have completely stopped drinking are called "recovering alcoholics". Recovering alcoholics can lead healthy, happy, productive lives.

Can family members make an alcoholic stop drinking?

No. It is important to know that an alcoholic needs help to stop drinking, but no one can be forced to accept the help, no matter how hard you try or what you do. It is also important to know that family members by themselves cannot provide the help that an alcoholic needs. An alcoholic needs the help of people trained to treat the disease.

I know I can't make my alcoholic parent stop drinking, so what can I do to make myself feel better?

Talk to someone you trust about the problem. Talk to a teacher, a Scout leader, a coach, a school counselor. Also, there is a group for kids who have alcoholic parents called Alateen. Alateen has meetings, like a club, and the kids share tips on how to make life easier. You can look for the phone number of Alateen in the phone book or call directory assistance for the number of Alateen. Someone at Al-Anon or the Alcoholics Anonymous answer line can probably tell you how to find the meetings too. Ask at school if there are any Alateen groups or school-sponsored support groups.

When Your Parent Has A Mental Illness

Growing up in any family can be challenging at times, but there are often special problems and challenges for families in which one or both parents have a mental illness. Children in these families often have to deal with instability or unpredictability. Often there is confusion in family roles and children have to take over many of the adult responsibilities, such as taking care of younger brothers and sisters or managing household duties normally managed by adults. They may even have the responsibility of taking care of the emotional or physical needs of their parents.

Children in these situations do not always receive the parental care and nurturing they need. Often they feel ashamed to talk about their situation with others and consequently may withdraw from relatives or friends who could help them or support them. Often unable to articulate their needs, even to themselves, these children frequently feel isolated and alone.

Children of mentally ill parents may also experience added difficulties as adults. These may include relationship difficulties:

> ♣ **It's A Fact!!**
>
> **How many children in the United States**
> **have at least one alcoholic parent?**
>
> About eleven million children in our country are growing up with at least one alcoholic parent. There are probably a few in your class right now. And remember, some adults grew up with alcoholic parents too.
>
> Source: © 2006; reprinted with permission by the National Association for Children of Alcoholics.

- difficulty in initiating relationships, and experiencing feelings of isolation
- difficulty in romantic relationships
- difficulty in maintaining friendships
- difficulty with trusting self and others
- difficulty balancing level of intimacy (excessive dependence or excessive avoidance)
- difficulty balancing taking care of self and taking care of others

  Difficulties may also include emotional concerns:

- guilt, resentment
- shame, embarrassment
- depression
- fear of inheriting parent's mental illness
- fear of discovery by partner, friends
- inability to express anger constructively, angry outbursts or repressed anger
- confusion about one's own identity
- negative outlook on life

- inability to deal with life unless it is chaotic or in crisis

- overly responsible or irresponsible in many areas of life such as commitments, money, alcohol, relationships, etc.

- self defeating thoughts, attitudes, and behaviors such as "I don't matter. I'm not worth much. It's no use trying."

- self defeating themes involving a tendency to equate achievement with worth as a person, such as: "Maybe I can matter if I can excel at something, be perfect in school, my job, my relationships. But if I fail, I'm worthless and it's terrible."

If you are experiencing any of these difficulties, you are not alone. It is helpful to recognize that these problematic feelings and behaviors helped you to cope and survive the more vulnerable years of childhood. Your recognition that they limit your life choices now is the beginning of your search for more rewarding and functional ways of relating.

How You Can Help Yourself

Acknowledge that you have a parent with a mental illness and acknowledge the effects this has had on you:

- Acknowledge previously inadmissible feelings such as anger, shame, guilt, etc.

- Grieve the parental support you never received.

- Remember that you are not responsible for causing your parent's problems or for fixing his/her condition.

Develop new ways of taking care of yourself:

- Recognize your own legitimate needs and begin taking care of them.

- Recognize the stressors in your life, and learn ways of managing them.

- Replace negative thoughts with more positive statements: "I am a worthwhile person. This truth does not depend on my successes or failures. My life has ups and downs, but my worth does not change."

Develop new ways of relating to others:

• Recognize old unhealthy family patterns of communicating, and practice new ways of relating to parents and other family members.

• Recognize the difficulties you have with relationships, and learn new ways of relating to others.

• Appreciate and enjoy stability in your relationships, recognizing that relationships don't have to be defined by crisis or dependency.

• Explore other resources.

Educate yourself about your parent's illness. This can help you understand what your parent is facing and what has caused problems for your family. It can also aid in relieving your feelings of guilt, resentment, embarrassment, and shame.

Consider seeing a mental health professional. A counselor an help you understand how your parent's illness impacts your life. Also a counselor can help you learn healthier ways of relating to others and caring for your own needs.

Consider joining a support group. A support group that addresses your specific situation can help reduce feelings of isolation. Seeking such support can be especially helpful when family members are either uncomfortable with or refuse to acknowledge the problem.

Part Two

Mood And Anxiety Disorders

Chapter 10

Depression

Lately Lindsay hasn't felt like herself. Her friends have noticed it, too. Kia was surprised when Lindsay turned down her invitation to go shopping last Saturday (she always loves to shop). There was really no reason not to go, but Lindsay just didn't feel like it. Instead, she spent most of Saturday sleeping.

But staying in more than usual isn't the only change in Lindsay. She's always been a really good student, but over the past couple of months her grades have fallen pretty dramatically, and she has trouble concentrating. She's even failed a couple of tests, and she hasn't yet turned in a paper that was due last week.

When she gets home from practice, she's not hungry for dinner. Though she usually manages to eat a little something with her family, she just doesn't have much of an appetite—and nothing seems to taste as good as it used to. After dinner, Lindsay goes to her room, does a bit of homework, and goes to bed. She's not even in the mood to talk on the phone with her friends.

About This Chapter: This information was provided by TeensHealth, one of the largest resources online for medically reviewed health information written for parents, kids, and teens. For more articles like this one, visit www.TeensHealth.org, or www.KidsHealth.org. © 2004 The Nemours Center for Children's Health Media, a division of The Nemours Foundation.

When her mother asks her what's wrong, Lindsay feels like crying but doesn't know why. Everything seems wrong, yet nothing particularly bad has happened. Lindsay just feels sad all the time and can't shake it. Lindsay may not realize it yet, but she is depressed.

Depression is very common and affects as many as one in eight people in their teen years. Depression affects people of every color, race, economic status, or age; however, it does seem to affect more females than males during adolescence and adulthood.

How Do People Respond To Someone Who's Depressed?

Sometimes friends or family members can recognize that a person is depressed. They may respond with love, kindness, or support, hoping that the sadness will soon pass. They may offer to listen if the person wants to talk—although depressed people often don't feel much like talking or can't find the words to describe what's wrong. If the depressed feeling doesn't pass with a little time, friends or loved ones may encourage the person to get help from a doctor or mental health professional.

But not everyone recognizes depression when it happens to someone they know; and some people have incorrect ideas about what it means to be depressed. People who don't understand may react to the depressed person's low energy with criticism, scolding them for acting lazy or not trying. Some people mistakenly believe that depression is simply an attitude a person can change or a mood they can shake. It's not that easy.

♣ It's A Fact!!

Sure, everybody feels sad or blue now and then. But if you're sad most of the time, and it's giving you problems with:

- your grades or attendance at school,

- your relationships with your family and friends,

- alcohol, drugs, or sex,

- controlling your behavior in other ways,

the problem may be depression.

Source: Excerpted from "Let's Talk about Depression," National Institute of Mental Health, 2001.

Many people just don't realize that depression can cause so many problems or so much pain. Sometimes even people who are depressed don't take their condition seriously enough. Some people have the mistaken belief that depression comes from weakness or is a character flaw. This myth causes some people to hide their depression. Feeling embarrassed, they may avoid getting help.

Occasionally, when depression causes physical symptoms, a person may see their doctor and be relieved to have a normal physical exam. Once in a while, even a well-meaning doctor may minimize or even overlook a person's depression by concluding that there's nothing wrong when medical tests come back normal.

Why Do People Get Depressed?

There is no single cause for depression. Many factors play a role including genetics, environment, medical conditions, life events, and certain thinking patterns that affect a person's reaction to events.

Research has revealed that depression runs in families and suggests that some people inherit genes that make it more likely for them to get depressed; but not everyone who has the genetic makeup for depression actually gets depression. And many people who have no family history of depression have the condition. So, although genes are one factor, they aren't the single cause of depression.

Life events—for example, the death of a close family member or friend—can go beyond normal grief and can sometimes lead to depression.

Family and social environment also play a role. For some teens, a negative, stressful, or unhappy family atmosphere can affect their self-esteem and lead to depression.

Social conditions like poverty, homelessness, and community violence can make it more likely for people to become depressed.

For some teens, undiagnosed learning disabilities may block school success, hormonal changes may affect mood, or physical illness may present challenges or setbacks. With or without the genetics for depression, any of these can set the stage for depression.

Substance abuse can cause chemical changes in the brain that affect mood—alcohol and some drugs are known to have depressant effects. The negative social and personal consequences of substance abuse can also lead to severe unhappiness and depression.

Certain medical conditions can affect hormone balance and therefore have an effect on mood. Some conditions, such as hypothyroidism, are known to cause a depressed mood in some people. When these medical conditions are diagnosed and treated by a doctor, the depression usually disappears.

What Happens In The Brain When Someone Is Depressed?

Depression involves the brain's delicate chemistry—specifically, it involves chemicals called neurotransmitters. These chemicals assist in transmitting messages between nerve cells in the brain.

Certain neurotransmitters regulate mood. When they are not available in sufficient quantities, the result can be depression.

The brain's response to stressful events, such as any of those described above, may alter the balance of neurotransmitters and result in depression.

Sometimes, a person may experience depression without any particular sad or stressful event that they can point to. People who have a genetic predisposition to depression may be more prone to the imbalance of neurotransmitter activity that is part of depression.

♣ It's A Fact!!

Sometimes people get seriously depressed after something like a divorce in the family, major financial problems, someone you love dying, a messed up home life, or breaking up with a boyfriend or girlfriend.

Other times—like with other illnesses—depression just happens. Often teenagers react to the pain of depression by getting into trouble: trouble with alcohol, drugs, or sex; trouble with school or bad grades; problems with family or friends. This is another reason why it's important to get treatment for depression before it leads to other trouble.

Source: Excerpted from "Let's Talk about Depression," National Institute of Mental Health, 2001.

Medications that are used to treat depression work by helping to restore the proper balance of neurotransmitters.

Types Of Depression

For some people, depression can be intense and occur in bouts that last for weeks at a time. For others, depression can be less severe but can linger at a low level for years.

Doctors who treat depression distinguish between these two forms, diagnosing the more severe, short-lasting form as major depression, and the longer-lasting but less severe form as dysthymia.

A third form of depression that may be diagnosed is called adjustment disorder with depressed mood. It refers to a depressive reaction to a specific life event (such as a death, divorce, or other loss) when the adjustment to the loss takes longer than the normally expected time frame or is more severe than expected and interferes with the person's daily activities.

Bipolar disorder (also sometimes called manic depressive illness) is another depressive condition that involves periods of major depression mixed with periods of mania. Mania is the term for abnormally high mood and extreme bursts of unusual activity or energy.

What Are The Symptoms Of Depression?

These are some symptoms that people have when they're depressed:

- depressed mood or sadness most of the time (for what may seem like no reason)

- lack of energy and feeling tired all the time

- inability to enjoy things that used to bring pleasure

- withdrawal from friends and family

- irritability, anger, or anxiety

- inability to concentrate

- significant weight loss or gain

- significant change in sleep patterns (inability to fall asleep, stay asleep, or get up in the morning)

- feelings of guilt or worthlessness

- aches and pains (even though nothing is physically wrong)

- pessimism and indifference (not caring about anything in the present or future)

- thoughts of death or suicide

When someone has five or more of these symptoms most of the time for two weeks or longer, that person is probably depressed. Sometimes people go through bouts where these symptoms are really intense; other times these same feelings could be present at a lower level all the time for years. Some people have just one episode of depression, or they may go on to have more than one after being better for a while. When a person has had more than one bout with major depression, a doctor will diagnose the person as having major depressive disorder.

Teens who are depressed may also show other warning signs or symptoms. They may have increased problems at school because of skipped classes, lack of interest or motivation, or poor concentration and low mental energy caused by depression. Some teens drop out altogether, expecting to fail because of their problems.

For depressed teens who are already feeling self-critical and experiencing low self-esteem, a failure experience at school may simply be more than they can bear. They may not realize that depression is causing concentration problems, and their negative thoughts are probably causing them to mistakenly conclude that they are stupid. They also may express feelings of anger or indifference by drinking or doing drugs.

Some teens with depression have other problems, too, that can intensify their feelings of worthlessness or inner pain. Teens who cut themselves, those who have extreme feelings of ugliness, and teens who have eating disorders may have unrecognized depression that needs attention.

Everyone has some ups and downs, and occasional sadness is a normal emotion. The normal stresses of life can cause teens to feel sad every once in a while. Things like an argument with a friend, a breakup, doing poorly on a test, not being chosen for a sport, a best friend moving out of town, or the death of a loved one can lead to feelings of sadness, hurt, disappointment, or grief. These reactions are usually brief and go away with a little time and care.

Depression is more than feeling blue, sad, or down in the dumps once in a while, though. Depression is a strong mood involving sadness, discouragement, despair, or hopelessness that lasts for weeks, months, or even longer, and interferes with a person's ability to participate in their normal activities.

Depression affects a person's thoughts, outlook, and behavior as well as their mood. In addition to a depressed mood, a person with depression may also experience other symptoms like tiredness, irritability, and appetite changes.

When a person has depression, the world looks bleak, and the person's thoughts reflect the hopelessness and helplessness they feel. People with depression tend to have negative and self-critical thoughts. Sometimes, despite their true value, people with depression can feel worthless and unlovable.

Depression can cloud everything, making even small problems seem overwhelming. People who are depressed can't see a bright future ahead and feel powerless to change things for the better. They may feel like giving up. They may cry at small things or cry for no apparent reason at all.

Because of their deep feelings of sadness and their low energy, people with depression sometimes pull away from people around them or from activities they once enjoyed. This only causes them to feel more lonely and isolated, making the depression worse.

Depression can be mild or severe. At its worst, depression can create such feelings of despair that a person thinks about suicide.

Depression can cause physical symptoms, too. Some people have an upset stomach, loss of appetite, weight gain or loss, headaches, and sleeping problems when they're depressed.

Getting Help

Depression is one of the most common emotional problems. The good news is that it's also one of the most treatable conditions. There are professionals who can help. In fact, about 80% of people who get help for their depression have a better quality of life—they function better and enjoy themselves in a way that they weren't able to before.

Treatment for depression can include talk therapy, medication, or a combination of both.

Talk therapy with a mental health professional is very effective in treating depression. Therapy sessions help people understand depression and what they can do about it.

Sometimes medicine may be prescribed for a person who has depression. When a doctor prescribes medicine, he or she will carefully monitor the person to make sure he or she gets the right dose. The doctor will adjust the dose as necessary. Medicines can take a few weeks before the person feels the medicine working. Because every person's brain is different, what works well for one person might not be good for another.

♣ It's A Fact!!
Be Able To Tell Fact From Fiction

Myths about depression often prevent people from doing the right thing. Some common myths are as follows:

Myth: It's normal for teenagers to be moody; teens don't suffer from real depression.

Fact: Depression is more than just being moody, and it can affect people at any age, including teenagers.

Myth: Telling an adult that a friend might be depressed is betraying a trust. If someone wants help, he or she will get it.

Fact: Depression, which saps energy and self-esteem, interferes with a person's ability or wish to get help. It is an act of true friendship to share your concerns with an adult who can help.

Myth: Talking about depression only makes it worse.

Fact: Talking through feelings with a good friend is often a helpful first step. Friendship, concern, and support can provide the encouragement to talk to a parent or other trusted adult about getting evaluated for depression.

Source: Excerpted from "Let's Talk about Depression," National Institute of Mental Health, 2001.

People who are depressed shouldn't wait and hope it will go away on its own because depression can be effectively treated. Friends or others need to step in if someone seems severely depressed and isn't getting help. Many teens find that opening up to parents or to other adults they trust can help. Simply saying, "I've been feeling really down lately and I think I'm depressed," can be a good way to open the discussion. Ask your parent to arrange an appointment with a therapist.

People who are extremely depressed and who may be thinking about hurting themselves or about suicide need help as soon as possible. When depression is this severe, it is a very real medical emergency, and an adult must be notified. Most communities have suicide hotlines where people can get guidance and support in an emergency.

Although it's important to be supportive, trying to cheer up a friend or reasoning with him or her probably won't work to help depression or suicidal feelings go away. Depression can be so strong that it outweighs a person's ability to respond to reason. Even if your friend has asked you to promise not to tell, this is a situation where telling can save a life. The most important thing a depressed person can do is to get the right treatment.

Depression—and the suffering that goes with depression—is real. Depression doesn't make a person "crazy." Just as things can go wrong in all other organs of the body, things can go wrong in the most important organ of all, the brain. Luckily, most teens who get help for their depression go on to have fulfilling, happy teen and adult years—and most importantly, to enjoy life and feel better about themselves.

♣ It's A Fact!!
What You Need To Know About Suicide

Most people who are depressed do not commit suicide. But depression increases the risk for suicide or suicide attempts. It is not true that people who talk about suicide do not attempt it. Suicidal thoughts, remarks, or attempts are always serious, if any of these happen to you or a friend, you must tell a responsible adult immediately, it's better to be safe than sorry.

Source: Excerpted from "Let's Talk about Depression,"
National Institute of Mental Health, 2001.

Chapter 11

Dysthymia

Dysthymia is a mild form of chronic depression, which leaves a person living a life where objectively they function reasonably but lack a sense of competence and self worth. Dysthymia literally means "ill humored" and captures well the subjective and objective experience of the disorders. Life lacks color and definition. A person suffering from dysthymia has a marked inability to derive pleasure from events or stimuli previously found pleasurable. Life lacks joy, color, vibrancy, and pleasure. People with dysthymia tend to be irritable, self-critical, and ruminate about past events, disappointments, or personal slights. Over time people with dysthymia become socially withdrawn and isolated. This is likely because of their inability to derive or give pleasure within social relationships.

Many people with dysthymia are unaware that they suffer from a treatable condition and will seek relief through alcohol and drugs, which only compounds their problem. This disorder robs people of life's pleasures and it can steal away their life. Research experts estimate anywhere from 3 to 12 percent of people with dysthymia end their suffering through suicide.

It is estimated that about three to five percent of the general population suffer from dysthymia and is slightly more prevalent among women than men. Children, teens, and the elderly can experience dysthymia but their

About This Chapter: Text in this chapter is from "Dysthymia," an undated fact sheet, © Mood Disorders Society of Canada (www.mooddisorderscanada.ca). Reprinted with permission.

mood will more often be irritable than depressed. For some it has been a life long experience, others report a single or multiple episodes over their lifetime. Some people go on to develop a major depressive disorders or others developing dysthymia following an acute episode of depression. This is important to note because it may be that there has been an incomplete response to treatment.

Dysthymia has been called many things including: neurotic depression, minor depression, intermittent depression, and depressive personality. In the past, it was felt this disorder was fairly fixed part of temperament but research supports the benefits of getting treatment. Getting a diagnosis of dysthymia can now open the door to relief from suffering.

What causes dysthymia?

The exact cause of dysthymia is not known. Like other depressive conditions may be precipitated by the interaction of a number of factors:

- Research has indicated that individuals can inherit a predisposition to develop depressive conditions. Individuals who have family members who have suffered from depression may have an increased risk of contracting such disorders themselves.

- Imbalances or impaired functioning in the brain chemistry is associated with mood and changes in brain neurotransmitters can have an effect on thoughts, emotions and behavior.

- Environmental factors may also give rise to depressive conditions. Disappointment, stress and/or trauma resulting from such things as unemployment, personal failure or tragedies, and family breakdown, can all precipitate depression.

> ♣ It's A Fact!!
> ## How is a diagnosed of dysthymia made?
>
> To receive a diagnosis of dysthymia a depressed mood must be present for over two years, occurring on an almost daily basis, and with at least two of the following symptoms:
>
> - poor appetite or overeating
> - insomnia or oversleeping
> - fatigue or low energy
> - low self-esteem
> - poor concentration
> - problems in decision making
> - hopelessness

- Psychological factors may contribute to the development of depression. For example, behavioral explanations have suggested that depression may be a product of "learned helplessness" that arises from a repeated loss of positive reinforcement and a, perhaps, increased rate of negative life events among other things.

- The way in which one views the world can worsen depression by maintaining negative and/or unrealistic beliefs and attitudes about one's self, the people around us and what the future holds.

- The success in treating dysthymia with antidepressant medication suggests it may have biological underpinnings. Researchers are currently exploring possible immunology, hormonal and neurotransmitter connections to dysthymia.

How is dysthymia treated?

The treatment for dysthymia is similar to the treatment of major depression and research shows that it requires just as aggressive a course and length of treatment. A combination of treatments is found to have the greatest effect.

- **Medication:** Research shows a positive response to antidepressant medication, especially to the newer generation of drugs such as Prozac, Zoloft, Paxil, Effexor and Serzone.

- **Cognitive therapy:** A unique form of talk therapy, cognitive therapy helps you understand how your thoughts affect your feelings and your feelings drive your behavior. Research suggests that cognitive therapy can help to treat depression and prevent illness relapse. Accessing cognitive therapy is difficult in more urban areas and often impossible in rural communities. However there are some excellent self-directed cognitive therapy handbooks available to guide you.

- **Interpersonal therapy:** A relatively new form of brief individual psychological therapy, IPT has been demonstrated to be effective in treating dysthymia. IPT focuses on treating dysthymia by addressing interpersonal relationship problems associated with, or affected by the depressive mood. It is based on the belief that strengthening patients' social support systems enhances their ability to cope. Ultimately, this helps to alleviate the depression.

• **Peer support:** Learning more about your disorder and seeking information and support in how cope with a mood disorders has been found to have a positive impact on recovery and prevention of relapse.

Chapter 12

Seasonal Affective Disorder

Maggie started off her junior year of high school with great energy. She had no trouble keeping up with her schoolwork and was involved in several after-school activities; but after the Thanksgiving break, she began to have difficulty getting through her assigned reading and had to work harder to apply herself. She couldn't concentrate in class, and after school all she wanted to do was sleep. Her grades began to drop, and she rarely felt like socializing. Even though Maggie was always punctual before, she began to have trouble getting up on time and was absent or late from school many days during the winter.

At first, Maggie's parents thought she was slacking off. They were upset with her, but they figured it was just a phase—especially since her energy finally seemed to return in the spring, but when the same thing happened the following November, they took Maggie to the doctor, who diagnosed her with a type of depression called seasonal affective disorder.

What Is Seasonal Affective Disorder?

Seasonal affective disorder (SAD) is a form of depression that appears at the same time each year. With SAD, a person typically has symptoms of

About This Chapter: This information was provided by TeensHealth, one of the largest resources online for medically reviewed health information written for parents, kids, and teens. For more articles like this one, visit www.TeensHealth.org, or www.KidsHealth.org. © 2005 The Nemours Center for Children's Health Media, a division of The Nemours Foundation.

depression and unexplained fatigue as winter approaches and daylight hours become shorter. When spring returns and days become longer again, people with SAD experience relief from their symptoms, returning to their usual mood and energy level.

What Causes SAD?

Experts believe that, with SAD, depression is somehow triggered by the brain's response to decreased daylight exposure. No one really understands how and why this happens. Current theories about what causes SAD focus on the role that sunlight might play in the brain's production of key hormones. Experts think that two specific chemicals in the brain, melatonin and serotonin, may be involved in SAD. These two hormones help regulate a person's sleep-wake cycles, energy, and mood. Shorter days and longer hours of darkness in fall and winter may cause increased levels of melatonin and decreased levels of serotonin, creating the biological conditions for depression.

♣ **It's A Fact!!**
In rare cases, SAD has a reverse seasonal pattern, with depression occurring only during the summer months.

Melatonin is linked to sleep. The body produces this hormone in greater quantities when it's dark or when days are shorter. This increased production of melatonin can cause a person to feel sleepy and lethargic. With serotonin, it's the reverse—serotonin production goes up when a person is exposed to sunlight, so it's likely that a person will have lower levels of serotonin during the winter when the days are shorter. Low levels of serotonin are associated with depression, whereas increasing the availability of serotonin helps to combat depression.

What Are The Symptoms Of SAD?

A person with SAD will show several particular changes from the way he or she normally feels and acts. These changes occur in a predictable seasonal pattern. The symptoms of SAD are the same as symptoms of depression, and a person with SAD may notice several or all of these symptoms:

- **Changes in mood:** A person may feel sad or be in an irritable mood most of the time for at least two weeks during a specific time of year. During that time, a guy or girl may feel a sense of hopelessness or worthlessness. As part of the mood change that goes with SAD, people can be self-critical; they may also be more sensitive than usual to criticism and cry or get upset more often or more easily.

- **Lack of enjoyment:** Someone with SAD may lose interest in things he or she normally likes to do and may seem unable to enjoy things as before. People with SAD can also feel like they no longer do certain tasks as well as they used to, and they may have feelings of dissatisfaction or guilt. A person with SAD may seem to lose interest in friends and may stop participating in social activities.

- **Low energy:** Unusual tiredness or unexplained fatigue is also part of SAD and can cause people to feel low on energy.

- **Changes in sleep:** A person may sleep much more than usual. Excessive sleeping can make it impossible for a student to get up and get ready for school in the morning.

- **Changes in eating:** Changes in eating and appetite related to SAD may include cravings for simple carbohydrates (think comfort foods and sugary foods) and the tendency to overeat. Because of this change in eating, SAD can result in weight gain during the winter months.

- **Difficulty concentrating:** SAD can affect concentration, too, interfering with a person's school performance and grades. A student may have more trouble than usual completing assignments on time or seem to lack his or her usual motivation. A person with SAD may notice that his or her grades may drop, and teachers may comment that the person seems to have less motivation or is making less effort in school.

- **Less time socializing:** People with SAD may spend less time with friends, in social activities, or in extracurricular activities.

The problems caused by SAD, such as lower-than-usual grades or less energy for socializing with friends, can affect self-esteem and leave a person feeling disappointed, isolated, and lonely—especially if he or she doesn't realize what's causing the changes in energy, mood, and motivation.

Who Gets SAD?

SAD can affect adults, teens, and children. It's estimated that about 6 in every 100 people (6%) experience SAD. The prevalence of SAD varies from region to region. One study of SAD in the United States found the rates of SAD were seven times higher among people in New Hampshire than in Florida, suggesting that the farther someone lives from the equator, the more likely they are to develop SAD. Interestingly, when people who get SAD travel to lower latitude areas during winter (those far south of the equator that experience longer daylight hours during winter months), they do not experience their seasonal symptoms. This supports the theory that SAD is related to light exposure.

♣ **It's A Fact!!**

Like other forms of depression, the symptoms of SAD can be mild, severe, or anywhere in between. Milder symptoms interfere less with someone's ability to participate in everyday activities, but stronger symptoms can interfere much more. It's the seasonal pattern of SAD—the fact that symptoms occur only for a few months each winter (for at least two years in a row) but not during other seasons—that distinguishes SAD from other forms of depression.

Most people don't experience seasonal depression (SAD), even if they live in areas where days are shorter during winter months. Experts don't fully understand why certain individuals are more likely to experience SAD than others. It may be that some people are more sensitive than others to variations in light, and therefore may experience more dramatic shifts in hormone production, depending on their exposure to light.

Like other forms of depression, females are about four times more likely than males to develop SAD, as are people with relatives who have experienced depression. Individual biology, brain chemistry, family history, environment, and life experiences may also make certain individuals more prone to SAD and other forms of depression.

Researchers are continuing to investigate what leads to SAD, as well as why some people are more likely than others to experience it.

How Is SAD Diagnosed And Treated?

Doctors and mental health professionals make a diagnosis of SAD after a careful evaluation. A medical checkup is also important to make sure that symptoms aren't due to a medical condition that needs treatment. Tiredness, fatigue, and low energy could be a sign of another medical condition such as hypothyroidism, hypoglycemia, or mononucleosis. Other medical conditions can cause appetite changes, sleep changes, or extreme fatigue.

Once a person's been diagnosed with SAD, doctors may recommend one of several treatments:

Increased Light Exposure: Because the symptoms of SAD are triggered by lack of exposure to light, and they tend to go away on their own when available light increases, treatment for SAD often involves increased exposure to light during winter months. For someone with mild symptoms, it may be enough to spend more time outside during the daylight hours, perhaps by exercising outdoors or taking a daily walk. Full spectrum (daylight) lightbulbs that fit in regular lamps can help bring a bit more daylight into your home in winter months and might help with mild symptoms.

Light Therapy: Stronger symptoms of SAD may be treated with light therapy (also called phototherapy). Light therapy involves the use of a special light that simulates daylight. A special light box or panel is placed on a tabletop or desk, and the person sits in front of the light for a short period of time every day (45 minutes a day or so, usually in the morning). The person should occasionally glance at the light (the light has to be absorbed through the retinas in order to work), but not stare into it for long periods. Symptoms tend to improve within a few days in some cases or within a few weeks in others. Generally, doctors recommend the use of light therapy until enough sunlight is available outdoors.

Like any medical treatment, light treatment should only be used under the supervision of a doctor. People who have another type of depressive disorder, skin that's sensitive to light, or medical conditions that may make the eyes vulnerable to light damage should use light therapy with caution. The lights that are used for SAD phototherapy must filter out harmful UV rays. Tanning beds or booths should not be used to alleviate symptoms of SAD. Some mild side effects of phototherapy might include headache or eyestrain.

Talk Therapy: Talk therapy (psychotherapy) is also used to treat people with SAD. Talk therapy focuses on revising the negative thoughts and feelings associated with depression and helps ease the sense of isolation or loneliness that people with depression often feel. The support and guidance of a professional therapist can be helpful for someone experiencing SAD. Talk therapy can also help someone to learn about and understand their condition as well as learn what to do to prevent or minimize future bouts of seasonal depression.

Medication: Doctors may also prescribe medications for teens with SAD. Antidepressant medications help to regulate the balance of serotonin and other neurotransmitters in the brain that affect mood and energy. Medications need to be prescribed and monitored by a doctor. If your doctor prescribes medication for SAD or another form of depression, be sure to let him or her know about any other medications or remedies you may be taking, including over-the-counter or herbal medicines. These can interfere with prescription medications.

Dealing With SAD

When symptoms of SAD first develop, it can be confusing, both for the person with SAD and family and friends. Some parents or teachers may mistakenly think that teens with SAD are slacking off or not trying their best. If you think you're experiencing some of the symptoms of SAD, talk to a parent, guidance counselor, or other trusted adult about what you're feeling.

If you've been diagnosed with SAD, there are a few things you can do to help:

• Follow your doctor's recommendations for treatment.

• Learn all you can about SAD and explain the condition to others so they can work with you.

• Get plenty of exercise, especially outdoors. Exercise can be a mood lifter.

• Spend time with friends and loved ones who understand what you're going through—they can help provide you with personal contact and a sense of connection.

• Be patient: Don't expect your symptoms to go away immediately.

• Ask for help with homework and other assignments if you need it. If you feel you can't concentrate on things, remember that it's part of the disorder and that things will get better again. Talk to your teachers and work out a plan to get your assignments done.

• Eat right: It may be hard, but avoiding simple carbohydrates and sugary snacks and concentrating on plenty of whole grains, vegetables, and fruits can help you feel better in the long term.

• Develop a sleep routine: Regular bedtimes can help you reap the mental health benefits of daytime light.

☞ Remember!!

Depression in any form can be serious. If you think you have symptoms of any type of depression, talk to someone who can help you get treatment.

Chapter 13

The Menstrual Cycle And Mood Changes

Premenstrual Mood Changes

Many women in their reproductive years experience temporary physical and emotional changes around the time of their period. In fact, at least 75% of women with regular menstrual cycles report unpleasant physical or mental symptoms before their periods. For the majority of women, these symptoms are mild and tolerable. However, for a certain group of women, these symptoms can be disabling and may cause significant disruption in their lives.

Premenstrual Syndrome (PMS)

First introduced in the 1950s, the term "PMS" has been widely used by the popular press. PMS typically refers to a general pattern of physical, emotional, and behavioral symptoms occurring 1–2 weeks before the start of a woman's period (menses). PMS is common, affecting from 30–80% of women of reproductive age. The most common physical symptoms include abdominal bloating, headaches, muscle and joint pain, and breast tenderness. The behavioral symptoms most commonly observed in women with PMS are fatigue, forgetfulness, poor concentration, and mild mood changes, including irritability and depressed mood.

About This Chapter: From "PMS and Premenstrual Dysphoric Disorder," © 2001 Center for Women's Mental Health at Massachusetts General Hospital. Reprinted with permission.

Premenstrual Dysphoric Disorder (PMDD)

Premenstrual dysphoric disorder (PMDD) is a more severe form of premenstrual syndrome affecting 3–8% of women in their reproductive years. In contrast to PMS, PMDD is characterized by more significant premenstrual mood disturbance. The most common symptom is irritability; however, many women also report depressed mood, anxiety, or mood swings. These symptoms emerge one to two weeks preceding menses, and the symptoms stop completely when the woman's period begins. By definition, this mood disturbance results in marked social or occupational impairment, with its most noticeable effects in interpersonal functioning.

PMDD is a psychiatric diagnosis and is considered to be one of the affective (mood) disorders. It is classified as a "depressive disorder not otherwise specified" in the system of classification published by the American Psychiatric Association in the *Diagnostic and Statistical Manual (DSM-IV-TR)*. The difference between PMDD and other affective disorders is related to the cyclical nature of the mood disturbance. Unlike other affective disorders, mood symptoms are only present for a specific period of time, during the phase of the menstrual cycle after ovulation and before a period begins. Additionally, these mood symptoms do not occur in the absence of a menstrual cycle (such as during pregnancy or menopause).

♣ It's A Fact!!
PMS Psychological Symptoms

- Depression
- Anger
- Irritability
- Anxiety
- Sensitivity to rejection
- Sense of feeling overwhelmed
- Social withdrawal

PMS Physical Symptoms

- Lethargy or fatigue
- Sleep disturbance (usually sleeping too much)
- Appetite disturbance (usually increased)
- Abdominal bloating
- Breast tenderness
- Headaches
- Muscle aches, joint pain
- Swelling of extremities

Diagnosis

It is important for healthcare providers to distinguish between PMDD and other medical and psychiatric conditions. Medical illnesses such as chronic fatigue syndrome, fibromyalgia, irritable bowel syndrome, and migraine disorder can have features that overlap with PMDD. Additionally, psychiatric disorders such as depression or anxiety disorders can worsen during the premenstrual period and thus mimic PMDD. An estimated 40% of women who seek treatment for PMDD actually have an underlying mood disorder that is made worse premenstrually. The best way to confirm the diagnosis of PMDD is by daily charting of symptoms. Women with PMDD should experience a symptom-free interval between menses and ovulation.

What Causes PMS And PMDD?

Although the cause of PMS and PMDD remains uncertain at present, researchers now agree that these disorders have a biological cause; they are not purely psychological. Recent research indicates that women who are vulnerable to premenstrual mood changes do not have abnormal levels of hormones. They also do not have problems with how their hormones are regulated. Instead, it seems that they have a particular sensitivity to normal cyclical hormonal changes. Fluctuations in the amount of two hormones—estrogen and progesterone—circulating in the body cause noticeable effects on central neurotransmission (how nerve cells communicate with each other). Three "pathways" of neurotransmission may be involved: the serotonergic (involving serotonin, a hormone that affects emotions and other brain functions), noradrenergic (involving noradrenaline—which is also called norepinephrine—a hormone that is involved in the body's response to stress and other physical functions), and dopaminergic (involving dopamine, a hormone involved in feelings of pleasure and other moods). In particular, accumulating evidence implicates the serotonergic system in the development of PMS and PMDD. Recent data suggest that women with premenstrual mood disorders have abnormal serotonin neurotransmission, which is thought to be associated with symptoms such as irritability, depressed mood, and carbohydrate craving. There may also be some role for gamma amino-butyric acid (GABA), the main inhibitory neurotransmitter, in the development of PMS/PMDD, however this remains to be defined. Likewise, the potential involvement of other systems in these disorders has yet to be made clear.

Non-Drug Treatment For PMS And PMDD

Lifestyle changes can help to improve the symptoms of PMS and PMDD. For women with mild symptoms, these approaches should be tried before medications. Although solid evidence is lacking, healthcare providers generally recommend that patients with PMS or PMDD decrease or eliminate the intake of caffeine, sugar, and sodium. Other helpful lifestyle modifications include decreasing alcohol and nicotine use [but remember, teens should not use alcohol or nicotine products at all] and ensuring adequate sleep. Also, regular aerobic exercise has been shown to have beneficial effects on both the emotional and physical symptoms of PMS/PMDD.

Certain nutritional supplements have also been shown to improve premenstrual symptoms. A large, multicenter trial of calcium supplementation found that 1200 mg calcium a day significantly reduced both the physical and emotional symptoms of PMS. Other studies have demonstrated that Vitamin B_6 in doses of 50–100 mg a day can have beneficial effects in women with PMS; however, patients must be cautioned that doses above 100 mg a day can cause peripheral neuropathy (nerve damage that can affect the arms, hands, legs, and feet). Limited evidence suggests that magnesium (200–360 mg a day) and Vitamin E (400 IU a day) can provide modest relief of symptoms.

Herbal remedies may have some role in the treatment of premenstrual symptoms. One recent double-blind, placebo-controlled trial concluded that *Agnus castus* fruit extract (1 tab a day), also known as chasteberry, significantly decreased premenstrual symptoms of irritability, anger, headache, and breast fullness when compared to placebo. In another study, gingko biloba was found to improve PMS symptoms, particularly breast tenderness and fluid retention. Though early evidence suggested that evening primrose oil was a useful treatment of PMS, a recent review of studies found that it was no more effective than placebo. Other botanical remedies used clinically but which require further investigation include black cohosh, St. John's wort and kava kava.

Psychotherapy offers another non-drug approach to the treatment of PMS and PMDD. A recent study found that cognitive-behavioral therapy was as effective as fluoxetine (20 mg daily), in the treatment of women with PMDD. Other limited studies suggest that cognitive approaches can be useful in helping to reduce premenstrual symptoms.

Medications PMS And PMDD

Psychotropic Medications: Selective serotonin reuptake inhibitors (SSRIs) are the first-line drugs for the treatment of premenstrual mood symptoms. A significant body of evidence, including multiple double-blind, randomized studies, supports the effectiveness of SSRIs in reducing both the emotional, as well as physical symptoms, of PMS and PMDD. In general, women respond to low doses of SSRIs, and this treatment response usually occurs rapidly, often within several days. SSRIs may be prescribed continuously throughout the menstrual cycle or may be given in intermittent fashion during the premenstrual phase of the cycle. Also, other non-SSRI antidepressants which inhibit serotonin reuptake, including clomipramine (a tricyclic antidepressant), nefazodone (Serzone), and venlafaxine (Effexor) have evidence to endorse their use in the treatment of premenstrual symptoms.

Among other psychotropic medications used in the treatment of PMS and PMDD, benzodiazepine alprazolam (Xanax) has been shown to have benefit in reducing premenstrual symptoms, in particular premenstrual anxiety. However, this medication should be prescribed cautiously, given its potential for addiction.

Hormonal Interventions: Hormonal treatments of PMS and PMDD are based on the principle that suppression of ovulation eliminates premenstrual symptoms. Results from studies using oral contraceptives (OCPs) to treat PMS and PMDD have been mixed. However, one recent study supported the usefulness of an oral contraceptive (Yasmin) containing drospirenone.

Gonadotropin-releasing hormone (GnRH) agonists, such as leuprolide, which suppress ovarian function, have been found to reduce premenstrual symptoms in most studies. These medications, however, cause estrogen to fall to menopausal levels and are thus associated with side effects such as hot flashes and vaginal dryness, as well as increased risk of osteoporosis. These side effects may be lessened by "add-back" therapy with estrogen and progesterone. Similarly, danazol, a synthetic androgen (male hormone), is an effective therapy for PMS/PMDD when given in doses high enough to inhibit ovulation. However, this medication is associated with significant androgenic side effects, including acne, hirsutism (growth of facial hair), and weight gain.

Treatment Approach

After the diagnosis of PMS or PMDD has been made by excluding other medical and psychiatric conditions and by the daily rating of symptoms, treatment can begin. For all women, simple lifestyle changes in diet, exercise, and stress management are encouraged. These lifestyle changes have no associated risks and may provide significant benefit. Additionally, all women should be advised to continue daily charting of their premenstrual symptoms after diagnosis, as this can help to determine treatment effectiveness and to give women a sense of control over their symptoms. For patients with mild physical and emotional symptoms of PMS, a trial of nutritional supplements, including calcium, magnesium, and vitamin B_6 may also be considered.

> ☞ **Remember!!**
>
> Many women experience certain behavioral and physical changes associated with phases of their menstrual cycles. In some women, these changes are severe, occur regularly, and include depressed feelings, irritability, and other emotional and physical changes. Called premenstrual syndrome (PMS) or premenstrual dysphoric disorder (PMDD), the changes typically begin after ovulation and become gradually worse until menstruation starts.
>
> Source: Excerpted from "Depression: What Every Woman Should Know," National Institute of Mental Health, NIH Publication No. 00-4779, updated 9/02/2005.

In determining whether or not to start medication therapy, patient preference, the severity of the patient's symptoms, as well as the associated medication side effects must all be considered. For patients with severe symptoms of PMS, or with a diagnosis of PMDD, SSRIs are the first-line treatment. These medications can be dosed on a continuous or intermittent schedule depending on the patient's preference and the severity of her symptoms. If a woman does not show improvement in symptoms after three menstrual cycles, a trial with a different SSRI should be begun. Additionally, if a patient has severely troubling side effects with one SSRI, she should be switched to a different medication.

For severe symptoms that fail to respond to any of the above strategies, medications that suppress ovulation, such as GnRH, may be considered. Because these medications induce a chemical menopause associated with troubling side effects and possible long-term consequence, they are not first-line agents for treatment of PMS or PMDD and should be used cautiously.

Chapter 14

Bipolar Disorder

At least 2 million Americans suffer from bipolar disorder, also known as manic-depressive illness. It is a mental illness involving episodes of serious mania and depression. The child's mood may swing from overly "high" and irritable to sad and hopeless, and then back again, with periods of normal mood in between.

Bipolar disorder typically begins in adolescence or early adulthood and continues throughout life. It is often not recognized as an illness, and children who have it may suffer needlessly for years or even decades. For those afflicted with the illness, it is extremely distressing and disruptive, and like other serious illnesses, bipolar disorder is also hard on other family members and friends. Family members of children with bipolar disorder often have to cope with serious behavioral problems and the lasting consequences of these behaviors.

Signs and symptoms of mania include discrete periods of the following:

• Increased energy, activity, restlessness, racing thoughts, and rapid talking

• Excessive "high" or euphoric feelings

About This Chapter: Reprinted with permission of the Center for the Advancement of Children's Mental Health, © 2003. All rights reserved. For additional information, contact The Center for the Advancement of Children's Mental Health at Columbia University, New York State Psychiatric Institute, 1051 Riverside Drive, Unit #78 New York, NY 10032, www.kidsmentalhealth.org.

- Extreme irritability and distractibility

- Decreased need for sleep

- Unrealistic beliefs in one's abilities and powers

- Uncharacteristically poor judgment

- A sustained period of behavior that is different from usual

- Increased sexual drive

- Abuse of drugs, particularly cocaine, alcohol, and sleeping medications

- Provocative, intrusive, or aggressive behavior

- Denial that anything is wrong

Signs and symptoms of depression include discrete periods of the following:

- Persistent sad, anxious, or empty mood

- Feelings of hopelessness or pessimism

- Feelings of guilt, worthlessness, or helplessness

- Loss of interest or pleasure in ordinary activities, including sex

- Decreased energy, a feeling of fatigue or of being "slowed down"

- Difficulty concentrating, remembering, making decisions

- Restlessness or irritability

- Sleep disturbances

♣ **It's A Fact!!**

Once the diagnosis of bipolar disorder is made, the treatment of children and adolescents is based mainly on experience with adults, since as yet there is very limited data on the efficacy and safety of mood stabilizing medications in youth. The essential treatment for this disorder in adults involves the use of appropriate doses of mood stabilizers, most typically lithium and/or valproate, which are often very effective for controlling mania and preventing recurrences of manic and depressive episodes. Research on the effectiveness of these and other medications in children and adolescents with bipolar disorder is ongoing. In addition, studies are investigating various forms of psychotherapy, including cognitive-behavioral therapy, to complement medication treatment for this illness in young people.

Source: Excerpted from "Child and Adolescent Bipolar Disorder: An Update from the National Institute of Mental Health, NIH Pub. No. 00-4778, 2000.

- Loss of appetite and weight, or weight gain
- Chronic pain or other persistent bodily symptoms that are not caused by physical disease
- Thoughts of death or suicide; suicide attempts

It may be helpful to think of the various mood states in manic-depressive illness as a spectrum or continuous range. At one end is severe depression, which shades into moderate depression; then come mild and brief mood disturbances that many people call "the blues," then normal mood, then hypomania (a mild form of mania), and then mania.

Some children with untreated bipolar disorder have repeated depressions and only an occasional episode of hypomania (bipolar II). In the other extreme, mania may be the main problem and depression may occur only infrequently. In fact, symptoms of mania and depression may be mixed together in a single "mixed" bipolar state.

The diagnosis of bipolar disorder in children and adolescents can be difficult. At present, it is not clear whether different criteria should be used to make the diagnosis in youngsters than in adults. For example, some experts have suggested that a mood state of continuous, rapidly changing mood states and irritability (but without euphoria, grandiosity, or discrete manic episodes) constitute the more typical manifestations of bipolar disorder in pre-pubertal children. However, this issue remains unresolved because of the lack of the necessary longitudinal research studies showing that such children in fact do show the more typical signs of bipolar disorder in adolescence or adulthood.

Perhaps in part because of its different manifestations in children and youth, manic-depressive illness is often not recognized by the patient, relatives, friends, or even physicians. An early sign of manic-depressive illness may be hypomania—a state in which the person shows a high level of energy, excessive moodiness or irritability, and impulsive or reckless behavior. Sometimes, hypomania may feel good to the person who experiences it. Thus, even when family and friends learn to recognize the mood swings, the individual often will deny that anything is wrong.

Recognition of the various mood states is essential so that the child who has manic-depressive illness can obtain effective treatment and avoid the harmful consequences of the disease, which include destruction of personal relationships and suicide.

In its early stages, bipolar disorder may masquerade as a problem other than mental illness. For example, it may first appear as alcohol or drug abuse, poor school or work performance, or attention-deficit/hyperactivity disorder. If left untreated, bipolar disorder tends to worsen, and the person experiences episodes of full-fledged mania and clinical depression.

What Causes Bipolar Disorder?

Bipolar disorder tends to run in families and is believed to be inherited in many cases. Despite vigorous research efforts, a specific genetic defect associated with the disease has not yet been detected. There are however, several theories being tested.

Cellular/Molecular: There are hypotheses that certain cells and/or molecules in the brain and a change in their activity cause the extreme highs and low associated with bipolar disorder. These theories involve studying specific chemical elements such as NA-, K-, -ATPase and guanine nucleotide binding proteins.

Genetic: Through twin studies and family studies (and even adoption studies), Bipolar disorder has shown strong hereditary tendencies. This is particularly true of early onset bipolar disorder.

Neurological: Brain imaging studies have suggested a correlation between structural abnormalities in the brain and having bipolar disorder. These abnormalities include a decrease in size of the medial temporal lobe and reduced total cerebral volume.

Psychological, Social, Environment: There are few studies concerning the impact of psychological, societal or environmental influences on bipolar disorder. Most studies that have been done are based on the theory of the mania being a defensive or compensatory reaction to severe depression. There is little evidence to support the notion that social or psychological factors "cause" bipolar disorder. However, some recent evidence suggests that social and environmental factors can be involved in triggering an episode.

✔ **Quick Tip**
Cautionary Note

Effective treatment depends on appropriate diagnosis of bipolar disorder in children and adolescents. There is some evidence that using antidepressant medication to treat depression in a person who has bipolar disorder may induce manic symptoms if it is taken without a mood stabilizer. In addition, using stimulant medications to treat attention deficit hyperactivity disorder (ADHD) or ADHD-like symptoms in a child with bipolar disorder may worsen manic symptoms. While it can be hard to determine which young patients will become manic, there is a greater likelihood among children and adolescents who have a family history of bipolar disorder. If manic symptoms develop or markedly worsen during antidepressant or stimulant use, a physician should be consulted immediately, and diagnosis and treatment for bipolar disorder should be considered.

Source: Excerpted from "Child and Adolescent Bipolar Disorder: An Update from the National Institute of Mental Health, NIH Pub. No. 00-4778, 2000.

Diagnosis

Bipolar illness can be diagnosed in children under age 12, although it is not common in this age bracket. It can be confused with attention deficit/hyperactivity disorder, so careful diagnosis is necessary.

Bipolar disorder involves cycles of mania and depression. Clinically, a patient is diagnosed as either bipolar I disorder or bipolar II disorder. bipolar I disorder is broken up into six subcategories. In the diagnosis of this disorder, whether bipolar I or bipolar II, the mental health practitioner must establish that the manic episode does not more accurately fit the criteria for schizoaffective disorder, or is not related to schizophrenia, schizophreniform disorder, delusional disorder, or another psychotic disorder.

Bipolar I Disorder: For a diagnosis of bipolar I disorder, a patient should have suffered from at least one manic episode. A manic episode is defined as an elevated, irritable or expansive mood which is not characteristic of the person and is sustained for at least one week.

Bipolar II Disorder: In order to be diagnosed with bipolar II disorder, a patient must be suffering from or have a history of suffering from at least one major depressive and hypomanic episode, and he/she must never have suffered a manic or mixed episode. In addition, the episode must cause significant distress or loss of functioning in the patient's life.

Chapter 15

Cyclothymia

Definition

Cyclothymic disorder, also called cyclothymia, is a mild form of bipolar disorder, characterized by alternating episodes of mood swings from mild or moderate depression to hypomania. Hypomania is defined as periods of elevated mood, euphoria, and excitement that do not cause the person to become disconnected from reality.

Causes, Incidence, And Risk Factors

The cause of cyclothymic disorder is unknown. Although the changes in mood are irregular and abrupt, the severity of the mood swings is far less extreme than that seen with bipolar disorder (manic depressive illness). Unlike in bipolar disorder, periods of hypomania do not progress into actual mania, in which the person may lose control over his or her behavior and go on spending binges, engage in highly risky sexual or drug-taking behavior and become detached from reality.

Hypomanic periods are energizing and a source of productivity for some people, while these periods cause others to become impulsive and unconcerned about the feelings of others, which can damage relationships. Because hypomania feels good, people with cyclothymia may not want to treat it.

Symptoms

- Alternating episodes of hypomania and mild depression lasting for at least two years

- Persistent symptoms (less than two consecutive symptom-free months)

Signs And Tests

The person's own description of the behavior usually leads to diagnosis of the disorder.

> ✔ Quick Tip
> **Support Groups**
>
> The stress of illness may be eased by joining a support group whose members share common experiences and problems.

Treatment

Cyclothymia is treated similarly to bipolar disorder. A combination of antimanic drugs, antidepressants, or psychotherapy can effectively treat this condition in many cases.

Expectations (Prognosis)

People may decline to seek treatment during their cheerful and uninhibited moods. There is likely to be a need for long-term treatment.

Complications

There is a potential for eventual progression to bipolar disorder.

Chapter 16

Anxiety And Anxiety Disorders

It's 1:15 A.M. and Morgan can't sleep because she's worried about the math test she has in the morning. Actually, it seems like she worries about almost everything these days. What if she oversleeps and misses the bus? Did she remember to put pads in her bag in case she gets her period tomorrow? Why hadn't Maya called her back tonight? How will she work at the store all day Saturday and still have time to write the paper that's due on Monday? It's another 45 minutes before Morgan is finally able to drift off.

It's completely normal to worry about your hectic, complicated life, but if the worries become overwhelming, you may feel that they're running your life. If you spend an excessive amount of time feeling anxious or you have difficulty sleeping because of your anxiety, pay attention to your thoughts and feelings. They may be symptoms of an anxiety problem or disorder.

What Is Anxiety?

Anxiety is a natural part of life, and most of us experience it from time to time. The word "anxiety" usually refers to worry, concern, stress, or nervousness.

About This Chapter: The text in this chapter is from "All About Anxiety," information provided by TeensHealth, one of the largest resources online for medically reviewed health information written for parents, kids, and teens. For more articles like this one, visit www.TeensHealth.org, or www.KidsHealth.org. © 2001 The Nemours Center for Children's Health Media, a division of The Nemours Foundation.

For most teens, anxiety is limited to particular situations such as tests, important dates (like the prom), or driving lessons.

Feeling anxious can sometimes be a good thing. Anxiety can actually help you by motivating you to prepare for a big test or by keeping you on your toes in potentially dangerous situations. Occasional anxiety isn't something to be concerned about.

But for some teens, anxiety is a constant factor in their lives. When a person has an anxiety disorder, it interferes with their ability to function normally on a daily basis. Anxiety disorders can cause teens to suffer from intense, long-lasting fear or worry, in addition to other symptoms.

Understanding Anxiety Disorders

Anxiety disorders are conditions that involve unrealistic fear and worry. Anxiety disorders are very common—it is estimated that that they affect about 13% of the U.S. population. Anxiety disorders affect people of all ages, including kids and teens.

A teen who has an anxiety disorder isn't "crazy," and certainly isn't alone. Many teens have anxiety disorders, and have feelings of fear, worry, panic, or intense stress that can sometimes make it hard to get through the day. Anxiety can also interfere with things as basic as sleep, concentration, and appetite, not to mention the ability to enjoy life and relax. The good news is that anxiety disorders are very treatable.

There are several types of anxiety disorders that can affect teens. They include:

- **Generalized anxiety disorder, or GAD,** for example, refers to constant, intense worry and stress about a variety of everyday things or situations. Teens with GAD may worry about school, health or safety of family members, the future, and whether they'll become ill or injured. They may always think of the worst that could happen. Along with the worry and dread, they may have physical symptoms, too, such as chest pain, headache, tiredness, tight muscles, stomachaches, or even vomiting. GAD can result in missed school days and avoidance of social activities.

- **Panic disorder** is characterized by panic attacks, or episodes of intense fear that occur for no apparent reason. With a panic attack a person may have a sense that things are unreal, and may have physical symptoms like a pounding heart, shortness of breath, dizziness, numbness, or tingling feelings. Sometimes a person having a panic attack mistakenly feels he may be dying or having a heart attack. The panic symptoms are caused by over activity of the body's normal fear response.

- **Agoraphobia** is an intense fear of having a panic attack. People with agoraphobia have had a panic attack before, and worry so much about having another that they avoid going anywhere they think it could possibly occur. They are often left with very few places they feel comfortable going outside their own home.

- **Social anxiety disorder** is an intense fear of social situations. Teens with social anxiety may feel too nervous to raise their hand or talk in class. They may fear making a mistake, saying the wrong answer, or looking foolish. They may feel extremely shy and anxious in situations where they have to interact with others, such as parties, the lunch table, or when they meet new people. They may be overly self-conscious about their clothes or hair, worrying that they might be criticized or teased, or that they might stand out or be noticed. With an extreme form of social anxiety called selective mutism, some kids and teens may be too anxious to talk at all in certain situations.

- **Obsessive-compulsive disorder (OCD)** is characterized by obsessions—thoughts or impulses that occur again and again and that a person feels he can't control—and compulsions—behaviors or rituals that a person feels he must perform to control disturbing thoughts and relieve the anxiety the thoughts trigger. With OCD a teen may, for example, have constant worry and fear about illness or germs, and may become stuck in a pattern of washing and cleaning that becomes time-consuming, distressing, and feels impossible to control. The worries (obsessions) with OCD are unrealistic, but are frightening to the person who has them. For example, a teen with illness obsessions may worry that just by reading about an illness or driving past a hospital he could become ill.

- **Posttraumatic stress disorder (PTSD)** refers to anxiety relating to a traumatic or terrifying past experience. With PTSD, a frightening, life-threatening event such as an accident, serious violence (such as rape, abuse, shooting, or gang violence), or a natural disaster (such as an earthquake, tornado, hurricane) causes such a severe fear response that the person may experience flashbacks, nightmares, or constant fear, worry, and stress after the fact. PTSD may occur within days or weeks after the life-threatening event, or it may be delayed and occur much later.

- **Specific phobias** are intense unrealistic fears relating to specific situations or things (that are not actually dangerous), such as heights, dogs, or flying in an airplane. Phobias usually cause people to avoid what they are afraid of. Some people can work around a phobia if it involves something they do not have to encounter in their everyday life. Other phobias may involve more common situations or things, and may be harder to steer clear of even if people do their best to avoid them. Avoiding these things or situations tends to make the fear stronger each time the person encounters them.

If you have an anxiety disorder, you may feel that it's ruling your life. In addition to worrying much of the time, you may be easily distracted and have trouble concentrating. You may feel stressed and tense or unable to relax. You may experience physical symptoms such as headaches, sweaty hands, upset stomach, pounding heart, and muscle tension. Like Morgan, you may find it nearly impossible to fall asleep. Some people have extremely intense symptoms—for example, people who are experiencing panic attacks may fear that they are having a heart attack or might even die.

But whether you think you might have an anxiety disorder or you know someone who does, understanding the disorder and its treatment can help.

Why Do People Get Anxiety Disorders?

There is no one cause for anxiety disorders. Several factors can play a role, including genetics, brain biochemistry, an overactive "fight or flight" response, life circumstances, and learned behavior.

Anxiety disorders tend to run in families, suggesting that there is a hereditary, or genetic, component to many of these conditions. A person who has a family member with an anxiety disorder has a greater chance of developing an anxiety disorder, though not necessarily the same type.

Genetics influence a person's brain biochemistry, and may make certain people more prone to problems with anxiety. The brain's biochemistry involves the brain's millions of nerve cells (called neurons) that constantly communicate with each other through chemicals called neurotransmitters.

Neurotransmitters are the brain's chemical messengers, and specific neurotransmitters help to regulate mood. Neurotransmitters are released from one neuron and attach to a receptor on another neuron. Sometimes there is interference with this process, such as if the receptor is blocked and unable to receive the neurotransmitter.

This interference can create an imbalance in the levels of the neurotransmitter in the brain, and can cause symptoms of anxiety. There are many kinds of neurotransmitters; two that are involved in anxiety are called serotonin and dopamine. When there's an imbalance of these chemicals, anxiety and other problems can occur.

Certain things that happen in a person's life can also set the stage for anxiety disorders. Frightening traumatic events that can lead to PTSD are a good example.

Early learning also plays a role. Growing up in a family where others are fearful or anxious can "teach" a child to view the world as a scary place. Likewise, if a child grows up in an environment that is actually scary or dangerous (if there is violence in the child's family or community, for example), the child may learn to be fearful or expect the worst.

The brain's automatic reaction to an anxiety-provoking situation also can fuel an anxiety disorder. Here's how this can happen: when a person senses danger (even if it doesn't turn out to be true danger), the brain quickly reacts by sending a signal to a small structure in the brain called the amygdala (pronounced: uh-mig-duh-luh). The amygdala immediately activates the body's automatic "fight or flight" response, and the body prepares itself for danger. This response is what triggers symptoms like sweating and a pounding heart.

Sometimes it turns out that as soon as the person processes the information in the thinking part of the brain (the cerebral cortex), which happens just moments later, the person realizes there's really no danger. The person then relaxes, and this fight or flight response stops.

But the amygdala is programmed to "remember" the trigger that set this process in motion in case it happens again. This is the brain's attempt to protect the person from future danger by keeping track of all cues that might signal danger. So, for example, if the person encounters the same thing that scared him once before (even if the person later realized it wasn't dangerous), the amygdala may activate the same anxiety reaction. It's possible for the amygdala to begin to overreact, and for the person to mistakenly interpret certain things as dangerous.

How Are Anxiety Disorders Diagnosed And Treated?

Some people go to their medical doctor because they're worried about the physical symptoms associated with anxiety. This is a good idea because symptoms like palpitations, chest pain, stomachaches, vomiting, shortness of breath, shakiness, numbness or tingling, or sleeping problems can be caused by certain medical illnesses.

A doctor can examine a person to determine whether he has any medical conditions that need treatment. But if the doctor doesn't find a medical cause for the symptoms, and sees that there's a certain pattern of physical symptoms, the doctor may diagnose anxiety and refer the person to a mental health specialist.

If you think you may have an anxiety disorder, you need to see a mental health specialist, such as a psychologist or psychiatrist, for an evaluation. Don't wait to ask for help—anxiety can be overwhelming, and it can prevent you from enjoying yourself, your friends, school, and social activities. There are treatments that can help teens with anxiety disorders feel much better, often fairly quickly.

Some people with anxiety try to medicate or relax themselves by using alcohol and drugs (even things like sleeping pills), which may seem to make the anxiety or stress go away temporarily. This is not a good solution for several reasons. Drugs and alcohol create only a false sense of relaxation, can be dangerous, and can lead to lots of other problems, which can make it that much harder to function.

☞ **Remember!!**
Dealing With An Anxiety Disorder

If you have an anxiety disorder, it may be difficult for your friends or family to understand just how you feel. Sometimes people give unrealistic advice like telling you to just stop worrying. Though they may have the best intentions, they may not understand that it's not that simple. You may have to explain this to them.

Because others may not always understand, sometimes people are reluctant to let loved ones know what they are going through. Some people may be concerned that their fear or behavior may be seen as childish, silly, or weird, but communication is the key. Close friends and family can be part of the solution, and their care and support can be valuable. Let them know what they can do to help.

You can expect the mental health specialist to ask about your medical history, your family situation, the symptoms you've been experiencing, and your general well-being. Don't be surprised if some of the questions are very personal—your responses will help the doctor to understand you more fully and create a treatment plan that's right for you.

Treatment for anxiety may include medication, cognitive-behavioral therapy or other types of talk therapy, and relaxation or biofeedback to control tense muscles. A combination of treatments may be prescribed.

When medications are part of the treatment for anxiety, often a certain class of medications called SSRIs is used. This is sometimes confusing to people with anxiety because the SSRI medications are commonly referred to as "antidepressants."

Here's the scoop to clear up the confusion: the SSRI medications were first developed as antidepressants, but it was recognized that they also have anti-anxiety effects. So, how could they work for both? Because depression and anxiety both involve, among other things, an imbalance of the neurotransmitter serotonin. SSRI medications help to restore the normal balance of serotonin, and therefore help with both depression and anxiety.

Though not every teen who has an anxiety disorder needs medication (in fact, most don't), the right medication can help to reduce symptoms of anxiety, and can be a great relief to someone whose anxiety symptoms are causing tremendous distress. Often when doctors prescribe medication, they begin with a very small dosage, and gradually increase to the dosage that works best. It may take some time to get the dosage that works best for you. And it may take several weeks before the full benefits of a certain medication are felt. As with any medication, it's very important to take it exactly as prescribed and to tell your doctor about any side effects.

In psychotherapy, or talk therapy, a teen talks with a mental health professional about the stresses and anxiety he's feeling. Getting support and sorting through problems by talking them through can be helpful to teens with anxiety.

In a particular type of talk therapy called cognitive-behavioral therapy (CBT), teens take an active role in "unlearning" some of their fear. CBT helps teens learn new ways to think and act when confronted with anxiety, and to manage and deal with stress so it doesn't get out of hand. In CBT, teens learn how to detect and measure their anxiety, recognize what triggers it, and practice ways to reduce it. They learn what makes their fear worse and what can ease it. Techniques vary, but may include relaxation and breathing exercises or exposure therapy, where a person is gradually exposed what triggers his fear. If it's done with proper support and new coping skills, exposure helps even intense fear fade away.

> **✔ Quick Tip**
>
> If you know someone who has an anxiety disorder, be a supportive friend. If she goes to a support group, you might offer to go to one of the meetings with her. Tell your friend you're there to listen if she'd like to talk. Learn as much as you can about the disorder so you can talk with her about it.

Don't hesitate to tell your doctor or therapist about what's working and what isn't—you're a member of your treatment team, and your ideas and feelings are important.

Chapter 17

Generalized Anxiety Disorder

Unlike the relatively mild, brief anxiety caused by a stressful event—such as giving an oral report or a first date—anxiety disorders are chronic, relentless, and can grow progressively worse if not treated. Each anxiety disorder has its own distinct features, but they are all bound together by the common theme of excessive, irrational fear and dread.

Generalized anxiety disorder (GAD) is much more than the normal anxiety people experience day to day. It's chronic and fills one's day with exaggerated worry and tension, even though there is little or nothing to provoke it. Having this disorder means always anticipating disaster, often worrying excessively about health, money, family, or work. Sometimes, though, the source of the worry is hard to pinpoint. Simply the thought of getting through the day provokes anxiety.

Some people have described GAD this way:

- "I always thought I was just a worrier. I'd feel keyed up and unable to relax. At times it would come and go, and at times it would be constant. It could go on for days. I'd worry about what I was going to fix for a party or what would be a great present for somebody. I just couldn't let something go."

About This Chapter: This chapter includes excerpts from "Anxiety Disorders," National Institute of Mental Health, 2000, updated 02/2006.

- "I'd have terrible sleeping problems. There were times I'd wake up wired in the middle of the night. I had trouble concentrating, even reading the newspaper or a novel. Sometimes I'd feel a little lightheaded. My heart would race or pound. And that would make me worry more. I was always imagining things were worse than they really were: when I got a stomachache, I'd think it was an ulcer."

- "When my problems were at their worst, I'd miss work and feel just terrible about it. Then I worried that I'd lose my job. My life was miserable until I got treatment."

People with GAD can't seem to shake their concerns, even though they usually realize that their anxiety is more intense than the situation warrants. Their worries are accompanied by physical symptoms, especially fatigue, headaches, muscle tension, muscle aches, difficulty swallowing, trembling, twitching, irritability, sweating, and hot flashes. People with GAD may feel lightheaded or out of breath. They also may feel nauseated or have to go to the bathroom frequently.

♣ **It's A Fact!!**
GAD affects about twice as many women as men. The disorder comes on gradually and can begin across the life cycle. It is diagnosed when someone spends at least 6 months worrying excessively about a number of everyday problems. There is evidence that genes play a modest role in GAD. (Source: NIMH, updated 2006.)

Individuals with GAD seem unable to relax, and they may startle more easily than other people. They tend to have difficulty concentrating, too. Often, they have trouble falling or staying asleep.

Unlike people with several other anxiety disorders, people with GAD don't characteristically avoid certain situations as a result of their disorder. When impairment associated with GAD is mild, people with the disorder may be able to function in social settings or on the job. If severe, however, GAD can be very debilitating, making it difficult to carry out even the most ordinary daily activities.

GAD is commonly treated with medications. GAD rarely occurs alone, however; it is usually accompanied by another anxiety disorder, depression, or substance abuse. These other conditions must be treated along with GAD.

How are other anxiety disorders different from generalized anxiety disorder?

Panic Disorder: People with panic disorder have feelings of terror that strike suddenly and repeatedly with no warning. They can't predict when an attack will occur, and many develop intense anxiety between episodes, worrying when and where the next one will strike. If you are having a panic attack, most likely your heart will pound and you may feel sweaty, weak, faint, or dizzy. Your hands may tingle or feel numb, and you might feel flushed or chilled. You may have nausea, chest pain or smothering sensations, a sense of unreality, or fear of impending doom or loss of control. You may genuinely believe you're having a heart attack or losing your mind, or on the verge of death.

Obsessive-Compulsive Disorder: OCD involves anxious thoughts or rituals you feel you can't control. If you have OCD, you may be plagued by persistent, unwelcome thoughts or images, or by the urgent need to engage in certain rituals.

Post-Traumatic Stress Disorder: PTSD is a debilitating condition that can develop following a terrifying event. Often, people with PTSD have persistent frightening thoughts and memories of their ordeal and feel emotionally numb, especially with people they were once close to.

Social Phobia: Social phobia, also called social anxiety disorder, involves overwhelming anxiety and excessive self-consciousness in everyday social situations. People with social phobia have a persistent, intense, and chronic fear of being watched and judged by others and being embarrassed or humiliated by their own actions.

Specific Phobias: A specific phobia is an intense fear of something that poses little or no actual danger. Some of the more common specific phobias are centered around closed-in places, heights, escalators, tunnels, highway driving, water, flying, and dogs.

What causes generalized anxiety disorder?

Researchers don't fully understand what causes GAD. Several parts of the brain are key actors in a highly dynamic interplay that gives rise to fear and anxiety. Using brain imaging technologies and neurochemical techniques, scientists are finding that a network of interacting structures is responsible for these emotions. Much research centers on the amygdala, an almond-shaped structure deep within the brain. The amygdala is believed to serve as a communications hub between the parts of the brain that process incoming sensory signals and the parts that interpret them. It can signal that a threat is present, and trigger a fear response or anxiety. It appears that emotional memories stored in the central part of the amygdala may play a role in disorders involving very distinct fears, like phobias, while different parts may be involved in other forms of anxiety.

By learning more about brain circuitry involved in fear and anxiety, scientists may be able to devise new and more specific treatments for anxiety disorders. For example, it someday may be possible to increase the influence of the thinking parts of the brain on the amygdala, thus placing the fear and anxiety response under conscious control.

How is generalized anxiety disorder treated?

In general, two types of treatment are available for an anxiety disorder—medication and specific types of psychotherapy (sometimes called "talk therapy"). Both approaches can be effective for most disorders. The choice of one or the other, or both, depends on the patient's and the doctor's preference.

Antidepressants: A number of medications that were originally approved for treatment of depression have been found to be effective for anxiety disorders. Some of the newest antidepressants are called selective serotonin reuptake inhibitors, or SSRIs. These medications act in the brain on a chemical messenger called serotonin. Venlafaxine, a drug closely related to the SSRIs, is useful for treating GAD. Antidepressant medications called tricyclics have been around longer than SSRIs and have been more widely studied for treating anxiety disorders. Clomipramine, prescribed for panic disorder and GAD, is an example of a tricyclic.

Anti-Anxiety Medications: High-potency benzodiazepines relieve symptoms quickly and have few side effects, although drowsiness can be a problem. Because people can develop a tolerance to them—and would have to continue increasing the dosage to get the same effect—benzodiazepines are

♣ It's A Fact!!

Approximately 6.8 million American adults, or about 3.1 percent of people age 18 and over, have generalized anxiety disorder (GAD) in a given year. GAD can begin across the life cycle, though the median age of onset is 31 years old.

Source: Excerpted from "The Numbers Count: Mental Disorders in America," National Institute of Mental Health, 2006.

generally prescribed for short periods of time. Benzodiazepines include clonazepam, which is used for social phobia and GAD, and alprazolam, which is helpful for panic disorder and GAD. Buspirone, a member of a class of drugs called azapirones, is a newer anti-anxiety medication that is used to treat GAD.

Psychotherapy: Psychotherapy involves talking with a trained mental health professional, such as a psychiatrist, psychologist, social worker, or counselor to learn how to deal with problems like GAD and other anxiety disorders.

Chapter 18

Obsessive-Compulsive Disorder

Obsessive-compulsive disorder (OCD) is a common anxiety disorder that affects about 1 to 2% of the population. As its name implies, the symptoms of OCD involve obsessions that lead to compulsions. Obsessions are recurrent and persistent ideas, thoughts, images, or impulses that may cause a great deal of anxiety or distress. People experiencing these obsessions typically find them to be disturbing and intrusive, and usually recognize that they don't make a lot of sense. In response to obsessions, people with OCD try to get rid of them by way of compulsions—acts that are done over and over again, and often according to certain personal rules. Also called rituals, compulsions are usually aimed at preventing or reducing distress and anxiety, or preventing some feared event or situation.

Obsessions and compulsions can take many forms. A few examples include: drivers who fear that they've hit a person every time they run over a pothole or bump on the road. In response to such an obsession, these persons may resort to compulsions such as retracing their routes to be sure no harm was done, or avoid the particular road altogether in the future. Individuals who fear or are obsessed with germs may wash their hands repeatedly throughout the day after touching any potentially "germy" objects, such as door handles,

About This Chapter: Text in this chapter was excerpted from "Obsessive Compulsive Disorder," from AAMFT Consumer Update, Copyright 2002 by the American Association for Marriage and Family Therapy. Reproduced with permission of the American Association for Marriage and Family Therapy, via Copyright Clearance Center.

money, or newspapers. Often, their hands are sore and raw from repeated washing, but they can't seem to stop washing. Others who might be obsessed with order and cleanliness may compulsively arrange items in a particular order, or clean their home floors many times a day. Those who fear burglary, fires, or floods may repeatedly check door locks, stove burners, and taps to ensure that their homes are safe. Over time, such repetitive actions work less and less effectively, and the persons may experience anxiety and often depression in response to the increasing obsessions and compulsions.

Besides causing a great deal of stress, OCD symptoms may take up a lot of time (more than an hour a day for some diagnosed people) and may significantly interfere with a person's work, social life, or relationships. OCD can be a challenging problem but fortunately, very effective treatments for OCD are now available to help individuals and families lead a more satisfying life.

♣ It's A Fact!!

If you have OCD, you may be plagued by persistent, unwelcome thoughts or images, or by the urgent need to engage in certain rituals.

You may be obsessed with germs or dirt, so you wash your hands over and over. You may be filled with doubt and feel the need to check things repeatedly. You may have frequent thoughts of violence, and fear that you will harm people close to you. You may spend long periods touching things or counting; you may be pre-occupied by order or symmetry; you may have persistent thoughts of performing sexual acts that are repugnant to you; or you may be troubled by thoughts that are against your religious beliefs.

The disturbing thoughts or images are called obsessions, and the rituals that are performed to try to prevent or get rid of them are called compulsions. There is no pleasure in carrying out the rituals you are drawn to, only temporary relief from the anxiety that grows when you don't perform them.

A lot of healthy people can identify with some of the symptoms of OCD, such as checking the stove several times before leaving the house. But for people with OCD, such activities consume at least an hour a day, are very distressing, and interfere with daily life.

Source: Excerpted from "Anxiety Disorders," National Institute of Mental Health, 2000.

What causes OCD?

There is no single, proven cause for OCD. There is, however, growing evidence that biological factors are a primary contributor to the disorder. Research suggests that OCD involves problems in communication between the front part of the brain (the orbital cortex) and deeper structures (the basal ganglia). These brain structures communicate with each other by using serotonin, a chemical messenger. It is possible that serotonin plays a significant role in the development or maintenance of OCD. Other psychological, familial, social and cultural factors may contribute to OCD, but it is not clear whether they cause the disorder.

What treatments are available for OCD?

There are several types of effective treatments for individuals with OCD and their families. The most common types of treatments are the following:

Cognitive Behavioral Therapy (CBT): This treatment has two parts: behavioral therapy and cognitive therapy. Behavioral therapy involves exposure and response prevention. Exposure is designed to reduce the negative emotions (anxiety and guilt) brought on by obsessions. It is based on the idea that anxiety usually decreases after lengthy contact with something feared. For example, people with obsessions about germs will be advised to stay in contact with "germy" objects, such as money. In order for exposure to be most helpful, it needs to be combined with response prevention (RP). In RP, the person's rituals (or compulsions) are blocked. For example, those who worry a lot about germs will be advised to stay in contact with "germy" objects, but avoid the compulsion to wash their hands excessively. This repeated exposure without rituals assists individuals to understand that coming into contact with certain objects or situations will not lead to the initial fear—in this case, becoming ill from the germs found on common objects.

CBT's second part is cognitive therapy (CT). It is often combined with behavioral therapy to help reduce the catastrophic thinking and exaggerated sense of responsibility often seen in OCD. In cognitive therapy, the therapist asks the client a series of questions to help him/her identify and evaluate the interpretations and beliefs that lead to typical OCD behavior. Once these beliefs are identified, the therapist will use a variety of strategies to assist the client in challenging the faulty assumptions that are seen in OCD.

Behavioral Family Treatment: Whenever possible, it is helpful for family members to participate in the treatment of OCD. Family members and persons with OCD both tend to benefit when the family members participate in psychoeducational groups. These groups educate family members about OCD and provide strategies that the family can use to assist and support the member with OCD.

Medication: Research shows that the use of medication, specifically serotonin reuptake inhibitors (SRIs), is beneficial for the treatment of OCD. Most research shows that medication alone does not get rid of OCD, but it reduces the force of obsessions and urges to engage in rituals (for example, excessive hand washing), thereby allowing the person with OCD to have more control over their thoughts and behaviors.

Chapter 19

Panic Disorder

Panic disorder is a serious condition that around one out of every 75 people might experience. It usually appears during the teens or early adulthood, and while the exact causes are unclear, there does seem to be a connection with major life transitions that are potentially stressful: graduating from college, getting married, having a first child, and so on. There is also some evidence for a genetic predisposition; if a family member has suffered from panic disorder, you have an increased risk of suffering from it yourself, especially during a time in your life that is particularly stressful.

Panic Attacks: The Hallmark Of Panic Disorder

A panic attack is a sudden surge of overwhelming fear that comes without warning and without any obvious reason. It is far more intense than the feeling of being 'stressed out' that most people experience. Symptoms of a panic attack include:

- racing heartbeat

- difficulty breathing, feeling as though you 'can't get enough air'

- terror that is almost paralyzing

- dizziness, lightheadedness, or nausea

- trembling, sweating, shaking

- choking, chest pains

- hot flashes, or sudden chills

- tingling in fingers or toes ('pins and needles')

- fear that you're going to go crazy or are about to die

You probably recognize this as the classic 'flight or fight' response that human beings experience when we are in a situation of danger. But during a panic attack, these symptoms seem to rise from out of nowhere. They occur in seemingly harmless situations— they can even happen while you are asleep.

> ### ✎ What's It Mean?
> There are three types of panic attacks:
>
> 1. Underexpected: The attack "comes out of the blue" without warning and for no discernible reason.
>
> 2. Situational: Situations in which an individual always has an attack (for example, upon entering a tunnel).
>
> 3. Situationally Predisposed: Situations in which an individual is likely to have a panic attack, but does not always have one. An example of this would be an individual who sometimes has attacks while driving.
>
> Source: Excerpted and reprinted with permission from "Panic Attack," © 2004 Anxiety Disorders Association of America (www.adaa.org).

In addition to the above symptoms, a panic attack is marked by the following conditions:

- it occurs suddenly, without any warning and without any way to stop it.

- the level of fear is way out of proportion to the actual situation; often, in fact, it's completely unrelated.

- it passes in a few minutes; the body cannot sustain the 'fight or flight' response for longer than that. However, repeated attacks can continue to recur for hours.

A panic attack is not dangerous, but it can be terrifying, largely because it feels 'crazy' and 'out of control.' Panic disorder is frightening because of the panic attacks associated with it, and also because it often leads to other complications such as phobias, depression, substance abuse, medical complications, even suicide. Its effects can range from mild word or social impairment to a total inability to face the outside world.

In fact, the phobias that people with panic disorder develop do not come from fears of actual objects or events, but rather from fear of having another attack. In these cases, people will avoid certain objects or situations because they fear that these things will trigger another attack.

How To Identify Panic Disorder

Please remember that only a licensed therapist can diagnose a panic disorder. There are certain signs you may already be aware of, though.

One study found that people sometimes see 10 or more doctors before being properly diagnosed, and that only one out of four people with the disorder receive the treatment they need. That's why it's important to know what the symptoms are, and to make sure you get the right help.

Many people experience occasional panic attacks, and if you have had one or two such attacks, there probably isn't any reason to worry. The key symptom of panic disorder is the persistent fear of having future panic attacks. If you suffer from repeated (four or more) panic attacks, and especially if you have had a panic attack and are in continued fear of having another, these are signs that you should consider finding a mental health professional who specializes in panic or anxiety disorders.

Causes Of Panic Disorder

Body: There may be a genetic predisposition to anxiety disorders; some sufferers report that a family member has or had a panic disorder or some other emotional disorder such as depression. Studies with twins have confirmed the possibility of 'genetic inheritance' of the disorder.

Panic disorder could also be due to a biological malfunction, although a specific biological marker has yet to be identified.

All ethnic groups are vulnerable to panic disorder. For unknown reasons, women are twice as likely to get the disorder as men.

Mind: Stressful life events can trigger panic disorders. One association that has been noted is that of a recent loss or separation. Some researchers liken the 'life stressor' to a thermostat; that is, when stresses lower your resistance, the underlying physical predisposition kicks in and triggers an attack.

Both: Physical and psychological causes of panic disorder work together. Although initially attacks may come out of the blue, eventually the sufferer may actually help bring them on by responding to physical symptoms of an attack.

For example, if a person with panic disorder experiences a racing heartbeat caused by drinking coffee, exercising, or taking a certain medication, they might interpret this as a symptom of an attack and, because of their anxiety, actually bring on the attack. On the other hand, coffee, exercise, and certain medications sometimes do, in fact, cause panic attacks. One of the most frustrating things for the panic sufferer is never knowing how to isolate the different triggers of an attack. That's why the right therapy for panic disorder focuses on all aspects—physical, psychological, and physiological—of the disorder.

People With Panic Disorder Can Lead Normal Lives

Can people with panic disorder lead normal lives? The answer to this is a resounding YES—if they receive treatment.

Panic disorder is highly treatable, with a variety of available therapies. These treatments are extremely effective, and most people who have successfully completed treatment can continue to experience situational avoidance or anxiety, and further treatment might be necessary in those cases. Once treated, panic disorder doesn't lead to any permanent complications.

Side Effects Of Panic Disorder

Without treatment, panic disorder can have very serious consequences.

The immediate danger with panic disorder is that it can often lead to a phobia. That's because once you've suffered a panic attack, you may start to avoid situations like the one you were in when the attack occurred.

Many people with panic disorder show 'situational avoidance' associated with their panic attacks. For example, you might have an attack while driving, and start to avoid driving until you develop an actual phobia towards it. In worst case scenarios, people with panic disorder develop agoraphobia—fear of going outdoors—because they believe that by staying inside, they can avoid all situations that might provoke an attack, or where they might not be able to get help. The fear of an attack is so debilitating, they prefer to spend their lives locked inside their homes.

Even if you don't develop these extreme phobias, your quality of life can be severely damaged by untreated panic disorder. A recent study showed that people who suffer from panic disorder:

- are more prone to alcohol and other drug abuse;

- have greater risk of attempting suicide;

- spend more time in hospital emergency rooms;

- spend less time on hobbies, sports and other satisfying activities;

- tend to be financially dependent on others;

- report feeling emotionally and physically less healthy than non-sufferers;

- are afraid of driving more than a few miles away from home.

✦ It's A Fact!!

Agoraphobia often, but not always, coincides with panic disorder. Agoraphobia is characterized by a fear of having a panic attack in a place from which escape is difficult. Many sufferers refuse to leave their homes, often for years at a time. Others develop a fixed route, or territory, from which they cannot deviate (for example, the route between home and work). It becomes impossible for these people to travel beyond what they consider to be their safety zones without suffering severe anxiety.

Source: Excerpted and reprinted with permission from "Panic Attack," © 2004 Anxiety Disorders Association of America (www.adaa.org).

Panic disorders can also have economic effects. For example, a recent study cited the case of a woman who gave up a $40,000 a year job that required travel for one close to home that only paid $14,000 a year. Other sufferers have reported losing their jobs and having to rely on public assistance or family members.

None of this needs to happen. Panic disorder can be treated successfully, and sufferers can go on to lead full and satisfying lives.

Treating Panic Disorder

Most specialists agree that a combination of cognitive and behavioral therapies are the best treatment for panic disorder. Medication might also be appropriate in some cases.

The first part of therapy is largely informational; many people are greatly helped by simply understanding exactly what panic disorder is, and how many others suffer from it. Many people who suffer from panic disorder are worried that their panic attacks mean they're 'going crazy' or that the panic might induce a heart attack. 'Cognitive restructuring' (changing one's way of thinking) helps people replace those thoughts with more realistic, positive ways of viewing the attacks.

Cognitive therapy can help the patient identify possible triggers for the attacks. The trigger in an individual case could be something like a thought, a situation, or something as subtle as a slight change in heartbeat. Once the patient understands that the panic attack is separate and independent of the trigger, that trigger begins to lose some of its power to induce an attack.

The behavioral components of the therapy can consist of what one group of clinicians has termed 'interoceptive exposure.' This is similar to the systematic desensitization used to cure phobias, but what it focuses on is exposure to he actual physical sensations that someone experiences during a panic attack.

People with panic disorder are more afraid of the actual attack than they are of specific objects or events; for instance, their 'fear of flying' is not that the planes will crash but that they will have a panic attack in a place, like a plane, where they can't get to help. Others won't drink coffee or go to an overheated room because they're afraid that these might trigger the physical symptoms of a panic attack.

Interoceptive exposure can help them go through the symptoms of an attack (elevated heart rate, hot flashes, sweating, and so on) in a controlled setting, and teach them that these symptoms need not develop into a full-blown attack. Behavioral therapy is also used to deal with the situational avoidance associated with panic attacks. One very effective treatment for phobias is in vivo exposure, which in its simplest terms means breaking a fearful situation down into small manageable steps and doing them one at a time until the most difficult level is mastered.

Relaxation techniques can further help someone 'flow through' an attack. These techniques include breathing retraining and positive visualization.

Some experts have found that people with panic disorder tend to have slightly higher than average breathing rates, learning to slow this can help someone deal with a panic attack and can also prevent future attacks.

In some cases, medications may also be needed. Anti-anxiety medications may be prescribed, as well as antidepressants, and sometimes even heart medications (such as beta blockers) that are used to control irregular heartbeats.

Finally, a support group with others who suffer from panic disorder can be very helpful to some people. It can't take the place of therapy, but it can be a useful adjunct.

If you suffer from panic disorder, these therapies can help you. But you can't do them on your own; all of these treatments must be outlined and prescribed by a psychologist or psychiatrist.

👉 Remember!!

Keep in mind that panic disorder, like any other emotional disorder, isn't something you can either diagnose or cure by yourself. An experience clinical psychologist or psychiatrist is the most qualified person to make this diagnosis, just as he or she is the most qualified to treat this disorder.

The text in this chapter was designed to answer your basic questions about panic disorder; a qualified mental health professional will be able to give you more complete information.

Panic disorder does not need to disrupt your life in any way!

Source: © 2005 American Psychological Association; reprinted with permission

Length Of Treatment

Much of the success of treatment depends on your willingness to carefully follow the outlined treatment plan. This is often multifaceted, and it won't work overnight, but if you stick with it, you should start to have noticeable improvement within about 10 to 20 weekly sessions. If you continue to follow the program, within one year you will notice a tremendous improvement.

If you are suffering from panic disorder, you should be able to find help in your area. You need to find a licensed psychologist or other mental health professional who specializes in panic or anxiety disorders. There may even be a clinic nearby that specializes in these disorders.

When you speak with a therapist, specify that you think you have panic disorder, and ask about his or her experience treating this disorder.

Chapter 20

Post-Traumatic Stress Disorder

A couple of months ago, a guy who'd been threatening Joe for a while pulled a gun on him as he walked to school. Luckily, the police arrived and no one was hurt; but lately Joe's noticed that he feels on edge a lot. Sudden noises send his heart racing, and he's changed the route he takes to school. The worst part is that the incident keeps popping into Joe's mind, even when he's trying to concentrate on something else. In fact, he finds it tough to concentrate at all these days, and stuff he used to love—like playing games online or getting together with his band—just doesn't seem like much fun.

Sometimes after experiencing a traumatic event—one that's especially frightening in a life-or-death kind of way—people have a strong and lingering reaction known as post-traumatic stress disorder.

What Is Post-Traumatic Stress Disorder?

Post-traumatic stress disorder (PTSD) is a very strong stress reaction that can develop in people who have lived through an extremely traumatic

About This Chapter: This information was provided by TeensHealth, one of the largest resources online for medically reviewed health information written for parents, kids, and teens. For more articles like this one, visit www.TeensHealth.org, or www.KidsHealth.org. © 2004 The Nemours Center for Children's Health Media, a division of The Nemours Foundation.

event, such as a serious car accident, a natural disaster like an earthquake, or an assault like rape. Physical or sexual abuse, manmade traumas such as shootings, and military combat can cause PTSD, too.

You don't have to be hurt to experience PTSD—for some people, simply witnessing or being threatened with great physical harm is enough to trigger it. Events that can lead to PTSD involve feelings of helplessness, fear, or horror, and a sense that life or safety is in danger.

It's normal to be stressed out and anxious after going through something traumatic. Strong emotions, jitters, and trouble sleeping, eating, or concentrating may all be part of a normal and temporary reaction to an overwhelming event, so might frequent thoughts and images of what happened, nightmares, or fears. Getting the right care and support after a traumatic experience can help these symptoms run their course and subside in a few days or weeks and allow a person to move on.

> ♣ **It's A Fact!!**
> **When does PTSD first occur?**
>
> PTSD can develop at any age, including in childhood. Symptoms typically begin within 3 months of a traumatic event, although occasionally they do not begin until years later. Once PTSD occurs, the severity and duration of the illness varies. Some people recover within 6 months, while others suffer much longer.
>
> Source: Excerpted from "Facts about Post-Traumatic Stress Disorder," National Institute of Mental Health, revised 2002.

But when a person has PTSD, the symptoms of a stress reaction are intense and last for longer than a month. For some people, the symptoms of PTSD begin soon after the trauma. Other people may have a delayed reaction that comes months—or even years—later. Delayed PTSD symptoms can be triggered by different things, such as the anniversary of an event or seeing someone who was involved in the situation.

What Are The Symptoms Of PTSD?

Whether it occurs right after the trauma or later on, PTSD has certain characteristic symptoms. These include:

- **Reliving the traumatic event:** Many people with PTSD have nightmares, flashbacks, or disturbing mental images about the trauma.

- **Avoiding reminders of the trauma:** People with PTSD may avoid people, places, or activities that remind them of the stressful event. They may also avoid talking about what happened.

- **Emotional numbness:** Many people with PTSD feel detached or apart from others, and describe feeling numb to some of the emotions they used to have. For example, loving or pleasure feelings may seem dulled. This could be caused by the overproduction of certain chemicals that block sensation during extreme stress.

- **Hyperalertness:** People with PTSD may be easily startled, on edge, jumpy, irritable, or tense. This may be due to high levels of stress hormones in the body. Normally, these hormones are part of the body's healthy fight or flight reaction to danger or stress. In cases of PTSD, however, the levels of these stress hormones may remain elevated long after they're needed, so the person constantly feels on edge. Difficulty concentrating and trouble sleeping may also be part of this hyperalert state.

Who Develops PTSD?

People of any age—kids, teens, and adults—can develop PTSD after facing an overwhelmingly frightening event that threatens life or safety; but not everyone who experiences a serious trauma develops PTSD. In fact, most people do not. Many recover from life-threatening traumas (after a normal reaction to the stressful event and the right support) without having a lasting problem. This ability to cope and bounce back is called resilience.

What makes some people more resilient to extremely stressful events when others have trouble coping? Researchers have found that certain things can help someone to be more resilient and to recover quicker from trauma. Everything from a person's belief in their ability to overcome problems to the types of hormones a person's body produces may play a role in resilience to stress.

Another factor in stress resilience is relationships: Having strong support from family and friends and getting counseling right after a traumatic event are two things that help. People who have little family or social support after a trauma, and those who have experienced past trauma, tend to be more vulnerable to PTSD.

The intensity or circumstances of a trauma can influence a person's vulnerability to PTSD, too. National disasters like the terrorist attacks of 9/11 or the Oklahoma City bombing can cause widespread anxiety and post-traumatic effects, even in people who didn't experience the trauma directly. These events can make people feel vulnerable and may trigger PTSD in some kids, teens, and adults.

How Is PTSD Treated?

Unfortunately PTSD often doesn't just go away on its own. Without treatment, some symptoms of PTSD can last for months or years, or they may come and go in waves. The right treatment and support, however, can help people of all ages to recover from PTSD.

Mental health professionals (such as psychologists, psychiatrists, and counselors) who specialize in treating anxiety problems are usually experienced in working with people who have PTSD. Therapy for PTSD may involve gradually talking it through in a safe environment and learning coping skills that help a person relieve anxiety, fear, or panic. These include relaxation techniques that help people with PTSD reset their stress response and techniques to resolve other problems, such as sleeping difficulties. Sometimes medications can help reduce symptoms of anxiety, panic, or depression in certain people.

♣ **It's A Fact!!**

It used to be believed that people who tend to be emotionally numb after a trauma were showing a healthy response, but now some researchers suspect that people who experience this emotional distancing may be more prone to PTSD.

Source: Excerpted from "Facts about Post-Traumatic Stress Disorder," National Institute of Mental Health, revised 2002.

Healing From Trauma

Sometimes people avoid seeking professional help because they're afraid that talking about an incident will bring back memories or feelings that are too painful. It can be difficult to talk about a traumatic event at first, but doing it in a safe environment with the help and support of a trained professional is the best way to ensure long-term healing. Working through the pain can help reduce symptoms like nightmares and flashbacks. It can also help people avoid potentially harmful behaviors and emotions, like extreme anger or self-injury.

So how do you find the right therapist or counselor for you? The best way is to ask a parent or adult you trust for help. People who are close to you know you well and understand your needs. (Having a support system of family and friends is key to recovering from PTSD.) A doctor or school counselor may also be able to help you find a mental health professional who specializes in anxiety problems; and there are lots of resources available to help locate therapists in your area.

Turning to a professional for help in overcoming PTSD doesn't mean you're weak, and it doesn't mean you're crazy. PTSD is like any physical illness: The body's systems aren't working properly and treatment is needed to fix the problem. In the case of PTSD, the stress response system isn't switching off as it should; instead, it's constantly (or frequently) vigilant when it no longer needs to be. A therapist can help a person deal with the feelings of guilt, shame, or anger that may accompany PTSD—and discover inner strengths that can promote healing.

PTSD can be treated successfully; but if it's not treated it may continue for a long time. Some people learn that in the process of healing from trauma they discover strengths they didn't know they had. Others find that treatment helps them develop new insights into life and how to cope with other problems.

Chapter 21

Fears and Phobias

The roller coaster hesitates for a split second at the peak of its steep track after a long, slow climb. You know what's about to happen, and there's no way to avoid it now. Terrified, you grip the handrail, palms sweating, heart racing, and brace yourself for the wild ride down.

We've all experienced that sudden rush of fear.

What is fear? What causes it? And why do some people seem fearless, seeking out horror flicks, thrill rides, and extreme sports, whereas other people avoid things that trigger any fear reaction? What can people do to conquer fears? What's the difference between fear and anxiety? When is a fear considered a phobia? Read on for the answers to these questions and more.

What is fear?

Fear is a normal human emotional reaction—it is a built-in survival mechanism with which we are all equipped. Even as babies, we possess the survival instincts necessary to respond when we sense danger. Fear is a reaction to danger that involves the mind and body. Fear serves a protective purpose—signaling us of danger and preparing us to deal with it.

About This Chapter: This information was provided by TeensHealth, one of the largest resources online for medically reviewed health information written for parents, kids, and teens. For more articles like this one, visit www.TeensHealth.org, or www.KidsHealth.org. © 2004 The Nemours Center for Children's Health Media, a division of The Nemours Foundation.

A fear reaction happens whenever we sense danger or when we're confronted with something new or unknown that seems potentially dangerous. Fear can be brief—like the startled reaction you have if a balloon unexpectedly pops or if you are surprised by something you didn't expect. This is often over in seconds, as soon as the brain gets enough data to realize there's no danger. If the brain doesn't receive the "all clear" signal, fear can last longer and feel more intense.

Most people tend to avoid the things they feel afraid of. There are, of course, exceptions—some people seek out the thrill of extreme sports, for example, because the rush of fear can be exciting. We all experience fear slightly differently and with more or less intensity. Some people even like it and find it exciting. During the scariest moments of the roller-coaster ride you may be telling yourself, "I'll never get on this thing again—that is, if I make it out alive!" Meanwhile, the friend sitting next to you may think, "This is awesome! As soon as it's over, I'm getting back on!"

Children tend to have more fears than adults because so much of what they experience is new and unfamiliar. Older children tend to have different fears than younger children, but it's normal for kids to have at least a handful of things that are scary to them. Whereas young children tend to fear things like the dark, monsters, loud thunder and lightning, getting lost, or big dogs, older kids are more likely to fear things like being bullied or getting hurt.

Teens have certain common fears, too. Most teens have some social fears like the fear of being embarrassed or rejected or fear of failing. They may also have personal fears, such as a fear of becoming ill or injured. Some may feel afraid of heights, dogs, snakes, or insects or of performing or public speaking. Because teens think about and care about the larger world community, they may also have global fears such as a fear of war or violence.

Some normal fears seem pretty much like a worry, or something you feel generally afraid of or uneasy about. Other times, fear comes as a sudden reaction to a sudden confrontation with danger. It's that sudden fear response that triggers the body's survival mechanism known as the fight or flight reaction. The fear reaction is known as "fight or flight" because that is exactly what the body is preparing itself to do—to fight off the danger or to run like crazy to get away.

What's happening in the body when you experience this reaction? The brain triggers a response that causes the heart rate to increase, blood to pump to large muscle groups to prepare for physical action (such as running or fighting), blood pressure to increase, skin to sweat to keep the body cool, and so forth. The body stays this way until the brain signals that it's safe to relax.

What's the difference between fear and anxiety?

Fear is a reaction to an actual danger signal—it involves physical and mental tension that helps you spring into action to protect yourself from something that is happening. The body suddenly gears up into fight or flight mode when, for example, the car in front of you swerves and you just miss it. Once you know the danger has passed, the fear goes away (though your knees may feel shaky for a few minutes).

The physical and mental tension of anxiety is very similar to fear but with one important difference. With anxiety, there isn't usually anything actually happening right then and there to trigger the feeling. The feeling is coming from the anticipation of future danger or something bad that could happen— there is no danger happening now.

Everyone experiences anxiety from time to time. It can be mild or intense or somewhere in between. A little anxiety helps us to stay on our toes and motivates us to do our best. For example, some anxiety about the possibility of doing poorly on a test can motivate you to study a little harder. A moderate amount of anxiety helps the body and mind get prepared to cope with something stressful or frightening.

Sometimes anxiety can get out of proportion and become too intense or too lasting, and it can interfere with a person's ability to do well. Teens who have a pattern of experiencing too much anxiety may be diagnosed with an anxiety disorder. There are several types of anxiety disorders a teen might experience—each type is named for the symptoms a teen might have or the particular way that anxiety affects him. Many teens with anxiety problems have symptoms that overlap into more than one category.

♣ It's A Fact!!

Agoraphobia is a disorder characterized by intense anxiety about having an panic episode in places or situations from which escape could be challenging or uncomfortable. Some people experience agoraphobia as a fear that stems from not being able to receive assistance during an anxiety attack. For instance, many people with agoraphobia fear leaving their homes alone, being in a large gathering of people, being on a bridge, or riding in various vehicles.

Agoraphobia frequently goes with other anxiety disorders, including panic disorder and specific phobias. Panic attacks are intense feelings of fear and often doom, which usually build and peak within about ten minutes of onset.

Some of the most typical symptoms of a panic attack include the following:

- chest pain and/or heart palpitations

- trembling

- feeling faint or dizzy

- shortness of breath or difficulty catching your breath

- fear of dying

- fear of losing control

- sweating

- feeling nauseated

- strange sensations: numbness, tingling, pricking, or burning

These attacks can be terrifying and physically overwhelming. (People experiencing panic attacks often rush to the emergency room convinced that they are having a heart attack.) Sometimes the attacks are prompted by a particular experience, and sometimes they seem to come out of the blue. Once a person has had some panic attacks, they may begin to fear having one in public and thus develop an additional panic reaction to these situations, and therefore, agoraphobia.

It's important to be as specific as possible when describing your experiences to your health care provider(s). This will help them to determine, with your help, what kinds of treatment approaches might be right for you. They're likely to ask you questions such as these:

- How long have you been experiencing these symptoms?

- Are there particular situations that cause you anxiety?

- How significantly do you feel your anxiety impairs your ability to function on a day-to-day basis?

- What are the treatments you've tried so far? What did you like about them, and what didn't seem to have an effect?

Also, keep in mind that although you may not have had much success with certain therapists or therapies, that doesn't mean that you couldn't find the right treatment with another therapist.

Some possibilities that you may want to consider with your health care provider include cognitive behavioral therapy and/or medication. Research has shown these treatments to be very effective in treating panic attacks and agoraphobia. Cognitive behavioral therapy is essentially just what it sounds like: an approach that aims to change behavior by helping a person adjust his or her way of thinking. It often includes real or imagined exposure (in a protected environment) to the situations or triggers that cause the fear. Over time, a person can learn to understand and therefore manage the fear that comes with being confronted with the traumatic object or situation and identify what maladaptive coping mechanisms have arisen. In doing so, that person can develop new, more reasonable ways of managing stress.

The National Institute of Mental Health (NIMH) reports that treatment can reduce or completely eliminate panic attacks in 70 to 90 percent of cases. (Early treatment can also help avoid the progression of panic disorder to agoraphobia.) The NIMH website (www.nihm.nih.gov) contains more information about treatment options and referrals to help find a therapist who specializes in treating agoraphobia. You can also contact the Anxiety Disorders Association of America (www.adaa.org) for more information.

Source: Excerpted and reprinted with permission from Go Ask Alice!, Columbia University's Health Q&A Internet Service, at www.goaskalice.columbia.edu. Copyright © 2006 by The Trustees of Columbia University.

♣ **It's A Fact!!**
Social Phobia

Social phobia, also called social anxiety disorder, involves overwhelming anxiety and excessive self-consciousness in everyday social situations. People with social phobia have a persistent, intense, and chronic fear of being watched and judged by others and being embarrassed or humiliated by their own actions. Their fear may be so severe that it interferes with work or school, and other ordinary activities. While many people with social phobia recognize that their fear of being around people may be excessive or unreasonable, they are unable to overcome it. They often worry for days or weeks in advance of a dreaded situation.

Social phobia can be limited to only one type of situation—such as a fear of speaking in formal or informal situations, or eating, drinking, or writing in front of others—or, in its most severe form, may be so broad that a person experiences symptoms almost anytime they are around other people. Social phobia can be very debilitating—it may even keep people from going to work or school on some days. Many people with this illness have a hard time making and keeping friends.

Physical symptoms often accompany the intense anxiety of social phobia and include blushing, profuse sweating, trembling, nausea, and difficulty talking. If you suffer from social phobia, you may be painfully embarrassed by these symptoms and feel as though all eyes are focused on you. You may be afraid of being with people other than your family.

People with social phobia are aware that their feelings are irrational. Even if they manage to confront what they fear, they usually feel very anxious beforehand and are intensely uncomfortable throughout. Afterward, the unpleasant feelings may linger, as they worry about how they may have been judged or what others may have thought or observed about them.

Social phobia affects about 5.3 million adult Americans. Women and men are equally likely to develop social phobia. The disorder usually begins in childhood or early adolescence, and there is some evidence that genetic factors are involved. Social phobia often co-occurs with other anxiety disorders or depression. Substance abuse or dependence may develop in individuals who attempt to "self-medicate" their social phobia by drinking or using drugs. Social phobia can be treated successfully with carefully targeted psychotherapy or medications.

Source: Excerpted from "Anxiety Disorders," National Institute of Mental Health, NIH Pub. No. 3879, 2000, updated August 2005.

What is a phobia?

A phobia is an intense, unreasonable fear of a thing or a situation that is far out of proportion to the actual danger or harm that is possible. The fear and distress lead the person to avoid the object or situation they fear.

Most people tend to avoid certain things they fear. If a person is afraid to jump from an airplane, he'll probably always avoid signing up for skydiving lessons. One could argue that this fear is somewhat reasonable and that skydiving is actually a risky activity. And not skydiving probably won't interfere much with the person's life. But if a phobia is related to an everyday object or situation, steering clear of it would cause greater disruption in someone's life. And if that fear is unreasonable—that is, most people would agree that there's not actually much, if any, danger—then the fear would probably be considered a phobia.

With a phobia, a person's fear is so intense that they do whatever they can to avoid coming into contact with the object of their fear, and often spend time thinking about whether they're likely to encounter it in a given situation. For a fear to be considered a phobia it has to be so extreme and cause so much distress that it gets in the way of a person's normal activities.

Phobias interfere with a person's life because the need to avoid the object of the phobia limits what a person feels comfortable doing. A teen with a phobia of dogs, for example, may avoid going to friends' homes because they have dogs or to the park because there might be a dog there. So although it may be totally normal for a teen to be somewhat afraid of a large growling dog he doesn't know, a teen with a phobia of dogs may be so fearful that seeing any dog is very frightening and merely thinking about encountering a dog might be distressing.

What causes phobias?

Some people may be more likely to develop phobias than others. Anxiety problems often run in families, and a phobia is one type of anxiety problem. Kids and teens who tend to be fearful and who worry a lot often have parents who have these traits. Anxiety that runs in families can partly be explained by biology and genetics. Certain biological traits passed down in families

✎ What's It Mean?

Acarophobia: Fear of small parasites, small particles, or of itching.

Acrophobia: Fear of heights.

Ailurophobia: Fear of or aversion to cats.

Androphobia: Fear of men, or of the male sex.

Anemophobia: Fear of wind.

Aquaphobia: Fear of water.

Arachnephobia: Fear of spiders (Syn: arachnophobia).

Astrapophobia: Fear of lightning.

Bathophobia: Fear of deep places or of looking into them.

Belonephobia: Fear of needles, pins, and other sharp-pointed objects.

Bromidrosiphobia: Fear of giving forth a bad odor from the body, sometimes with the belief that such an odor is present.

Brontophobia: Fear of thunder (Syn: tonitrophobia).

Claustrophobia: Fear of being in a confined place.

Cremnophobia: Fear of precipices or steep places.

Cynophobia: Fear of dogs.

Entomophobia: Fear of insects.

Eremophobia: Fear of deserted places or of solitude.

Ereuthophobia: Fear of blushing.

Gephyrophobia: Fear of crossing a bridge.

Gerontophobia: Fear of old persons.

Gynephobia: Fear of women or of the female sex.

Hamartophobia: Fear of error or sin.

Haphephobia: A morbid dislike or fear of being touched.

Helminthophobia: Fear of worms.

Hylephobia: Fear of forests.

Hypengyophobia: Fear of responsibility.

Hypnophobia: Fear of falling asleep.

Ichthyophobia: Fear of fish.

Laliophobia: Fear of speaking or stuttering.

Mechanophobia: Fear of machinery.

Necrophobia: Fear of corpses.

Neophobia: Morbid aversion to, or dread of, novelty or the unknown.

Noctiphobia: Morbid dread of night and its darkness and silence.

Nosophobia: An inordinate dread and fear of disease.

Ochlophobia: Fear of crowds.

Onomatophobia: Abnormal dread of certain words or names because of their supposed significance.

Ophidiophobia: Fear of snakes.

Phasmophobia: Fear of ghosts.

Pnigophobia: Fear of choking.

Pyrophobia: Morbid dread of fire.

Radiophobia: Fear of radiation, as from x-rays or nuclear energy.

Scopophobia: Morbid dread of being stared at.

Spectrophobia: Fear of mirrors or of one's mirrored image.

Taphophobia: Fear of being buried alive.

Thanatophobia: Fear of death.

Toxicophobia: Fear of being poisoned (Syn: toxiphobia).

Trichophobia: Morbid disgust caused by the sight of loose hairs on clothing or elsewhere.

Triskaidekaphobia: Superstitious dread of the number 13.

Xenophobia: Fear of strangers.

Zoophobia: Fear of animals.

Source: From *Stedman's Medical Dictionary, 27th Edition*, copyright © 2000 Lippincott Williams & Wilkins. All rights reserved.

may affect the brain's chemical regulation of mood and can affect how sensitive someone is or how strongly they react to fear cues.

Some people are born with a natural tendency to be more cautious and inhibited; others have an inborn tendency to be more bold and uninhibited. Having a cautious style may make it more likely for someone to develop phobias or anxiety.

Learning also plays a role in helping phobias develop and linger. Children learn by watching how their parents and others react to the world around them—this is part of how kids learn what's safe and what's dangerous. If parents are overcautious or overemphasize danger, children may more easily learn to see the world this way, too.

When someone develops a phobia, they quickly learn that they feel anxious when they are near the object or situation they fear—and that they feel relief when they avoid it. Learning that avoidance can reduce their anxiety (at least for the moment) and increases the likelihood that they will avoid the feared situation or object next time. The difficulty is that these avoidance behaviors have to keep increasing and happening even sooner to provide the same relief. Pretty soon, a person finds himself spending time worrying about the possibility of encountering the feared situation and avoiding anything that might bring him into contact with it. With a phobia, the pattern of anxiety, avoidance, and worry about the possibility of contact tends to grow bigger and interferes more with life over time.

What are specific phobias?

The term specific phobia is used for an intense unreasonable fear of a specific object or situation. Someone may have a specific phobia of snakes, heights, elevators, or blood, for example.

Specific phobias may develop when a person has an encounter with an object or situation that involves or provokes fear. A brain structure called the amygdala (pronounced: uh-mig-duh-luh), which keeps track of memory and emotions, remembers when that person encounters the object the next time that it provoked fear in the past. The amygdala then signals that the object might be dangerous.

How are specific phobias treated?

Gradual exposure to the object or situation is a very effective way to help people overcome specific phobias. Exposure is a technique based on certain principles of learning and behavior. The idea is that the brain can learn to adapt to something that seems dangerous at first, but isn't actually dangerous, by gradually having time to encounter that thing in a controlled, gradual, supported way. Just as kids can learn to overcome their fear of the dark by gradually getting used to it with the right support and reassurance of safety, gradual exposure can introduce someone slowly to the feared object or situation, allowing the brain to adjust. With this gradual exposure, anxiety decreases as the person faces the fear—first from a distance, then gradually closer and more fully. Exposure may even begin by having the person simply imagine the object or look a picture of it because with phobias this can be enough to trigger the intense fear.

Exposure is usually combined with techniques that help people to relax while they are imagining or encountering the object. Relaxation techniques may include things like specific ways of breathing, muscle relaxation training, guided mental imagery, or soothing self-talk. Pairing a relaxing sensation with an object that has triggered fear can help the brain to neutralize the fear the object used to be associated with.

Part Three

Behavioral, Personality, And Psychotic Disorders

Chapter 22

Behavior Disorders

Disruptive Behavior Disorders

Disruptive behavior disorders involve consistent patterns of behaviors that "break the rules." Young people of all ages break some rules, especially less important ones. More serious oppositional behavior is a normal part of childhood for children two and three years old and for young teenagers. At other times, when young people are routinely very, very oppositional and defiant of authority, a mental health disorder may be identified.

Oppositional Defiant Disorder: In oppositional defiant disorder, the rules broken are usually those in the family and the school. Oppositional defiant disorder may occur in children of any age and in adolescents. Sometimes oppositional defiant disorder leads to conduct disorder. Between one and six percent of children and adolescents have oppositional defiant disorder.

About This Chapter: This chapter begins with "Disruptive Behavior Disorders—Children and Adolescents," © 2006 Mental Health Association of Westchester (http://mhawestchester.org); reprinted with permission. "Questions and Answers About Conduct Disorder," is excerpted from "Children and Adolescents with Conduct Disorder," National Mental Health Information Center, April 2003. "Antisocial Behavior" is excerpted from "Child and Adolescent Violence Research at the NIMH," National Institute of Mental Health, 2000, updated September 2005.

The following are examples of oppositional defiant disorder behaviors:

- Frequent defiance of the authority of parents, teachers and others
- Arguing and refusing to obey rules at home and school
- Failure to take responsibility for bad behavior or mistakes
- Resentment and looking for revenge
- Regular temper tantrums

Conduct Disorder Behaviors: In conduct disorder, the rules broken include the regulations and laws made by society. Conduct disorder usually occurs in older children and adolescents. Between one and four percent of young persons seven to seventeen have conduct disorder.

Examples of conduct disorder behaviors include the following:

- Aggressive behaviors that threaten or harm people or animals
- Behaviors that destroy property such as fire setting, breaking windows or graffiti
- Stealing, bullying, or lying to get something
- Serious violations of rules, including school truancy and running away from home

What causes disruptive behavior disorders?

Research has identified both biological and environmental causes for disruptive behavior disorders. Youngsters most at risk for oppositional defiant and conduct disorders are those who have low birth weight, neurological damage, or attention deficit/hyperactivity disorder. Youngsters may also be at risk if they were rejected by their mothers as babies, separated from their parents and not given good foster care, physically or sexually abused, raised in homes with mothers who were abused, or living in poverty.

How can disruptive behavior disorders be treated?

Because so many of the factors that cause disruptive behavior disorders happen very early in a child's life, it is important to recognize the problems as early as possible and get treatment. The treatment that has shown the best results involves a combination of the following elements:

Signs Of Conduct Disorder

Symptoms of conduct disorder include:

- Aggressive behavior that harms or threatens other people or animals;

- Destructive behavior that damages or destroys property;

- Lying or theft;

- Truancy or other serious violations of rules;

- Early tobacco, alcohol, and substance use and abuse; and

- Precocious sexual activity.

Children with conduct disorder or oppositional defiant disorder also may experience:

- Higher rates of depression, suicidal thoughts, suicide attempts, and suicide;

- Academic difficulties;

- Poor relationships with peers or adults;

- Sexually transmitted diseases;

- Difficulty staying in adoptive, foster, or group homes; and

- Higher rates of injuries, school expulsions, and problems with the law.

Source: Excerpted from "Children and Adolescents with Conduct Disorder," National Mental Health Information Center, April 2003.

- Specialized parent skills training

- Behavior therapies to teach young people how to control and express feelings in healthy ways

- Coordination of services with the young person's school and other involved agencies

- Parent training and therapy with the child or adolescent, most effective when done in the family home

No medications have been consistently useful in reducing the symptoms of oppositional defiant or conduct disorders. Medications may be helpful to some young people, but they tend to have side effects that must be monitored carefully.

Questions And Answers About Conduct Disorder

How common is conduct disorder?

Conduct disorder affects 1 to 4 percent of 9- to 17-year-olds, depending on exactly how the disorder is defined. The disorder appears to be more common in boys than in girls and more common in cities than in rural areas.

Who is at risk for conduct disorder?

Research shows that some cases of conduct disorder begin in early childhood, often by the preschool years. In fact, some infants who are especially "fussy" appear to be at risk for developing conduct disorder. Other factors that may make a child more likely to develop conduct disorder include:

- Early maternal rejection;

- Separation from parents, without an adequate alternative caregiver;

- Early institutionalization;

- Family neglect;

- Abuse or violence;

- Parental mental illness;

- Parental marital discord;

- Large family size;

- Crowding; and

- Poverty.

What help is available for families?

Although conduct disorder is one of the most difficult behavior disorders to treat, young people often benefit from a range of services that include:

- Training for parents on how to handle child or adolescent behavior.

♣ **It's A Fact!!**
Some Signs of Hyperactivity, Impulsivity, And Inattention

- Feeling restless, often fidgeting with hands or feet, or squirming while seated

- Running, climbing, or leaving a seat in situations where sitting or quiet behavior is expected

- Blurting out answers before hearing the whole question

- Having difficulty waiting in line or taking turns

- Often becoming easily distracted by irrelevant sights and sounds

- Often failing to pay attention to details and making careless mistakes

- Rarely following instructions carefully and completely losing or forgetting things like pencils, books, and tools needed for a task

- Often skipping from one uncompleted activity to another

Source: Excerpted from "Attention Deficit Hyperactivity Disorder," National Institute on Mental Health, 2003.

- Family therapy.

- Training in problem solving skills for children or adolescents.

- Community-based services that focus on the young person within the context of family and community influences.

Antisocial Behavior

The National Institute of Mental Health (NIMH) has gathered information about risk factors, experiences, and processes that are related to the development of aggressive, antisocial, and violent behavior, including mental health problems, associated with childhood and adolescence. NIMH research points to the importance of a nurturing social environment in childhood, good early education, and success in academic areas. It has been learned that the influence of peers, whether positive or negative, is of critical importance. Research also suggests that current policies and approaches grouping or housing troubled adolescents together may be the wrong approach, and it is clear that there are no quick, inexpensive answers. This overview highlights what is known about risk factors for the development of antisocial and problem behavior, and the often underutilized early prevention and intervention strategies.

What are the risk factors for antisocial behavior?

Many studies indicate that a single factor or a single defining situation does not cause child and adolescent antisocial behavior. Rather, multiple factors contribute to and shape antisocial behavior over the course of development. Some factors relate to characteristics within the child, but many others relate to factors within the social environment (for example, family, peers, school, neighborhood, and community contexts) that enable, shape, and maintain aggression, antisocial behavior, and related behavior problems.

The research on risk for aggressive, antisocial, and violent behavior includes multiple aspects and stages of life, beginning with interactions in the family. Such forces as weak bonding, ineffective parenting (poor monitoring, ineffective, excessively harsh, or inconsistent discipline, inadequate supervision), exposure to violence in the home, and a climate that supports aggression and violence puts children at risk for being violent later in life. This is particularly so for youth with problem behavior, such as early conduct and attention problems, depression, anxiety disorders, lower cognitive and verbal abilities, etc. Outside of the home, one of the major factors contributing to youth violence is the impact of peers. In the early school years, a good deal of mild aggression and violence is related to peer rejection and competition for status and attention. More serious behavior problems and violence are associated with smaller numbers of youths who are failing academically and who band together, often with other youth rejected by prosocial peers. Successful early adjustment at home increases the likelihood that children will overcome such individual challenges and not become violent. However, exposure to violent or aggressive behavior within a family or peer group may influence a child in that direction.

Does antisocial behavior occur with other mental health disorder?

There is strong evidence for the co-occurrence of two or more syndromes or disorders among children with behavioral and emotional problems. Many people think that children either act out or turn their feelings inward, but the truth is more complex. The obviously angry adolescent has other conditions such as anxiety disorders and depression (as seen in the quiet withdrawn young person) more often than would occur by chance. Research in this area indicates that very young children with conduct problems and anxiety disorders or depression display more serious aggression than youths with only conduct problems. It is not entirely clear whether depression precipitates acting out, whether impairments and predispositions for acting out lead to depression, or whether there are underlying causal factors that are responsible for the joint display of such problems.

It is very common for youth with conduct problems to also display symptoms of attention deficit hyperactivity disorder (ADHD), the most commonly diagnosed behavioral disorder of childhood. The diagnosis is made by the presence of persistent age-inappropriate inattention and impulsivity, often coexisting with hyperactivity. This co-occurrence is often associated with an early onset of aggression and impairment in personal, interpersonal, and family functioning. Furthermore, academic underachievement is common in youth with early onset conduct problems, ADHD, and adolescents who display delinquent behavior.

Is there a genetic cause of antisocial behavior?

Our understanding of the nature of genetic influences on antisocial behavior is incomplete. Many twin and adoption studies indicate that child and adolescent antisocial behavior is influenced by both genetic and environmental factors, suggesting that genetic factors directly influence cognitive and temperamental predispositions to antisocial behavior. These predisposing child factors and socializing environments, in turn, influence antisocial behavior.

Research suggests that for some youth with early onset behavior problems, genetic factors strongly influence temperamental predisposition, particularly oppositional temperament, which can affect experiences negatively. When antisocial behavior emerges later in childhood or adolescence, it is suspected that genetic factors contribute less, and such youths tend to engage in delinquent behavior primarily because of peer influences and lapses in parenting. The nature of the child's social environment regulates the degree to which heritable early predisposition results in later antisocial behavior. Highly adaptive parenting is likely to help children who may have a predisposition to antisocial behavior. Success in school and good verbal ability tend to protect against the development of antisocial behavior, pointing to the importance of academic achievement.

Do parental and family factors cause antisocial behavior?

Research has demonstrated that youths who engage in high levels of antisocial behavior are much more likely than other youths to have a biological parent who also engages in antisocial behavior. This association is believed to reflect both the genetic transmission of predisposing temperament and the maladaptive parenting of antisocial parents.

The importance of some aspects of parenting may vary at different ages. For example, inadequate supervision apparently plays a stronger role in late childhood and adolescence than in early childhood. There is evidence from many studies that parental use of physical punishment may play a direct role in the development of antisocial behavior in their children. In longitudinal studies, higher levels of parental supervision during childhood have been found to predict less antisocial behavior during adolescence. Other researchers

☞ **Remember!!**

Recent years have witnessed a strong growth in our understanding of the risk factors and processes that contribute to and shape child and adolescent antisocial behavior. Yet gaps remain in our scientific understanding of how child, family, school/community, and peer factors interact, and which are the most appropriate targets for prevention and early intervention in different settings. We are also learning that being "at risk" does not doom any one child to become violent; conversely, the apparent absence of certain risk does not necessarily protect any one child from problem behavior. The development of serious behavior problems is best understood as a dynamic interaction between child predispositions and various influences on children's lives (family, peer, and school/community) that change over critical periods of development.

Successful programs that produce long-term sustained effects may need to involve long-term intense interventions to target the multiple factors that can lead to negative outcomes such as family conflict, depression, social isolation, school failure, substance abuse, delinquency, and violence.

Source: National Institute of Mental Health, updated September 2005.

have observed that parents often do not define antisocial behavior as something that should be discouraged, including such acts as youths bullying or hitting other children or engaging in "minor" delinquent acts such as shoplifting.

Research examining the mental health outcomes of child abuse and neglect has demonstrated that childhood victimization places children at increased risk for delinquency, adult criminality, and violent criminal behavior. Findings from early research on trauma suggest that traumatic stress can result in failure of systems essential to a person's management of stress response, arousal, memory, and personal identity that can affect functioning long after acute exposure to the trauma has ended. One might expect that the consequences of trauma can be even more profound and long lasting when they influence the physiology, behavior, and mental life of a developing child or adolescent.

Do peer influences cause antisocial behavior?

Antisocial children with earlier ages of onset tend to make friends with children similar to themselves. Consequently, they reinforce one another's antisocial behavior. Children with ADHD are often rejected due to their age-inappropriate behavior, and thus are more likely to associate with other rejected and/or delinquent peers. The influence of delinquent peers on late-onset antisocial behavior appears to be quite strong. Association with antisocial peers has been shown to be related to the later emergence of new antisocial behavior during adolescence among youths who had not exhibited behavior problems as children.

Less adult supervision allows youths to spend more time with delinquent peers. Thus, improving parental supervision may be an important way to reduce the effects of delinquent peer influence. Ongoing research is examining how neighborhood effects on antisocial behavior are mediated by the willingness of neighbors to supervise youths and possibly reduce the likelihood of association with delinquent peers in the neighborhood.

Do socioeconomic factors cause antisocial behavior?

An inverse relationship of family income and parental education with antisocial behavior has been found in many population-based studies. Across gender and ethnicity, much of the inverse relationship between family income and antisocial behavior is accounted for by less parental monitoring at lower levels of socioeconomic status.

Chapter 23

Adjustment Disorder

Definition

Adjustment disorder is an abnormal and excessive reaction to a life stressor, such as starting school, getting divorced, or grief.

Causes, Incidence, And Risk Factors

Symptoms of adjustment disorder typically begin within three months of the identifiable stressor and usually do not last longer than six months. Adults often develop adjustment disorder related to marital or financial problems.

In adolescents, common stressors include school problems, family conflict, or sexuality issues. Other stressors for people of any age include the death of a loved one, general life changes, or unexpected catastrophes.

There is no way to predict which people are likely to develop adjustment disorder, given the same stressor. Financial conditions, social support, and career and recreational opportunities can influence how well a person reacts to stress. A given person's susceptibility to stress may be influenced by such factors as social skills, intelligence, flexibility, genetic factors, and coping strategies.

Symptoms

To receive a diagnosis of adjustment disorder, symptoms must be severe enough to effect a person's work or social life. Some of the symptoms that can occur include:

- Depression
- Palpitations
- Agitation
- Conduct disturbances
- Trembling or twitching
- Physical complaints

Signs And Tests

The following criteria need to be met to establish a diagnosis:

- The person must have a psychological evaluation
- The symptoms clearly follow a psychosocial stressor
- The symptoms are more severe than would be expected
- There do not appear to be other underlying disorders

♣ **It's A Fact!!**
There is no known way to prevent this disorder. Strong support from friends and family can help.

Treatment

The primary goal of treatment is to relieve symptoms and help the person return to the level of functioning the person had before the stressful event.

Most mental health professionals recommend a form of psychosocial treatment for this disorder. Treatments include individual psychotherapy, family therapy, behavior therapy, and self-help groups.

When medications are used, they are usually in addition to other forms of treatment.

Expectations (Prognosis)

Adjustment disorders usually resolve quickly without any remaining symptoms.

Calling Your Health Care Provider

Call for an appointment with your health care provider if symptoms suggestive of adjustment disorder develop.

Chapter 24

Body-Focused Repetitive Behaviors

What exactly are body-focused repetitive behaviors (BFRBs)?

These are a group of behaviors in which an individual damages his or her appearance or causes physical injury through:

- Hair pulling to the point of having seriously thinned hair or bald spots, missing eyebrows, or eyelashes

- Skin picking, resulting in scabs, sores that never heal, holes in the skin, and scarring

- Nail and/or cuticle biting, causing bleeding or infected fingertips

- Blemish picking or squeezing, causing scarring and infections

- Biting the inside of the cheek

These behaviors may be performed when the individual is stressed or excited, or bored or inactive. Hours may be spent in these activities, taking individuals away from family or work activities. Depression, shame, and

About This Chapter: Excerpted from "Hair Pulling, Skin Picking and Biting: Body-focused Repetitive Disorders," from AAMFT Consumer Update, Copyright 2002 by the American Association for Marriage and Family Therapy. Reproduced with permission of the American Association for Marriage and Family Therapy, via Copyright Clearance Center.

isolation can also result. BFRBs most often begin in late childhood or in the early teens, and may affect at least 1 out of 20 people. While once thought to be rare and impossible to treat, we now know that neither of these ideas is true. While it is not always easy to find practitioners who can treat these disorders, there are a growing number of resources, and the picture is gradually improving.

♣ **It's A Fact!!**
Trichotillomania may be classified as an impulse control disorder, obsessive-compulsive spectrum disorder, or habit/stereotypy. Hair-pulling may exist as either a habit or goal-directed behavior. Habits are repetitive behaviors or routine actions occurring without conscious effort.

Source: Excerpted from "Meeting Summary: Scientific Advances in Trichotillomania and Related Body-Focused Repetitive Behaviors," National Institute of Mental Health, April 2005.

What are other signs of BFRBs?

Many of the signs of BFRBs can be well hidden, and only revealed by accident. Many sufferers do such things as styling their hair to cover bald spots, wearing wigs or hair weaves, penciling in eyebrows, wearing clothing that hides skin damage, or keeping their hands behind their backs or in their pockets as much as possible, to name a few. Sufferers may go to great lengths to not undress or take their hair down in front of spouses. Children may suddenly refuse to go to school, to avoid being teased or reprimanded by their teachers. Adults may shy away from social situations, work, or job interviews. Feelings of depression are also very common.

When should someone seek help?

It is important for sufferers to find help when it becomes evident that the behavior is out of control and is starting to limit their lives or affect the sufferer's relationships. It may be clear at this point, that different attempts at stopping have not worked, and are not going to work. Along with these, there may also be emotional problems such as depression, substance abuse, or the avoidance of school, social events, or work that can also be warning signs. Frequent family fights or disputes over the behavior should also be indicators that some type of help is needed.

How are BFRBs treated?

There are three main types of help. These are behavioral therapy, medication, and family therapy. Ordinary talk therapy alone has not been shown to be of much help. Behavioral therapy usually consists of two approaches: Habit reversal therapy (HRT), which teaches the sufferer a set of alternative behaviors that can help them focus themselves, interrupt, and block the behavior, and stimulus control (SC), which teaches them how to identify, change, and control the different triggers present in their routines, environments, and moods that lead to the behaviors. Medication can be of help in some cases, although it does not seem to be equally effective for everyone. It should be regarded as a tool to help with behavior therapy. Medicinal use is advised when the urge to do the behaviors is so strong that the individual feels it's irresistible and cannot follow behavioral therapy instructions. Family therapy can be extremely valuable in a number of ways, and can make important contributions in healing the family, and aiding the sufferer's recovery. First, it can help family members to accept the problem, to not blame the sufferer, and to not become over-involved in the symptoms or treatment. It can also be of help in calming situations where fighting and conflict have resulted. Another contribution family therapy can make is to help those close to the sufferer to be patient about setbacks and lapses, which are not unusual.

Consumer Resources

1. *The Hair Pulling Problem: A Complete Guide to Trichotillomania*, Fred Penzel, Ph.D., Oxford University Press, New York, 2003. This represents the latest, largest, and most comprehensive self-help book for hair pullers now available.

2. The Trichotillomania Learning Center (TLC) (http://www.trich.org/), Santa Cruz, CA. A nonprofit foundation, TLC is the premiere organization for BFRB sufferers, and provides support, information, and referrals.

3. "Bad Hair Life," Without question, the definitive video documentary on TTM. This is a must-see for all those with the disorder, and their significant others. It is available from Fanlight Productions (http://www.fanlight.com/) 800-937-4113.

4. *Obsessive-Compulsive Disorders: A Complete Guide to Getting Well and Staying Well*, Fred Penzel, Ph.D., Oxford University Press, New York, 2000. A compendium of self-help information for those who suffer from OCD, BDD, Trichotillomania, Compulsive Skin Picking, and Compulsive Nail Biting.

5. *The Hair-Pulling "Habit" and You (Revised Ed.)*, Ruth Golomb and Sherrie Vavrichek, Writers' Cooperative of Greater Washington, Silver Spring, Maryland, 2000. A very good self-help workbook for children with trichotillomania.

6. *Help for Hair Pullers: Understanding and Coping with Trichotillomania*, Nancy J. Keuthen, Ph.D., Dan J. Stein, M.D., and Gary A. Christenson, M.D., New Harbinger Publications, Oakland, CA, 2001. An excellent guide written by three acknowledged experts and top researchers in the field of TTM.

Chapter 25

Self-Injury

Emma's mom first noticed the cuts when Emma was doing the dishes one night. Emma told her mom that their cat had scratched her. Her mom seemed surprised that the cat had been so rough, but she didn't think much more about it.

Emma's friends had noticed something strange as well. Even when the weather was hot, Emma wore long-sleeved shirts. She had become secretive, too, like something was bothering her, but Emma couldn't seem to find the words to tell her mom or her friends that the marks on her arms were from something that she had done. She was cutting herself with a razor when she felt sad or upset.

What Is Cutting?

Injuring yourself on purpose by making scratches or cuts on your body with a sharp object—enough to break the skin and make it bleed—is called cutting. Cutting is a type of self-injury, or SI. Cutting is more common among girls, but guys sometimes self-injure, too. People may cut themselves on their wrists, arms, legs, or bellies. Some people self-injure by burning their skin with the end of a cigarette or lighted match.

About This Chapter: This information was provided by TeensHealth, one of the largest resources online for medically reviewed health information written for parents, kids, and teens. For more articles like this one, visit www.TeensHealth.org, or www.KidsHealth.org. © 2005 The Nemours Center for Children's Health Media, a division of The Nemours Foundation.

When cuts or burns heal, they often leave scars or marks. People who injure themselves usually hide the cuts and marks and sometimes no one else knows.

Self-injury is not new. It's also not a very common behavior, but lately people are talking about it more. As guys and girls hear about cutting, they may feel curious about it and why people do it. Because it seems a little bit forbidden, some younger teens may think that cutting might make them seem daring, grown up, or popular.

♣ It's A Fact!!

The dangers of cutting are obvious, such as the risk of losing too much blood or getting an infection, but there are hidden emotional dangers to cutting, too. It can become enough of a habit that some people feel they are "addicted" to cutting.

With all the talk about it, cutting can almost seem like the latest fad, but cutting is a serious problem.

Why Do People Cut Themselves?

It can be hard to understand why people cut themselves on purpose. Cutting is what experts call an unhealthy coping mechanism. This means that the people who do it have not developed healthy ways of dealing with strong emotions, intense pressure, or upsetting relationship problems.

There are lots of good, healthy ways to cope with difficulties, such as talking problems over with parents, other adults, or friends; putting problems in perspective; and getting plenty of exercise, but people who cut haven't developed these skills. When emotions don't get expressed in a healthy way, tension can build up—sometimes to a point where it seems almost unbearable. Cutting may be an attempt to relieve that extreme tension. It's a confused way of feeling in control. That's one of the reasons why younger teens are more likely to cut.

The urge to cut might be triggered by strong feelings the person can't express—such as anger, hurt, shame, frustration, or depression. People who cut sometimes say they feel they don't fit in or that no one understands them. A person might cut because of losing someone close or to escape a sense of emptiness. Cutting might seem like the only way to find relief, or the only way to express personal pain over relationships or rejection.

People who cut or self-injure sometimes have other mental health problems that contribute to their emotional tension. Cutting is sometimes (but not always) associated with depression, bipolar disorder, eating disorders, obsessive thinking, or compulsive behaviors. It can also be a sign of mental health problems that cause people to have trouble controlling their impulses or to take unnecessary risks. Some people who cut themselves have problems with drug or alcohol abuse.

Some people who cut have had a traumatic experience, such as living through violence, a disaster, or abuse. Self-injury may feel like a way of "waking up" from a sense of numbness after a traumatic experience. Or it may be a way of reinflicting the pain they went through, expressing anger over it, or trying to get control of it.

What Can Happen To People Who Cut?

Although cutting may provide some temporary relief from a terrible feeling, even people who cut agree that cutting isn't a good way to get that relief. For one thing, the relief doesn't last—the troubles that triggered the cutting remain, they're just masked over.

People don't usually intend to hurt themselves permanently when they cut, and they don't usually mean to keep cutting once they start, but both can happen. It's possible to misjudge the depth of a cut, making it so deep that it requires stitches (or, in extreme cases, hospitalization). Cuts can become infected if a person uses nonsterile or dirty cutting instruments—razors, scissors, pins, or even the sharp edge of the tab on a can of soda.

Most people who cut aren't attempting suicide. Cutting is usually a person's attempt at feeling better, not ending it all. Although some people who cut do attempt suicide, it's usually because of the emotional problems and pain that lie behind their desire to self-harm, not the cutting itself.

Cutting can be habit forming. It can become a compulsive behavior—meaning the more a person does it, the more he or she feels the need to do it. The brain starts to connect the false sense of relief from bad feelings to the act of cutting, and it craves this relief the next time tension builds. When cutting becomes a compulsive behavior, it can seem impossible to stop. So cutting can seem almost like an addiction. A behavior that starts as an attempt to feel more in control can end up controlling you.

How Does Cutting Start?

Cutting often begins on an impulse. It's not something the person thinks about ahead of time. Shauna says, "It starts when something's really upsetting and you don't know how to talk about it or what to do; but you can't get your mind off feeling upset, and your body has this knot of emotional pain. Before you know it, you're cutting yourself, and then somehow, you're in another place. Then, the next time you feel awful about something, you try it again—and slowly it becomes a habit."

Natalie, an eleventh grader who started cutting in middle school, explains that it was a way to distract herself from feelings of rejection and helplessness she felt she couldn't bear. "I never looked at it as anything that bad at first—just my way of getting my mind off something I felt really awful about. I guess part of me must have known it was a bad thing to do, though, because I always hid it. Once a friend asked me if I was cutting myself and I even lied and said 'no.' I was embarrassed."

Sometimes self-injury affects a person's body image. Jen says, "I actually liked how the cuts looked. I felt kind of bad when they started to heal—and so I would 'freshen them up' by cutting again. Now I can see how crazy that sounds, but at the time, it seemed perfectly reasonable to me. I was all about those cuts—like they were something about me that only I knew. They were like my own way of controlling things. I don't cut myself any more, but now I have to deal with the scars."

You can't force someone who self-injures to stop. It doesn't help to get mad at a friend who cuts, reject that person, lecture her, or beg him to stop. Instead, let your friend know that you care, that he or she deserves to be healthy and happy, and that no one needs to bear their troubles alone.

Cutting—The New Cool?

Girls and guys who self-injure are often dealing with some heavy troubles. Many work hard to overcome difficult problems. So they find it hard to believe that there are some teens who cut just because they think it's a way to seem tough and rebellious.

♣ It's A Fact!!

Some people with very dramatic personalities cut as a way to call attention to themselves. Kirsty used to cut in the school bathroom so her friends could find her. When they showed fear or panic at the sight of Kirsty bleeding, it reinforced her cutting. Fortunately, a school counselor helped Kirsty get the assistance she needed.

Tia tried cutting because a couple of the girls at her school were doing it. They pressured her. "It seemed like if I didn't do it, they would think I was afraid or something. So I did it once, but when I walked away, I thought about how lame it was to do something like that to myself for no good reason. Next time they asked I just said, 'no thanks, it's not for me.'"

If you have a friend who suggests you try cutting, say what you think. Why get pulled into something you know isn't good for you? There are plenty of other ways to express who you are. (Not giving in to peer pressure is one of them.)

Lindsay had been cutting herself for three years because of abuse she suffered as a child. She's 16 now and hasn't cut herself in more than a year. "I feel proud of that," Lindsay says. "So when I hear girls talk about it like it's a fad, it really gets to me."

Getting Help

There are better ways to deal with troubles than cutting—healthier, long-lasting ways that don't leave a person with emotional and physical scars. The first step is to get help with the troubles that led to the cutting in the first place. Here are some ideas for doing that:

1. **Tell someone:** People who have stopped cutting often say the first step is the hardest—admitting to or talking about cutting; but they also say that after they open up about it, they often feel a great sense of relief. Choose someone you trust to talk to at first (a parent, school counselor, teacher, coach, doctor, or nurse). If it's too difficult to bring up the topic in person, write a note.

2. **Identify the trouble that's triggering the cutting:** Cutting is a way of reacting to emotional tension or pain. Try to figure out what feelings or situations are causing you to cut. Is it anger? Pressure to be perfect? Relationship trouble? A painful loss or trauma? Mean criticism or mistreatment? Identify the trouble you're having, then tell someone about it. Many people have trouble figuring this part out on their own. This is where a mental health professional can be helpful.

3. **Ask for help:** Tell someone that you want help dealing with your troubles and the cutting. If the person you ask doesn't help you get the assistance you need, ask someone else. Sometimes adults try to downplay the problems teens have or think they're just a phase. If you get the feeling this is happening to you, find another adult (such as a school counselor or nurse) who can make your case for you.

4. **Work on it:** Most people with deep emotional pain or distress need to work with a counselor or mental health professional to sort through strong feelings, heal past hurts, and to learn better ways to cope with life's stresses. One way to find a therapist or counselor is to ask at your doctor's office, at school, or at a mental health clinic in your community.

✔ Quick Tip

Every (yes, every) urge passes if you give it time—but only if you don't act on it. Whenever you act on an urge, you're actually making it stronger and more likely to show up the next time the same tension is present.

Resisting The Urge To Cut

Lots of people who deal with the troubles that caused them to cut still feel the urge. So it can help to have some ideas on how to resist for those times when your emotional tension surges. First, be aware of which situations are likely to trigger your urge to cut. Make a commitment that this time you will not follow the urge, but will do something else instead. Then make a plan for what you will do instead of cutting when you feel this urge. Experts recommend these alternatives as ways to get past the urge to cut:

- rub an ice cube on your skin instead of cutting it

- drink a glass of water

- call a friend

- take a shower

- go for a walk or a run

- exercise

- watch TV

- play with a pet

- draw, scribble, or color designs on paper

- rip up some paper

- listen to music that will shift your mood

- wear a rubber band around your wrist and snap it against your skin

- draw on the skin with a red pen in the place you might usually cut

Remember!!

Although cutting can be a difficult pattern to break, it is possible. Getting professional help to overcome the problem doesn't mean that a person is weak or crazy. Therapists and counselors are trained to help people discover inner strengths that help them heal. These inner strengths can then be used to cope with life's other problems in a healthy way.

Chapter 26

Eating Disorders

Facts About Eating Disorders

What are eating disorders?

Eating disorders are extreme expressions of food and weight issues experienced by many individuals, particularly girls and women. They include anorexia nervosa, bulimia nervosa, and binge eating. Eating disorders are dangerous behaviors that result in big health problems.

Girls with eating disorders can do major damage to their bodies. Restricting what you eat can make you sick—like feeling nauseous, tired, dizzy, or irritable. If this behavior goes on too long, it can mess up your menstrual cycle, dry out your hair and skin, and might even cause early osteoporosis—a disease of the bones. The physical consequences can become life threatening.

The physical problems are only half the story. The emotional problems can be serious too. An unhealthy attitude about food and body image is the main problem. Some girls use food to make themselves feel better; others

About This Chapter: Text in this chapter is from the following BodyWise publications produced by the U.S. Department of Health and Human Services (www.girlpower.gov) and the National Women's Health Information Center (www.womenshealth.gov): "What Are Eating Disorders?" "Anorexia Nervosa," Bulimia Nervosa," "Binge Eating Disorder," "Statistics," "Could You or Your Friend Have an Eating Problem?" "Where to Go for Help," and "Treatment," 2004, and "How to Help a Friend," Office on Women's Health, 2004.

stop eating to feel like they are "in control" of their life. Both behaviors leave people feeling bad about what they are eating. And worst of all, the more people begin to obsess over what they are eating (or not eating), the less they care about other things—like school, friends, or other activities.

How do people get eating disorders?

Experts don't know exactly how people develop eating disorders, but it is likely the result of many factors. Many people who suffer from eating disorders have low self-esteem. Most people with eating disorders share certain traits such as a fear of becoming fat, feelings of not measuring up to other people's expectations, or feeling helpless. Some people with eating disorders feel they have to be perfect in every way—having a perfect body, getting perfect grades, and being an excellent athlete. People who suffer from eating disorders may be depressed or feel they lack control over their lives. Sometimes, they also feel like they don't fit in or don't belong. Often, the problems begin when a person is dealing with a difficult transition, shock, or loss.

♣ It's A Fact!!

Being a teenager can be tough, and sometimes teens who are healthy try to lose weight even though they don't need to. You may feel a lot of pressure to look a certain way. Acting on this pressure may lead to eating disorders like anorexia nervosa or bulimia nervosa.

Anorexia nervosa is a form of self-starvation where a person does not eat enough food to keep healthy and does not maintain a healthy weight.

Bulimia nervosa is when a person eats a lot of food and then vomits or uses other methods, such as fasting or over-exercising, to avoid gaining weight after overeating.

Source: National Institute of Diabetes and Digestive and Kidney Diseases, December 2001.

Girls often experiment with different ways to lose as much weight as possible or to keep their weight down. Here are some examples of unsafe methods girls use to control their weight:

- Diuretics (or water pills) make your body lose water but also important nutrients. In extreme cases, this can cause heart problems.

- Laxatives can cause stomachaches and cramps as well as other serious problems to your digestive system. Laxatives can become habit-forming.

- Self-induced vomiting, even once in a while, can pop blood vessels in your face and swell up your neck glands. Because your food isn't being digested right, you may suffer stomachaches, constipation, heartburn, or diarrhea. Also, repeated vomiting can ruin your teeth and give you cavities.

- Diet pills can cause your heart to beat faster and make you jittery. They also are habit-forming. Once they wear off, you become hungry and want to eat, so you reach for another pill to control your appetite.

- Serious over exercising is another unhealthy way some people control their weight. Exercising for long periods of time when it is not part of a program (like with your school coach) is not smart. Over exercising will make you feel tired and increase your chance of injuries.

Anorexia Nervosa: The Relentless Pursuit Of Thinness

People who suffer from this disorder have an intense and irrational fear of gaining weight because they see themselves as being fat, even when everyone else doesn't. Anorexics feel that they are heavier than the rest of the people around them and want to do something about it. They feel the need to become thinner and thinner and that the quickest way to lose weight is to not eat at all. Food, calories, and body weight take control of the person's life. Anorexics often become isolated. They stop seeing friends and having fun.

Signs And Symptoms

- Missing periods

- Strange eating habits, like restricting certain foods or drastically reducing how much food you eat

- Feeling moody

- Denying hunger

- Extreme concern with body weight and shape

- Over exercising

- Significant or extreme weight loss

Cindy's Story

Cindy was 12 when she developed anorexia nervosa. A rather shy, studious girl, she tried hard to please everybody. She was attractive, but just a little bit overweight. She was afraid that she wasn't pretty enough to get the attention of boys in her class. Her father jokingly told her that she would never get a boyfriend if she didn't lose some weight. She took him seriously, though, and began to diet. "I thought that being thin was the most important thing. I thought it was the only way to get people to like me or notice me. I started worrying that if I ever gained weight I'd become ugly."

Soon after the pounds started dropping off, Cindy's periods stopped. She became obsessed with dieting and food, and she developed strange eating habits. She stopped eating all fast food and anything with fat in it. Every day she weighed all the food she would eat on the kitchen scale, cutting solids into tiny pieces and measuring liquids exactly. Cindy knew the calorie and fat counts of everything. She put her daily ration in small containers lining them up in neat rows. She also exercised all the time, sometimes as much as three hours a day to burn lots of calories. "I'd inline skate, do exercise tapes, or run eight miles a day." She never took an elevator if she could walk up steps.

Cindy managed to push away her friends and was mostly alone. "Every day I counted calories and fat grams, weighed myself and stood in front of a mirror looking for any fat." Cindy was constantly freezing, even when she wore tights and two pairs of wool socks under her jeans. She didn't have much energy and her grades started slipping. No one was able to convince Cindy that she was in danger.

Finally, her doctor insisted that she be hospitalized for treatment of her illness. While in the hospital, she secretly continued her exercise routine in the bathroom, doing lots of sit-ups and knee bends. It took several hospital-izations and a good deal of family therapy for Cindy to face and solve her problems. Now, Cindy is in therapy and is making headway. Her weight is up and her eating habits are healthier. Cindy's advice to other girls: "If you like yourself, you won't change for others—even to be thin. People who like you only because you're thin aren't worth it."

Bulimia Nervosa: The Diet-Binge-Purge Disorder

People who suffer from bulimia eat large amounts of food in a quick, automatic, and helpless fashion. This is called a binge. This may numb their feelings for a little bit, but eventually people suffering from bulimia feel physi-cal discomfort and anxiety about gaining weight. As a result, they purge the food they have eaten by making themselves vomit, using laxatives, over exer-cising, or limiting their diets. Some people use a combination of all these forms of purging.

Signs And Symptoms

- Sneaking food

- Making excuses to go to the bathroom after meals

- Eating large amounts of food on the spur of the moment

- Taking laxatives, vomiting, and/or over exercising to "purge" food

- Extreme concern with body weight and image

- Enamel on teeth begins to wear away, causing cavities

Karen's Story

Karen developed bulimia nervosa at 14, and like Cindy, her strange eat-ing behaviors began when she started to diet. Karen would diet and exercise to lose weight, but unlike Cindy, she regularly ate huge amounts of food and maintained her normal weight by forcing herself to vomit. Karen often felt angry, frightened, and depressed. "My looks were everything to me," Karen said. "I felt guilty if I ate anything with fat in it and was afraid I'd gain a lot of weight, so I would make myself vomit. But at the same time, eating a lot of food was the only thing that made me feel better."

Unable to understand her own behavior, she thought no one else would either. She felt isolated and lonely. Typically, when things were not going well, she would be overcome with an uncontrollable desire for sweets. "After a bad day at school all I could think about was coming home and eating," Karen said. She would sneak the food into her room and even had hiding places for it so her family would not catch on. "I would eat pounds of candy and cake at a time and not stop until I was exhausted or in severe pain." Then, feeling really guilty and disgusted, she would make herself vomit.

Karen's eating habits embarrassed her so much that she kept them secret, until a teacher heard her vomiting in the school bathroom. The teacher referred her to a doctor where she became involved in group therapy and had regular visits with a doctor. Karen learned how to treat her illness and gained understanding from others with the same problem. "Now when I have a bad day, I call a friend instead of turning to food," Karen said. "Sometimes it's still hard, but I now have the confidence in myself to do it."

Binge Eating Disorder: Compulsive Eating

Binge eating is another type of eating disorder. Here, a person eats an amount of food larger than what others would eat in the same amount of time. When someone is bingeing, she usually doesn't have much control over how much she is eating. Binge eating is different from anorexia and bulimia because people do not regularly vomit, over exercise, or abuse laxatives after they have eaten.

Signs And Symptoms

- Eating large amounts of food, even when not hungry
- Eating faster than normal
- Eating alone or in secret
- Eating until uncomfortably full

Statistics On Eating Disorders

Today, eating disorders affect almost 5 percent of all young women in the United States, and as many as 15 percent of young women have unhealthy attitudes and behaviors about food. Most cases of eating disorders occur in women, with many reporting that their disorders started before they were 20 years old. One study recently found that 70 percent of sixth-grade girls surveyed said that they first became concerned about their weight between the ages of 9 and 11. That same study found that a lot of girls (30 to 55 percent) started dieting when they were in middle school.

In a study of children aged 8 to 10, approximately half the girls and one-third of the boys were unhappy with their size.

In a study of girls aged 9 to 15, slightly more than half reported exercising to lose weight, slightly less than half reported eating less to lose weight, and approximately 1 out of 20 reported using diet pills or laxatives to lose weight.

Research has shown that approximately 40 percent of fourth graders have been on a "diet" once in awhile. Research from Anorexia Nervosa and Related Eating Disorders, Inc. (ANRED) suggests that about one percent of female adolescents have anorexia. That means that about one out of every 100 females between the ages of 10 and 20 are not eating enough and should be seeing a doctor.

Bulimia affects 1 to 3 percent of middle and high school girls.

Boys and men develop eating disorders, too. Research from ANRED suggests that 5 to 10 percent of people with anorexia or bulimia are males.

Could You Or Your Friend Have An Eating Problem?

Here are some things to look for if you think you or a friend might have a problem.

- You stop eating or feel guilty when eating certain foods.

- You don't like to eat in front of other people and may even stop going to fun events because there might be fattening foods.

- You weigh yourself a lot and feel fat even when you aren't.

- You often count calories and/or fat grams and worry about what you'll eat next.

- You purposely don't eat for awhile, and then overeat and feel guilty.

- You occasionally purge by making yourself vomit, using laxatives, or over exercising.

Where To Go For Help

If you think that you or somebody you know may have an eating disorder, get help. Don't wait and don't try to deal with the problem by yourself. Talk to a parent or other trusted adult like a counselor, coach, relative, or teacher.

Confronting someone who has an eating disorder is very hard. Your friend

---

♣ It's A Fact!!
Research Shows Bulimic Teens Likely
To Suffer From Depression

Teen-agers suffering from bulimia may in fact be fighting a two-front war, coping with the effects of a devastating eating disorder while struggling with a chronic form of depression, reveals research by Texas A&M University psychologist Marisol Perez, who says the finding has critical implications for the way the disorder is treated.

Often masked by the bulimia itself, dysthymia—a lower-level, chronic form of depression—is often present in bulimics and may even predispose them to the eating disorder, shows the research by Perez and her colleagues Thomas E. Joiner Jr. of Florida State University and Peter M. Lewinsohn of the Oregon Research Institute.

Dysthymia, Perez explains, is different from the more familiar major depression in terms of its duration, severity and persistence of mood disturbance, all factors that can impact the course and treatment of eating disorders.

"As pernicious as major depression can be, it tends to remit, even if untreated," she notes. "By contrast, dysthymia is unrelenting, often lasting decades, with the average episode length lasting more than ten years."

It's this long-lasting nature, Perez says, that makes dysthymia, rather than major depression, more likely to be associated with bulimia, which is characterized by unrelenting negative feelings about one's self.

Bulimics, she says, tend to have chronic low self-esteem. Previous models, she notes, have proposed that high perfectionism when dashed by low self-worth is predictive of bulimia. Because of this, the chronic and pervasive self-esteem may not want to admit she has a problem and may get angry with you for trying to help. If you think a friend has an eating disorder, let her know that you care about her, you're worried, and you want to help. Urge her to tell a trusted adult about her eating disorder. If she won't do it, you need to talk to an adult yourself. She needs as much support and understanding from the people in her life as possible. Reaching out to get help could save your friend's life.

problems associated with dysthymia may make dysthymic people vulnerable to bulimia, she says.

The relationship between bulimia and dysthymia might be the struggle to regulate unrelenting negative moods stemming from the depression and the feelings of low self-esteem associated with the eating disorder, Perez speculates.

Individuals who suffer from simultaneously existing disorders, such as bulimia and dysthymia, usually have a worse course and prognosis in treatment than those who only suffer from one disorder, Perez says. She believes that her findings can provide additional information to create more focused and effective treatments for teens with bulimia. Knowledge of the co-existence of bulimia and dysthymia in teens can help therapists assess specifically for dysthymia in bulimic patients and choose a treatment that will combat both disorders, she says.

Perez says that it is possible for adults to suffer from both disorders, but she notes that the patterns between bulimia and dysthymia may change from adolescence to adulthood, making major depression more likely to co-exist in adults than dysthymia.

She reasons that as the course of bulimia progresses, the social support network and resources of a bulimic person may start to diminish, making negative life events harder to overcome. The binges and purges that serve as a type of coping mechanism in the beginning of the disorder may, over time, lose their comforting aspects while their harmful ones continue to be amplified. This, in turn, may cause the intensity of the depression to increase, making the occurrence of major depression and bulimia more common in adults, she says.

Treatment

Eating disorders are treatable and people do recover from them. They are most successfully treated when treated early. While most patients can be treated as outpatients, some need hospitalized care. Because eating disorders are both an emotional and physical problem, a range of professionals are important for recovery. A therapist helps with the underlying emotional issues and a nutritionist or doctor helps with choosing nutritious foods to maintain a normal weight. A doctor also treats any medical complications of an eating disorder.

♣ It's A Fact!!
How are eating disorders treated?

- **Anorexia nervosa:** The first goal for the treatment of anorexia is to ensure the person's physical health, which involves restoring a healthy weight (NIMH, 2002). Reaching this goal may require hospitalization. Once a person's physical condition is stable, treatment usually involves individual psychotherapy and family therapy during which parents help their child learn to eat again and maintain healthy eating habits on his or her own. Behavioral therapy also has been effective for helping a person return to healthy eating habits. Supportive group therapy may follow, and self-help groups within communities may provide ongoing support.

- **Bulimia nervosa:** Unless malnutrition is severe, any substance abuse problems that may be present at the time the eating disorder is diagnosed are usually treated first. The next goal of treatment is to reduce or eliminate the person's binge eating and purging behavior (NIMH, 2002). Behavioral therapy has proven effective in achieving this goal. Psychotherapy has proven effective in helping to prevent the eating disorder from recurring and in addressing issues that led to the disorder. Studies have also found that Prozac, an antidepressant, may help people who do not respond to psychotherapy (APA, 2002). As with anorexia, family therapy is also recommended.

- **Binge-eating disorder:** The goals and strategies for treating binge-eating disorder are similar to those for bulimia. Binge-eating disorder was recognized only recently as an eating disorder, and research is under way to study the effectiveness of different interventions (NIMH, 2002).

Source: From "Eating Disorders," National Mental Health Information Center, Substance Abuse and Mental Health Services Administration, 2003.

How To Help A Friend

If you are reading this, chances are that you are worried about someone who might have an eating disorder. You might be worried about a friend at school, or possibly a sister or brother. Maybe you have seen your friend throw away food instead of eating. Maybe you have seen your friend vomit on purpose or take laxatives or diet pills. Perhaps your friend seems sad or complains about being fat or feeling worthless. This information can help you approach a friend who may need your help.

A person who is not eating enough may need help: Most of us grow up hearing about family members and friends who are trying to lose weight, and we do not think much about it. However, some people go too far. Being obsessed with body fat or losing weight can be a sign of stress or depression. People who develop eating disorders, such as anorexia or bulimia, often remember that their problems started when they began dieting.

- People who have anorexia eat very little even though they are thin. They have an intense fear of body fat and weight gain.

- People with bulimia will get rid of food that they have just eaten by vomiting or taking laxatives or diuretics (water pills). They also have a fear of body fat even though their size or weight may be normal for them.

- Over-exercising is when someone feels driven to exercise as a way to burn calories from food that she or he has just eaten. People with anorexia or bulimia may over-exercise.

A person who is eating too much may need help: Your friend may need help if she or he is binge eating. Binge eating means eating large amounts of food in a short period of time, usually alone, without being able to stop when full. People with binge eating disorder do not try to get rid of the food they have eaten.

We all overeat sometimes—at parties, on holidays, or when we eat a favorite food. Children and teens may eat a lot because they are growing and are very hungry. But your friend may have a problem if she or he feels out of control when overeating. People with binge eating disorder may feel disgusted with themselves or feel depressed or very guilty after overeating.

Your Friend's Health May Be In Danger

- Not eating enough can make someone feel cold, tired, moody, or grumpy. Not eating can cause dry hair and skin, interfere with a girl's menstrual cycle, and weaken young people's bones.

- Vomiting can damage your throat and teeth, and using laxatives can hurt your intestines and other parts of your body.

- Binge eating can lead to obesity or being overweight.

If You Are Concerned About Your Friend, Don't Keep Your Suspicions To Yourself

In a calm and caring way, tell your friend what you saw or heard. Use "I" statements, and let your friend know that you are concerned. Here are some suggestions:

- "I'm worried about you because you haven't eaten lunch this week."

- "I heard you talking about taking laxatives (or diet pills) and that scares me."

♣ **It's A Fact!!**
What is required for a formal diagnosis of an eating disorder?

Anorexia nervosa: Weighs at least 15 percent below what is considered normal for others of the same height and age; misses at least three consecutive menstrual cycles (if a female of childbearing age); has an intense fear of gaining weight; refuses to maintain the minimal normal body weight; and believes he or she is overweight though in reality is dangerously thin (American Psychiatric Association [APA], 1994; NIMH, 2002).

Bulimia nervosa: At least two binge/purge cycles a week, on average, for at least three months; lacks control over his or her eating behavior; and seems obsessed with his or her body shape and weight (APA, 1994; NIMH, 2002).

Binge-eating disorder: At least two binge-eating episodes a week, on average, for six months; and lacks control over his or her eating behavior (NIMH, 2002).

Source: From "Eating Disorders," National Mental Health Information Center, Substance Abuse and Mental Health Services Administration, 2003.

- "Are you O.K.? Were you vomiting after lunch? I am concerned about you."

Listen carefully to what your friend says. Think about how your friend might feel. Your friend might feel ashamed or scared. Your friend may feel unimportant or think that life doesn't matter. Feeling out of control also is common. Not eating or eating too much may be your friend's way of coping with problems at home or at school.

What if they get mad or deny it? It is very common for people with problems to say that there is nothing wrong. They might beg you not to tell. Or they may promise they won't do it anymore. Your friend may get angry because of fear, shame, or other strong emotions.

Tell Your Friend That You Want To Help

What your friend is doing is scary and unhealthy. Tell your friend that you care and that you want her or him to get help. Encourage your friend to talk to a grownup. Say you would be willing to go along to provide support.

Tell your friend that you want to help and don't want to keep your concern a secret. Your friend's health might be in danger. You may decide to tell your friend that you want to talk to a grownup about it.

Tell An Adult About Your Concern

Being worried about your friend and wanting to help is a good thing. Consider telling your parents or your friend's parents, a teacher, or the school nurse or counselor what you know. Tell someone who will understand and can get help for your friend. It is not "tattling" or "ratting" on your friend if you are worried about her or his health.

Here are some suggestions of what to say:

- "I'm worried about ___ because I saw her (him) throw up on purpose/ take a laxative/talk about taking diet pills/throw away her (his) lunch."

- "I'm concerned about ___ because she (he) always complains about being too fat/seems so sad/says she (he) never can do anything right."

You Are Doing The Right Thing

Being healthy means accepting and nourishing your body. Someone who is not eating or eating too much may need help.

You can't solve your friend's problems, but you can help. Honestly share your concerns and tell a grownup so your friend can get professional help if needed.

Knowing what your friend is doing and telling someone about it might be stressful for you. You might decide to talk to someone, such as a counselor, about your experience with trying to help your friend.

You are doing the right thing. Others will be glad to know and want to help you as well.

Chapter 27

Body Dysmorphic Disorder

Many of us spend a lot of time and effort on our appearance. We wear makeup, work out at the gym, buy flattering clothes, and style our hair, all done in hope of looking more attractive. Individuals with body dysmorphic disorder (BDD) are beset by a more extreme version of these normal appearance concerns. Although we don't know what causes BDD, most likely there are multiple sources including biological, psychological, and sociocultural factors. Both medication and cognitive/behavioral therapy have been helpful in moderating the symptoms.

What are the symptoms?

The defining features of body dysmorphic disorder are a distressing and time-consuming preoccupation with an imaginary defect in one's appearance, or excessive concern about a slight physical anomaly. This preoccupation causes significant distress or impairs school, work, personal, or social functioning. Although virtually any body part can become the source of preoccupation, BDD most commonly involves the eyes, ears, nose, skin, chin, jaw or other facial features. Other areas of concern include hands, feet, breasts and genitals. People with body dysmorphic disorder are ashamed of their

About This Chapter: Text in this chapter is from "About Body Dysmorphic Disorder," by Naomi Weinshenker, M.D. Reprinted with permission from the New York University Child Study Center, http://www.aboutourkids.org, © 2001. All rights reserved.

"defect" and invent elaborate means to hide their deformity from the world. Camouflaging behaviors include excessive hair combing and hair removal, ritualized application of makeup, and avoidance of situations that might expose the perceived defect. Anxiety, shame, and secondary depression are frequent consequences of this disorder. In one case series of individuals with BDD, 30% were so impaired as to remain housebound.

The most frequent co-occurring psychiatric disorders are obsessive-compulsive disorder, social anxiety disorder, and depression. Suicidal thinking and gestures are, unfortunately, not uncommon consequences of BDD.

♣ It's A Fact!!
Real Life Stories

For 17-year-old James, the simple act of looking in a mirror is torture. Ever since a friend made a casual comment about his appearance, James has been obsessed with the size and shape of his nose. "It's just not right... it just doesn't fit my face," he will state. James is unable to be reassured that there is nothing objectively wrong with his nose and will spend at least an hour per day checking himself in various reflections. He has begun to consult with cosmetic surgeons about the possibility of rhinoplasty (plastic surgery intended to change the size or shape of the nose).

"I wish I could convince my parents to take me to a plastic surgeon" said 15-year-old Kristin. She is preoccupied with her "large" jaw, "small" breasts and "uneven" skin and will ask her mother whether she looks okay at least a dozen times per day. She has begun to use heavy makeup and has also started wearing long sleeves and pants at all times in order to cover her skin. Kristin's appearance concerns are so time-consuming and distressing that she has ceased to spend time with her friends and has dropped her extracurricular activities.

Both James and Kristin have body dysmorphic disorder.

Who is likely to have it?

Body dysmorphic disorder often begins as early as adolescence and may remain undiagnosed for years. It is rare for children under 12 to be diagnosed with BDD. Although there have been no formal studies of the frequency of BDD in the general population, it is estimated to affect 1–2 % of the United States population. If BDD were simply an extreme form of normal attention to appearance, it would probably be much more common in females because women show more obvious outward signs of appearance concerns. However, BDD appears to affect roughly equal numbers of males and females. Research to date suggests that although the symptoms echo normal appearance concerns, BDD is far more complex and serious a disorder.

Why does it happen?

At this time, theories about the cause(s) of BDD are speculative. Most likely there are multiple factors, including biological, psychological, and sociocultural, that contribute to its etiology. Neurochemical factors, such as abnormalities in the brain chemical serotonin, may make some people more likely to express the symptoms of BDD. However, psychological factors such as teasing about one's appearance during childhood, family's or peers' emphasis on appearance, or trauma or sexual abuse might also be risk factors for the expression of symptoms. Finally, media messages about appearance might worsen the condition in some vulnerable individuals with BDD.

How is it treated?

Psychopharmacology: The antidepressants known as SSRIs (selective serotonin reuptake inhibitors) are the cornerstone of medication treatment for body dysmorphic disorder. Examples of SSRIs include Prozac, Zoloft, and Paxil. The SSRIs are a type of antidepressant used successfully in the treatment of both depression and obsessive-compulsive disorder. People who respond to an SSRI generally experience improvement in several ways. They spend less time thinking about the defect and the thoughts are less intrusive and painful. Compulsive behaviors, such as checking or camouflaging, often diminish. Patients often report that associated anxiety and depression have lessened. Ultimately, self-confidence and self-esteem are enhanced.

Psychotherapy: Although research is still in the early stages, cognitive-behavioral therapy (CBT) appears to be another good treatment for body dysmorphic disorder. A particular type of CBT known as exposure and response prevention has been shown, thus far, to be the most useful type of therapy for BDD. Exposure consists of having the individual expose the physical defect in feared and/or avoided situations (for example, in school or social situations) while response prevention involves helping the individual refrain from performing compulsive behaviors related to the defect. The goal is that, over time, anxiety associated with the feared defect and situation will decrease and the associated behaviors will lessen in frequency. This type of therapy is often recommended in addition to medication.

Chapter 28

Personality Disorders

Personality traits are patterns of thinking, perceiving, reacting, and relating that are relatively stable over time and in various situations. Personality disorders occur when these traits are so rigid and maladaptive that they impair interpersonal or vocational functioning. Personality traits and their potential maladaptive significance are usually evident from early adulthood and persist throughout much of life.

Mental coping mechanisms (defenses) are used unconsciously at times by everyone. But in persons with personality disorders, coping mechanisms tend to be immature and maladaptive. Repetitious confrontation in prolonged psychotherapy or by peer encounters is usually required to make such persons aware of these mechanisms.

Without environmental frustration, persons with personality disorders may or may not be dissatisfied with themselves. They may seek help because of symptoms (for example, anxiety, depression) or maladaptive behavior (for example, substance abuse, vengefulness) that results from their personality disorder. Often they do not see a need for therapy, and they are referred by their peers, their families, or a social agency because their maladaptive behavior causes

About This Chapter: From *The Merck Manual of Diagnosis and Therapy, Edition 17*, pp. 1549-1554, edited by Mark H. Beers and Robert Berkow. Copyright © 1999 by Merck & Co., Inc., Whitehouse Station, NJ. Reviewed in April 2006 by Dr. David A. Cooke, MD, Diplomate, American Board of Internal Medicine.

difficulties for others. Because these patients usually view their difficulties as discrete and outside of themselves, mental health professionals have difficulty getting them to see that the problem is really based on who they are.

Persons with severe personality disorders are at high risk of hypochondriasis, alcohol or drug abuse, and violent or self-destructive behaviors. They may have inconsistent, detached, overemotional, abusive, or irresponsible styles of parenting, leading to medical and psychiatric problems for their children. Persons with a personality disorder are less likely to comply with a prescribed treatment regimen. Even when they do, their symptoms—whether psychotic, depressive, or anxious—are far less responsive to drugs. Persons with personality disorders are often very frustrating to those around them, including physicians—who have to deal with their unrealistic fears, excessive demands, sense of entitlement, unpaid bills, noncompliance, and angry vilification. Such persons can also cause stress for other patients who are exposed to their dramatic or demanding behaviors.

Diagnosis And Classification

Diagnosis is based on observing repetitive patterns of behavior or perception that cause distress and impair social functioning, even when the patient lacks insight about these patterns and despite the fact that the patient often resists change.

The *Diagnostic and Statistical Manual of Mental Disorders, Fourth Edition (DSM-IV)*, divides personality disorders into three clusters: A) odd/eccentric, B) dramatic/erratic, and C) anxious/inhibited.

Cluster A

Paranoid personality: Persons with this personality disorder are generally cold and distant in interpersonal relationships or are controlling and jealous if they become attached. They tend to react with suspicion to changes in situations and to find hostile and malevolent motives behind other people's trivial, innocent, or even positive acts. Often these hostile motives represent projections of their own hostilities onto others. When they believe they have confirmed their suspicions, they sometimes react in ways that surprise or scare others. They then use the resulting anger of or rejection by others (for example, projective identification) to justify their original feelings. Paranoid persons tend to take legal action against others, especially when they feel a sense of righteous indignation. However, they cannot see their role in a conflict. In their occupations, these persons may be highly efficient and conscientious, although they usually need to work in relative isolation.

Paranoid tendencies may develop among persons who feel particularly alienated because of a defect or handicap. For example, a person with chronic deafness may mistakenly think he is being talked about or laughed at.

Schizoid personality: Persons with this personality disorder are introverted, withdrawn, solitary, emotionally cold, and distant. They are most often absorbed in their own thoughts and feelings and fear closeness and intimacy with others. They are reticent, are given to daydreaming, and prefer theoretic speculation to practical action.

Schizotypal personality: Like schizoid persons, persons with this personality disorder are socially isolated and emotionally detached, but in addition, they express oddities of thinking, perception, and communication, such as magical thinking, clairvoyance, ideas of reference, or paranoid ideation. These oddities suggest schizophrenia but are never severe enough to meet its criteria. Nonetheless, persons with this personality disorder are believed to have a muted phenotypic expression (spectrum variant) of the genes that cause schizophrenia.

Cluster B

Borderline personality: Persons with this personality disorder—predominantly women—are unstable in their self-image, mood, behavior, and interpersonal relationships. This personality disorder becomes evident in early adult years, but it tends to become milder or to stabilize with age. Such persons believe they were deprived of adequate care during their childhood and consequently feel empty, angry, and entitled to nurturance. As a result, they are relentless seekers of care. This personality disorder is by far the most common type seen in psychiatric and all other types of health care services.

When persons with a borderline personality feel cared for, they appear like lonely waifs, who seek help for depression, substance abuse, eating disorders, and past mistreatments. However, when they fear the loss of the caring person, their mood shifts dramatically and is frequently expressed as inappropriate and intense anger. The shift in mood is accompanied by extreme changes in their view of the world, themselves, and others—from black to white, from hated to loved, or vice versa. Their view is never neutral. When they feel abandoned (or all alone), they dissociate or become desperately impulsive. At times, their concept of reality is so poor that they have brief episodes of psychotic thinking, such as paranoid ideas and hallucinations.

Such persons have far more dramatic and intense interpersonal relationships than those with cluster A personality disorders. Their thought processes are disturbed more than those of persons with an antisocial personality, and aggression is more often turned against the self. They are more angry, more impulsive, and more confused about identity than those with a histrionic personality. They tend to evoke intense, initially nurturant responses in caretakers. But after repeated crises, vague unfounded complaints, and failures to comply with therapeutic recommendations, caretakers—including the physician—often become very frustrated with them and view them as help-rejecting complainers. Splitting, acting out, hypochondriasis, and projection are common coping mechanisms.

Antisocial personality (previously called psychopathic or sociopathic): Persons with this personality disorder callously disregard the rights and feelings of others. They exploit others for materialistic gain or personal gratification (unlike narcissistic persons, who exploit others because they think their superiority justifies it). Characteristically,

♣ It's A Fact!!

Antisocial personality disorder is often associated with alcoholism, drug addiction, infidelity, promiscuity, failure in one's occupation, frequent relocation, and imprisonment. In Western culture, more men have this personality disorder than women, and more women have a borderline personality; these two disorders have much in common. In the families of patients with both personality patterns, the prevalence of antisocial relatives, substance abuse, divorces, and childhood abuse is high. Often, the patient's parents have a poor relationship, and the patient was severely emotionally deprived in his formative years. Life expectancy is decreased, but among survivors, the disorder tends to diminish or stabilize with age.

they act out their conflicts in impulsive and irresponsible ways, sometimes with hostility and serious violence. They tolerate frustration poorly. Often they do not anticipate the negative consequences of their antisocial behaviors and typically do not feel remorse or guilt afterward. Many of them have a well-developed capacity for glibly rationalizing their behavior or for blaming it on others. Dishonesty and deceit permeate their relationships. Punishment rarely modifies their behavior or improves their judgment and foresight; it usually confirms their harshly unsentimental view of the world.

Narcissistic personality: Persons with this personality disorder are grandiose; or, they have an exaggerated sense of superiority. Their relationships with others are characterized by their need to be admired, and they are extremely sensitive to criticism, failure, or defeat. When confronted with a failure to fulfill their high opinion of themselves, they can become enraged or seriously depressed. Because they believe themselves to be superior, they often believe others envy them and feel entitled to have their needs attended to without waiting. Thus they can justify exploiting others whose needs or beliefs they consider less important. Such characteristics often offend persons they encounter, including their physicians. This personality disorder occurs in high achievers but may also occur in persons with few achievements.

Histrionic (hysterical) personality: Persons with this personality disorder conspicuously seek attention, are conscious of appearance, and are dramatic. Their expression of emotions often seems exaggerated, childish, and superficial and, like other dramatic behaviors, often evokes sympathetic or erotic attention from others. Thus relationships are often easily established but tend to be superficial and transient. These persons may combine sexual provocativeness or sexualization of nonsexual relationships with unexpected sexual inhibitions and dissatisfactions. Behind their sexually seductive behaviors and their tendency to exaggerate somatic problems (like hypochondriasis) often lie more basic wishes for dependency and protection.

Cluster C

Dependent personality: Persons with this disorder surrender responsibility for major areas of their lives to others and allow the needs of those they depend on to supersede their own needs. They lack self-confidence and feel intensely insecure about their ability to take care of themselves. They often protest that they cannot make decisions and do not know how or what to do. This behavior is due partly to a belief that others are more capable and partly to a reluctance to express their views for fear of offending persons they need with their aggressiveness (a form of aggression against self). Dependency occurs in other personality disorders where it may be hidden by obvious behavioral problems; for example, histrionic or borderline behaviors mask underlying dependency.

Avoidant personality: Persons with this personality disorder are hypersensitive to rejection and fear starting relationships or anything new because they may fail or be disappointed. This personality disorder is a spectrum variant of generalized social phobia. Because of their strong conscious desire for affection and acceptance, persons with an avoidant personality disorder, unlike those with a schizoid personality disorder, are openly distressed by their isolation and inability to relate comfortably to others. Unlike those with a borderline personality disorder, they respond to rejection with withdrawal, not temper tantrums. Persons with an avoidant personality disorder tend to have an incomplete or a weak response to anxiolytic drugs.

♣ It's A Fact!!

Treating a personality disorder takes a long time. Personality traits such as coping mechanisms, beliefs, and behavior patterns take many years to develop, and they change slowly. Changes usually occur in a predictable sequence, and different treatment modalities are needed to facilitate them. Reducing environmental stress can quickly relieve symptoms such as anxiety or depression. Behaviors, such as recklessness, social isolation, lack of assertiveness, or temper outbursts, can be changed in months. Group therapy and behavior modification, sometimes within day care or designed residential settings, are effective. Participation in self-help groups or family therapy can also help change socially undesirable behaviors. Behavioral change is most important for patients with borderline, antisocial, or avoidant personality disorder.

Obsessive-compulsive personality: Persons with this personality disorder are conscientious, orderly, and reliable, but their inflexibility often makes them unable to adapt to change. Because they are cautious and weigh all aspects of a problem, they may have difficulty making decisions. They take responsibilities seriously, but because they hate mistakes and incompleteness, they can become entangled with details and forget the purpose of or have trouble completing their tasks. As a result, their responsibilities cause them anxiety, and they rarely enjoy much satisfaction from their achievements.

> ♣ **It's A Fact!!**
> Most obsessive-compulsive traits are adaptive, and as long as they are not too marked, persons who have them often achieve much, especially in the sciences and other academic fields in which order, perfectionism, and perseverance are desirable. However, they can feel uncomfortable with feelings, interpersonal relationships, and situations in which they lack control or must rely on others or in which events are unpredictable.

Other Personality Types

Passive-aggressive, cyclothymic, and depressive types of personality disorders are not classified in the *DSM-IV*. Yet, they can be useful diagnoses.

Passive-aggressive (negativistic) personality: Persons with this personality disorder typically appear inept or passive, but these behaviors are covertly designed to avoid responsibility or to control or punish others. Passive-aggressive behavior is often evident in procrastination, inefficiency, or unrealistic protests of disability. Frequently, such persons agree to perform tasks they do not want to perform and then subtly undermine completion of the tasks. Such behavior usually serves to deny or conceal hostility or disagreements.

Cyclothymic personality: In persons with this personality disorder, high-spirited buoyancy alternates with gloom and pessimism; each mood lasts weeks or longer. Characteristically, the rhythmic mood changes are regular and occur without justifiable external cause. This personality disorder is a spectrum variant of manic-depressive illness (bipolar disorder), but most cyclothymic persons do not develop bipolar disorder. Cyclothymic personality is considered a temperament, present in many gifted and creative people.

Depressive (masochistic) personality: Persons with depressive personality disorder are chronically morose, worried, and self-conscious. Their pessimistic outlook impairs their initiative and disheartens persons who spend much time with them. To them, self-satisfaction is undeserved and sinful. They unconsciously believe their suffering is a badge of merit needed to earn the love or admiration of others. This personality disorder is considered a temperament that usually does not result in social dysfunction.

Chapter 29

Dissociative Disorders

Dissociative disorders are so-called because they are marked by a disso-ciation from or interruption of a person's fundamental aspects of waking consciousness (such as one's personal identity, one's personal history, etc.). Dissociative disorders come in many forms, the most famous of which is dissociative identity disorder (formerly known as multiple personality disorder). All of the dissociative disorders are thought to stem from trauma experienced by the individual with this disorder. The dissociative aspect is thought to be a coping mechanism—the person literally dissociates himself from a situation or experience too traumatic to integrate with his conscious self. Symptoms of these disorders, or even one or more of the disorders themselves, are also seen in a number of other mental illnesses, including post-traumatic stress disorder, panic disorder, and obsessive compulsive disorder.

Types Of Dissociative Disorders

Dissociative amnesia is characterized by a blocking out of critical per-sonal information, usually of a traumatic or stressful nature. Dissociative amnesia, unlike other types of amnesia, does not result from other medical trauma (for example, a blow to the head).

About This Chapter: Reprinted with permission from "Dissociative Disorders," a fact sheet from the NAMI, The Nation's Voice on Mental Illness. Reviewed by Jack D. Maser, Ph.D. Copyright © 2005 NAMI. All rights reserved. For additional information, contact the NAMI Information Helpline at 1-800-950-NAMI, or visit http://www.nami.org.

206 Mental Health Information For Teens, Second Edition

✎ What's It Mean?

Dissociative amnesia has several subtypes:

Localized amnesia is present in an individual who has no memory of specific events that took place, usually traumatic. The loss of memory is localized with a specific window of time. For example, a survivor of a car wreck who has no memory of the experience until two days later is experiencing localized amnesia.

Selective amnesia happens when a person can recall only small parts of events that took place in a defined period of time. For example, an abuse victim may recall only some parts of the series of events around the abuse.

Generalized amnesia is diagnosed when a person's amnesia encompasses his or her entire life.

Systematized amnesia is characterized by a loss of memory for a specific category of information. A person with this disorder might, for example, be missing all memories about one specific family member.

Dissociative fugue is a rare disorder. An individual with dissociative fugue suddenly and unexpectedly takes physical leave of his or her surroundings and sets off on a journey of some kind. These journeys can last hours, or even several days or months. Individuals experiencing a dissociative fugue have traveled over thousands of miles. An individual in a fugue state is unaware of or confused about his identity, and in some cases will assume a new identity (although this is the exception).

Dissociative identity disorder (DID), which has been known as multiple personality disorder, is the most famous of the dissociative disorders. An individual suffering from DID has more than one distinct identity or personality state that surfaces in the individual on a recurring basis. This disorder is also marked by differences in memory which vary with the individual's "alters," or other personalities.

Depersonalization disorder is marked by a feeling of detachment or distance from one's own experience, body, or self. These feelings of depersonalization are recurrent. Of the dissociative disorders, depersonalization is the one most easily identified with by the general public; one can easily relate to feeling as they in a dream, or being "spaced out." Feeling out of control of one's actions and movements is something that people describe when intoxicated. An individual with depersonalization disorder has this experience so frequently and so severely that it interrupts his or her functioning and experience. A person's experience with depersonalization can be so severe that he or she believes the external world is unreal or distorted.

Treatment

Since dissociative disorders seem to be triggered as a response to trauma or abuse, treatment for individuals with such a disorder may stress psychotherapy, although a combination of psychopharmacological and psychosocial treatments is often used. Many of the symptoms of dissociative disorders occur with other disorders, such as anxiety and depression, and can be controlled by the same drugs used to treat those disorders. A person in treatment for a dissociative disorder might benefit from antidepressants or antianxiety medication.

Chapter 30

Psychosis

About This Information

This information is from a series of fact sheets for parents, teachers, and young people entitled *Mental Health and Growing Up*. The aims of these fact sheets are to provide practical, up-to-date information about mental health problems (emotional, behavioral, and psychiatric disorders) that can affect children and young people. The text in this chapter describes different types of serious mental illnesses, and how and why they might affect you. It also offers some practical advice about how to get help.

Introduction

The term *psychosis* is used to describe when a person loses touch with reality. Teenagers often worry that they may be *going mad* when they are feeling stressed, confused, or very upset. In fact, feelings like these are very rarely a sign of mental illness. They can often get a lot better if you talk them through with someone you trust.

Psychosis is much more serious and affects people of all ages, but becomes increasingly common as you reach young adulthood.

About This Chapter: "Psychotic Illness," reprinted with permission from *Mental Health and Growing Up, 3rd Edition*, a publication of the Royal College of Psychiatrists, http://www.rcpsych.ac.uk. Copyright © 2004 Royal College of Psychiatrists. All rights reserved.

When a young person has a psychotic breakdown, not due to drug use, it can be difficult to know what the long-term effects will be, and a definite diagnosis may not be possible.

Psychosis

Schizophrenia is the most common form of psychosis. Symptoms include delusions, thought disorder and hallucinations.

Delusions are unshakable beliefs that are obviously untrue. For example, an ill person might strongly believe that there is a plot to harm them—that they are being spied on through the TV or being taken over by aliens.

♣ It's A Fact!!
The symptoms of schizophrenia are sometimes mistaken as moodiness or teenage rebellion. In young people, hearing voices is not necessarily a sign of schizophrenia, but may be due to anxiety, stress, or depression.

Thought disorder is when someone is not thinking straight and it is hard to make sense of what they are saying. Their ideas may be jumbled up, but it is more than being muddled or confused.

Hallucinations are when someone sees, hears, smells, or feels something that isn't really there. The most common hallucination that people have is hearing voices. In schizophrenia, hallucinations are totally real to the person having them. This can be very frightening and can make them believe that they are being watched or picked on. People who are having these experiences may act strangely. For example, they may talk or laugh to themselves as if talking to somebody that you can't see.

Bipolar Affective Disorder

The main feature of bipolar affective disorder is extreme changes of mood. When someone is high, they can become very overactive and loud, and lose their inhibitions. They can also suffer from delusions, for example, that they are famous, or have special powers. Mania can alternate with periods of depression. Some people with bipolar disorder experience delusions and hallucinations.

❧ **It's A Fact!!**

If the psychosis is due to drug use, a young person may need help with this.

What Causes Psychotic Illness?

This is still not fully understood. In both schizophrenia and bipolar affective disorder, there are abnormalities in the chemistry of the brain. This causes changes in thoughts, feelings and behavior.

There are a number of reasons that can make a person more likely to develop a psychotic illness:

• genetic factors play a part; probably by increasing the risk of an imbalance in brain chemistry.

• Having a parent or close relative with schizophrenia or bipolar disorder means that a person will have a slightly greater than normal chance of developing the condition.

Getting Help

The person with the illness may not notice that there is a problem and deny that there is anything wrong. Your general practitioner or school nurse can give you good advice. They will be able to get you specialist help, if it is needed. A psychiatrist may need to visit the person to find out whether or not they are ill and to offer the treatment required.

Medication is an important part of treatment and often needs to be taken for a long time in order to stay well. As with medication of any kind, there may be side-effects; the doctor will be able to advise on what they are and about what can be done to help.

Other forms of treatment are also important. Both the patient and their family will need help to understand the condition, to cope successfully, and to prevent the illness recurring. Support is often needed to rebuild the confidence needed to continue with school, college, or work.

The young person may need to be treated in hospital or in a specialist in-patient service. Talking treatments can be helpful, but need to be in addition to medication.

Chapter 31

Schizophrenia

What is schizophrenia?

Schizophrenia is a chronic, severe, and disabling brain disorder. It affects about 1 percent of people all over the world (including 3.2 million Americans) and has been recognized throughout recorded history.

People with schizophrenia may hear voices other people don't hear or believe that others are reading their minds, controlling their thoughts, or plotting to harm them. These experiences are terrifying and can cause fearfulness, withdrawal, or extreme agitation. People with schizophrenia may not make sense when they talk, may sit for hours without moving or talking much, or can seem perfectly fine until they talk about what they are really thinking. Since many people with schizophrenia have difficulty holding a job or caring for themselves, the burden on their families and society is significant as well.

Available treatments can relieve many of the disorder's symptoms, but most people who have schizophrenia must cope with some residual symptoms as long as they live. Nevertheless, this is a time of hope for people with schizophrenia and their families. Many people with the disorder now lead

About This Chapter: Text in this chapter is excerpted from "Schizophrenia," National Institute of Mental Health, 2005. The full text of this document, including references, is available online at http://www.nimh.nih.gov/publicat/schizoph.cfm.

rewarding and meaningful lives in the community. Researchers are developing more effective medications and using new research tools to understand the causes of schizophrenia and find ways to prevent and treat it.

When does it start and who gets it?

Psychotic symptoms (such as hallucinations and delusions) usually emerge in men in their late teens and early twenties and in women in their mid-twenties to early thirties. They seldom occur after age 45 and only rarely before puberty, although cases of schizophrenia in children as young as five have been reported. In adolescents, the first signs can include a change of friends, a drop in grades, sleep problems, and irritability. Since many normal adolescents exhibit these behaviors as well, a diagnosis can be difficult to make at this stage. In young people who go on to develop the disease, this is called the "prodromal" period.

Research has shown that schizophrenia affects men and women equally and occurs at similar rates in all ethnic groups around the world.

♣ It's A Fact!!

Ranking among the top 10 causes of disability worldwide, schizophrenia, at any age, exacts a heavy toll on patients and their families. Children with schizophrenia experience difficulty in managing everyday life. They share with their adult counterparts psychotic symptoms (hallucinations, delusions), social withdrawal, flattened emotions, increased risk of suicide and loss of social and personal care skills. They may also share some symptoms with—and be mistaken for—children who suffer from autism or other pervasive developmental disabilities, which affect about 1 in 500 children. Although they tend to be harder to treat and have a worse prognosis than adult-onset schizophrenia patients, researchers are finding that many children with schizophrenia can be helped by the new generation of antipsychotic medications.

Source: Excerpted from "Childhood-Onset Schizophrenia: An Update from the NIMH," National Institute of Mental Health, 2003.

What are the symptoms of schizophrenia?

The symptoms of schizophrenia fall into three broad categories: positive symptoms, negative symptoms, and cognitive symptoms (or cognitive deficits).

What are positive symptoms?

Positive symptoms are easy-to-spot behaviors not seen in healthy people and usually involve a loss of contact with reality. They include hallucinations, delusions, thought disorder, and disorders of movement. Positive symptoms can come and go. Sometimes they are severe and at other times hardly noticeable, depending on whether or not the individual is receiving treatment.

Hallucinations: A hallucination is something a person sees, hears, smells, or feels that no one else can see, hear, smell, or feel. "Voices" are the most common type of hallucination in schizophrenia. Many people with the disorder hear voices that may comment on their behavior, order them to do things, warn them of impending danger, or talk to each other (usually about the patient). They may hear these voices for a long time before family and friends notice that something is wrong. Other types of hallucinations include seeing people or objects that are not there, smelling odors that no one else detects (although this can also be a symptom of certain brain tumors), or feeling things like invisible fingers touching their bodies when no one is close by.

Delusions: Delusions are false personal beliefs that are not part of the person's culture and do not change, even when other people present proof that the beliefs are not true or logical. People with schizophrenia can have delusions that are quite bizarre, such as believing that neighbors can control their behavior with magnetic waves, people on television are directing special messages to them, or radio stations are broadcasting their thoughts aloud to others. They may also have delusions of grandeur and think they are a famous historical figure. People with paranoid schizophrenia can believe that others are deliberately cheating, harassing, poisoning, spying upon, or plotting against them or the people they care about. These beliefs are called delusions of persecution.

Thought Disorder: People with schizophrenia often have unusual thought processes. One dramatic form is disorganized thinking where the person may have difficulty organizing his thoughts or connecting them logically. Speech may be garbled or hard to understand. Another form is "thought blocking" where the person stops abruptly in the middle of a thought. When asked, sometimes the person says it felt as if the thought had been taken out of his head. Finally, the individual might make up unintelligible words, so-called "neologisms."

Disorders Of Movement: People with schizophrenia can be clumsy and uncoordinated. They may also show involuntary movements and may show grimacing or unusual mannerisms. They may repeat certain motions over and over or, in extreme cases, may become catatonic. Catatonia is a state of immobility and unresponsiveness that was more common when treatment for schizophrenia was not available; fortunately, it is now rare.

> ♣ **It's A Fact!!**
> **When is schizophrenia diagnosed in children and teens?**
>
> A child's stage of development must be taken into account when considering a diagnosis of mental illness. Behaviors that are normal at one age may not be at another. Rarely, a healthy young child may report strange experiences—such as hearing voices—that would be considered abnormal at a later age. Clinicians look for a more persistent pattern of such behaviors. Parents may have reason for concern if a child of 7 years or older often hears voices saying derogatory things about him or her, or voices conversing with one another, talks to himself or herself, stares at scary things—snakes, spiders, shadows—that are not really there, and shows no interest in friendships. Such behaviors could be signs of schizophrenia.
>
> Fortunately, schizophrenia is rare in children, affecting only about 1 in 40,000, compared to 1 in 100 in adults.
>
> Source: Excerpted from "Childhood-Onset Schizophrenia: An Update from the NIMH," National Institute of Mental Health, 2003.

What are negative symptoms?

The term "negative symptoms" refers to reductions in normal emotional and behavioral states. These include:

- flat affect (immobile facial expression, monotonous voice),

- lack of pleasure in everyday life,

- diminished ability to initiate and sustain planned activity, and

- speaking infrequently, even when forced to interact.

People with schizophrenia often neglect basic hygiene and need help with everyday living activities. Because it is not as obvious that negative symptoms are part of a psychiatric illness, people with schizophrenia are often perceived by others as lazy and not willing to better their lives.

What are cognitive symptoms?

Cognitive symptoms are subtle and are often detected only when neuropsychological tests are performed. They include:

- poor executive functioning (the ability to absorb and interpret information and make decisions based on that information),

- inability to sustain attention, and

- problems with working memory (the ability to keep recently learned information in mind and use it right away).

Cognitive impairments often interfere with the patient's ability to lead a normal life and earn a living, and can cause great emotional distress.

Are people with schizophrenia violent?

People with schizophrenia are not especially prone to violence and often prefer to be left alone. Studies show that if people have no record of criminal violence before they develop schizophrenia and are not substance abusers, they are unlikely to commit crimes after they become ill. Most violent crimes are not committed by people with schizophrenia, and most people with schizophrenia do not commit violent crimes. Substance abuse always increases violent behavior, whether or not the person has schizophrenia. If someone with paranoid schizophrenia becomes violent, their violence is most often directed at family members and takes place at home.

♣ It's A Fact!!
Schizoaffective Disorder

Schizoaffective disorder is one of the more common, chronic, and disabling mental illnesses. As the name implies, it is characterized by a combination of symptoms of schizophrenia and an affective (mood) disorder. There has been a controversy about whether schizoaffective disorder is a type of schizophrenia or a type of mood disorder. Today, most clinicians and researchers agree that it is primarily a form of schizophrenia. Although its exact prevalence is not clear, it may range from two to five in a thousand people (that is, 0.2% to 0.5%). Schizoaffective disorder may account for one-fourth or even one-third of all persons with schizophrenia.

To diagnose schizoaffective disorder, a person needs to have primary symptoms of schizophrenia (such as delusions, hallucinations, disorganized speech, disorganized behavior) along with a period of time when he or she also has symptoms of major depression or a manic episode.

Differentiating schizoaffective disorder from schizophrenia and from mood disorder can be difficult. The mood symptoms in schizoaffective disorder are more prominent, and last for a substantially longer time than those in schizophrenia. Schizoaffective disorder may be distinguished from a mood disorder by the fact that delusions or hallucinations must be present in persons with schizoaffective disorder for at least two weeks in the absence of prominent mood symptoms. The diagnosis of a person with schizophrenia or mood disorder may change later to that of schizoaffective disorder, or vice versa.

Source: Excerpted and reprinted with permission from "Schizoaffective Disorder," a fact sheet from the NAMI, The Nation's Voice on Mental Illness. Reviewed by Dilip Jeste, M.D., November 2003. Copyright © 2005 NAMI. All rights reserved. For additional information, contact the NAMI Information Helpline at 1-800-950-NAMI, or visit http://www.nami.org.

✤ It's A Fact!!
Schizophrenia And Substance Abuse

Some people who abuse drugs show symptoms similar to those of schizophrenia, and people with schizophrenia may be mistaken for people who are high on drugs. While most researchers do not believe that substance abuse causes schizophrenia, people who have schizophrenia abuse alcohol and/or drugs more often than the general population.

Substance abuse can reduce the effectiveness of treatment for schizophrenia. Stimulants (such as amphetamines or cocaine), PCP, and marijuana may make the symptoms of schizophrenia worse, and substance abuse also makes it more likely that patients will not follow their treatment plan.

Source: NIMH, 2005.

Is there a link between schizophrenia and suicide?

People with schizophrenia attempt suicide much more often than people in the general population. About 10 percent (especially younger adult males) succeed. It is hard to predict which people with schizophrenia are prone to suicide, so if someone with schizophrenia talks about or tries to commit suicide, professional help should be sought right away.

Can schizophrenia be inherited?

Scientists have long known that schizophrenia runs in families. It occurs in 1 percent of the general population, but is seen in 10 percent of people with a first degree relative (a parent, brother, or sister) with the disorder. People who have second degree relatives (aunts, uncles, grandparents, or cousins) with the disease also develop schizophrenia more often than the general population. The identical twin of a person with schizophrenia is most at risk, with a 40–65 percent chance of developing the problem.

Our genes are located on 23 pairs of chromosomes that are found in each cell. We inherit two copies of each gene, one from each parent. Several of these genes are thought to be associated with an increased risk of schizophrenia, but scientists currently believe that each gene has a very small effect and is not responsible for causing the disease by itself. It is still not possible to predict who will develop the disease by looking at their genetic material.

Although there is a genetic risk for schizophrenia, genes alone are not likely to be sufficient to cause the disorder. Interactions between genes and the environment are thought to be necessary for schizophrenia to develop. Many environmental factors have been suggested as risk factors, such as exposure to viruses or malnutrition in the womb, problems during birth, and psychosocial factors, like stressful environmental conditions.

Do people with schizophrenia have faulty brain chemistry?

It is likely that an imbalance in the complex, interrelated chemical reactions of the brain involving the neurotransmitters dopamine and glutamate (and possibly others) plays a role in schizophrenia. Neurotransmitters are substances that allow brain cells to communicate with one another. Basic knowledge about brain chemistry and its link to schizophrenia is expanding rapidly and is a very promising area of research.

♣ It's A Fact!! Schizophrenia And Nicotine

People with schizophrenia are addicted to nicotine at three times the rate of the general population (75–90 percent vs. 25–30 percent). Research has revealed that the relationship between smoking and schizophrenia is complex. People with schizophrenia seem to be driven to smoke, and researchers are exploring whether there is a biological basis for this need. In addition to its known health hazards, several studies have found that smoking interferes with the action of antipsychotic drugs. People with schizophrenia who smoke may need higher doses of their medication.

Source: NIMH, 2005.

Do the brains of people with schizophrenia look different?

The brains of people with schizophrenia look a little different than the brains of healthy people, but the differences are small. Sometimes the fluid-filled cavities at the center of the brain, called ventricles, are larger in people with schizophrenia, overall grey matter volume is lower, and some areas of the brain have less or more metabolic activity. Microscopic studies of brain tissue after death have also revealed small changes in the distribution or characteristics of brain cells in people with schizophrenia. It appears that many of these changes were prenatal because they are not accompanied by glial cells, which are always present when a brain injury occurs after birth. One theory suggests that problems during brain development lead to faulty connections that lie dormant until puberty. The brain undergoes major changes during puberty, and these changes could trigger psychotic symptoms.

The only way to answer these questions is to conduct more research. Scientists in the U.S. and all over the world are studying schizophrenia and trying to develop new ways to prevent and treat the disorder.

♣ It's A Fact!!

Unlike most adult-onset patients, children who become psychotic prior to puberty show conspicuous evidence of progressively abnormal brain development. In the first longitudinal brain imaging study of adolescents, magnetic resonance imaging (MRI) scans revealed fluid filled cavities in the middle of the brain enlarging abnormally between ages 14 and 18 in teens with early-onset schizophrenia, suggesting a shrinkage in brain tissue volume. These children lost four times as much gray matter, neurons and their branch-like extensions, in their frontal lobes as normally occurs in teens. This gray matter loss engulfs the brain in a progressive wave from back to front over 5 years, beginning in rear structures involved in attention and perception, eventually spreading to frontal areas responsible for organizing, planning, and other "executive" functions impaired in schizophrenia. Since losses in the rear areas are influenced mostly by environmental factors, the researchers suggest that some non-genetic trigger contributes to the onset and initial progression of the illness. The final loss pattern is consistent with that seen in adult schizophrenia. Adult-onset patients' brains may have undergone similar changes when they were teens that went unnoticed because symptoms had not yet emerged, suggest the researchers.

Source: Excerpted from "Childhood-Onset Schizophrenia: An Update from the NIMH," National Institute of Mental Health, 2003.

How is schizophrenia treated?

Since the causes of schizophrenia are still unknown, current treatments focus on eliminating the symptoms of the disease.

Antipsychotic Medications: Antipsychotic medications have been available since the mid-1950s. They effectively alleviate the positive symptoms of schizophrenia. While these drugs have greatly improved the lives of many patients, they do not cure schizophrenia.

Everyone responds differently to antipsychotic medication. Sometimes several different drugs must be tried before the right one is found. People with schizophrenia should work in partnership with their doctor to find the medications that control their symptoms best with the fewest side effects.

Length Of Treatment: Like diabetes or high blood pressure, schizophrenia is a chronic disorder that needs constant management. At the moment, it cannot be cured but the rate or recurrence of psychotic episodes can be decreased significantly by staying on medication. Although responses vary from person to person, most people with schizophrenia need to take some type of medication for the rest of their lives and use other approaches, such as supportive therapy or rehabilitation, as well.

Relapses occur most often when people with schizophrenia stop taking their antipsychotic medication because they feel better, or only take it occasionally because they forget or don't think taking it regularly is important. It is very important for people with schizophrenia to take their medication on a regular basis and for as long as their doctors recommend. If they do so, they will experience fewer psychotic symptoms.

♣ **It's A Fact!!**

Antipsychotic medications can produce unpleasant or dangerous side effects when taken with certain other drugs. For this reason, the doctor who prescribes the antipsychotics should be told about all medications (over-the-counter and prescription) and all vitamins, minerals, and herbal supplements the patient takes. Alcohol or other drug use should also be discussed.

Source: NIMH, 2005.

Psychosocial Treatment: Numerous studies have found that psychosocial treatments can help patients who are already stabilized on antipsychotic medication deal with certain aspects of schizophrenia, such as difficulty with communication, motivation, self-care, work, and establishing and maintaining relationships with others. Learning and using coping mechanisms to address these problems allows people with schizophrenia to attend school, work, and socialize. Patients who receive regular psychosocial treatment also adhere better to their medication schedule and have fewer relapses and hospitalizations. A positive relationship with a therapist or a case manager gives the patient a reliable source of information, sympathy, encouragement, and hope, all of which are essential for recovery. By explaining the nature and causes of schizophrenia and the need for medication, the therapist can also help patients acknowledge the reality of their disorder and adjust to the limitations it imposes.

Illness Management Skills: People with schizophrenia can take an active role in managing their own illness. Once they learn basic facts about schizophrenia and the principles of schizophrenia treatment, they can make informed decisions about their care. If they are taught how to monitor the early warning signs of relapse and make a plan to respond to these signs, they can learn to prevent relapses. Patients can also be taught more effective coping skills to deal with persistent symptoms.

Integrated Treatment For Co-occurring Substance Abuse: Substance abuse is the most common co-occurring disorder in people with schizophrenia, but ordinary substance abuse treatment programs usually do not address this population's special needs. When schizophrenia treatment programs and drug treatment programs are integrated, better outcomes result.

Rehabilitation: Rehabilitation emphasizes social and vocational training to help people with schizophrenia function more effectively in the community. Because people with schizophrenia frequently become ill during the critical career-forming years of life (ages 18–35), and because the disease often interferes with normal cognitive functioning, most patients do not receive the training required for skilled work. Rehabilitation programs can include vocational counseling, job training, money management, learning to use public transportation, and practicing social and workplace communication skills.

Family Education: Patients with schizophrenia are often discharged from the hospital into the care of their families, so it is important that family members know as much as possible about the disease in order to prevent relapses. Family members should be able to use different kinds of treatment adherence programs and have an arsenal of coping strategies and problem-solving skills to manage their ill relative effectively. Knowing where to find outpatient and family services that support people with schizophrenia and their caregivers is also valuable.

Cognitive Behavioral Therapy: Cognitive behavioral therapy is useful for patients with symptoms that persist even when they take medication. The cognitive therapist teaches people with schizophrenia how to test the reality of their thoughts and perceptions, how to "not listen" to their voices, and how to shake off the apathy that often immobilizes them. This treatment appears to be effective in reducing the severity of symptoms and decreasing the risk of relapse.

What is the role of the patient's support system?

Support for someone with a mental disorder can come from family, a professional residential or day program caregiver, shelter operators, friends or roommates, professional case managers, or anyone else in their community or place of worship that is concerned for their welfare. There are many situations in which people with schizophrenia will need help from other people.

> ✔ **Quick Tip**
>
> Self-help groups for people with schizophrenia and their families are becoming increasingly common. Although professional therapists are not involved, the group members are a continuing source of mutual support and comfort for each other, which is also therapeutic. People in self-help groups know that others are facing the same problems they face and no longer feel isolated by their illness or the illness of their loved one. The networking that takes place in self-help groups can also generate social action. Families working together can advocate for research and more hospital and community treatment programs, and patients acting as a group may be able to draw public attention to the discriminations many people with mental illnesses still face in today's world.
>
> Support groups and advocacy groups are excellent resources for people with many types of mental disorders.
>
> Source: NIMH, 2005.

Getting Treatment: People with schizophrenia often resist treatment, believing that their delusions or hallucinations are real and psychiatric help is not required. If a crisis occurs, family and friends may need to take action to keep their loved one safe.

The issue of civil rights enters into any attempt to provide treatment. Laws protecting patients from involuntary commitment have become very strict, and trying to get help for someone who is mentally ill can be frustrating. These laws vary from state to state, but generally, if a person is dangerous to himself or others because of mental illness and refuses to seek treatment, family members or friends may have to call the police to transport the person to the hospital if he/she will not go of his own accord. In the emergency room, a mental health professional will assess the patient and determine whether a voluntary or involuntary admission is needed.

People with mental illnesses who do not want treatment may hide their strange behavior or ideas from a professional, so family members and friends should ask to speak privately with the person conducting the patient's examination and explain what has been happening at home. The professional will then be able to question the patient and hear the patient's distorted thinking for themselves. Professionals must personally witness bizarre behavior and hear delusional thoughts before they can legally recommend commitment, and family and friends can give them the information they need to do so.

Caregiving: Ensuring that people with schizophrenia continue to get treatment and take their medication after they leave the hospital is also important. If patients stop taking their medication or stop going for follow-up appointments, their psychotic symptoms will return. If these symptoms become severe enough, they can become unable to care for their own basic needs for food, clothing, and shelter; neglect personal hygiene; and end up on the street or in jail, where they rarely receive the kind of help they need.

Family and friends can also help patients set realistic goals and regain their ability to function in the world. Each step towards these goals should be small enough to be attainable, and the patient should pursue them in an atmosphere of support. People with a mental illness who are pressured and criticized usually regress and their symptoms worsen. Telling them what they are doing right is the best way to help them move forward.

✔ Quick Tip

How should you respond when someone with schizophrenia makes statements that are strange or clearly false?

Since these bizarre beliefs or hallucinations are very real to the patient, it will not be useful to say they are wrong or imaginary. Going along with the delusions will not be helpful, either. It is best to calmly say that you see things differently than the patient does, but acknowledge that everyone has the right to see things in their own way. Being respectful, supportive, and kind without tolerating dangerous or inappropriate behavior is the most helpful way to approach people with this disorder.

Source: NIMH, 2005.

What is the outlook for the future?

The outlook for people with schizophrenia has improved over the last 30 years or so. Although we still do not have a cure, effective treatments have been developed, and many people with schizophrenia improve enough to lead independent, satisfying lives.

This is a very exciting time for schizophrenia research. The explosion of knowledge in genetics, neuroscience, and behavioral research are all being used to understand the causes of the disorder, how to prevent it, and how to develop better treatments to allow those with schizophrenia achieve their full potential.

Part Four

Getting Help For Mental Illness

Chapter 32

Psychiatrists And Other Mental Health Care Providers

What is a psychiatrist?

A psychiatrist is a medical physician who specializes in the diagnosis, treatment, and prevention of mental illnesses, including substance abuse and addiction. Psychiatrists are uniquely qualified to assess both the mental and physical aspects of psychological disturbance. Their medical education has given them a full working knowledge of the many causes for a patient's feelings and symptoms. Armed with this understanding, psychiatrists can make a complete, accurate diagnosis and then recommend or provide treatment.

Why do people go to a psychiatrist?

People seek psychiatric help for many reasons. Life's usual round of trials may become overwhelming. Relationships may become troubled, or the pangs of anxiety—easily dismissed before as simple "nerves"—may grow sharper and last longer. The fresh-faced young newcomer down the hall at work may seem to threaten a secure job, and headaches may start to come literally one

About This Chapter: This chapter includes "What is a Psychiatrist?" "What are the differences between psychiatrists and other types of professionals who provide mental health care?" and "What are the most common treatments psychiatrists use?" © 2006 American Psychiatric Association; reprinted with permission from www.healthy minds.org and American Psychiatric Association.

after the other. The emotions that arise in reaction to everyday stresses and strains may blow badly out of proportion, or may be strangely absent. Eating may become a refuge, and sleep may begin to seem either irresistible or elusive. Alcohol or drug use may get out of control.

The problems can be sudden, such as a panic attack or as frightening hallucinations, thoughts or suicide, or "voices" that whisper intrusive and incomprehensible things. Or they may be more long-term-such as a pall of gloom that never seems to lift, causing everyday life to feel distorted, out of control, not worth living.

How does one become a psychiatrist?

A person wanting to become a psychiatrist must complete high school and college before entering medical school. While there is no requirement for a particular major, college students headed for medical school take required courses in the biological and physical sciences (general and organic chemistry, physics, biology, mathematics) as well as liberal arts courses. The prospective psychiatrist may also study social and psychological sciences and psychobiology. Most psychiatrists and other physicians feel that a liberal arts college education is the best preparation for medical school.

Medical students follow a standard curriculum, with only a few opportunities for choice. In addition to chemistry, biochemistry and physiology, students take courses in psychiatry, behavioral science, and neuroscience in the first two years of medical school. In the last two years, students are assigned to medical specialty "clerkships,"

♣ It's A Fact!!

How do psychiatrists tell what is wrong with their patients?

Because they are physicians, psychiatrists can order or perform a full range of medical laboratory and psychological tests that provide a complete picture of a patient's physical and mental state. Their education and years of clinical experience equip them to understand the complex relationship between emotional and other medical illnesses, evaluate all the medical and psychological data, make a diagnosis, and develop a treatment plan.

where they study and work with physicians in at least five different medical specialties. Medical students taking a psychiatry clerkship take care of patients with mental illnesses in the hospital and in outpatient settings. They also have an opportunity to work with medical and surgical patients who may have psychiatric problems or who have difficulty coping with their illnesses. Because modern psychiatry places special emphasis on the relationship between mind and body, students pay special attention to issues of stress and physical illness, prevention and behavior change, in addition to learning to care for severely mentally ill patients. Newly graduated physicians take written examinations for a state license to practice medicine. After graduation, doctors spend the first year of residency training in a hospital taking care of patients with a wide range of medical illnesses. The psychiatrist-in-training then spends at least three additional years in a psychiatric residency learning the diagnosis and treatment of mental illnesses, gaining valuable skills in various forms of psychotherapy and in the use of psychiatric medicines and other treatments.

After completing their residency training, most psychiatrists take a voluntary examination given by the American Board of Psychiatry and Neurology, to become a "board certified" psychiatrist.

Can psychiatrists become "sub specialists"?

Yes. Many psychiatrists continue training beyond the initial four years. They may study child and adolescent psychiatry, geriatric psychiatry, forensic (legal) psychiatry, administrative psychiatry, alcohol and substance abuser psychiatry, emergency psychiatry, psychiatry in general medical settings (called "consultation/liaison psychiatry"), mental retardation psychiatry, community psychiatry and public health, military psychiatry and psychiatric research. Some choose additional training in psychoanalysis at special psychoanalytic institutes.

What are the differences between psychiatrists and other types of professionals who provide mental health care?

Only the psychiatrist is a medical doctor who can order medical tests and prescribe medication. It takes many years of education and training to become a psychiatrist. After earning a bachelor's degree, he or she must graduate from medical school and go on to complete four years of residency training in the field of psychiatry.

Other professionals who care for people with mental illness or provide mental health services undergo different types of training whose length and core emphases differ according to the field of study. Here is a brief summary:

Psychologist: Most clinical psychologists have a master's or doctoral degree; on the doctoral level, the degree is usually a Ph.D. (doctor of philosophy) or Psy.D. (doctor of psychology, which is not a medical doctor). A psychologist applies psychological principles to the treatment of mental, emotional, and behavioral disorders and developmental disabilities through a broad range of psychotherapies. A psychologist is commonly trained in advanced psychology, abnormal psychology, statistics, testing theory, psychological testing, psychological theory, research methods, psychotherapeutic techniques, and psychosocial evaluation.

Licensed clinical social worker: A licensed clinical social worker (L.C.S.W.) is also trained in psychotherapy and helps individuals deal effectively with a variety of mental health and daily living problems to improve overall functioning. A social worker usually has a master's degree in social work (M.S.W.). and has studied, among others, sociology, growth and development, mental health theory and practice, human behavior/social environment, psychology, research methods.

Psychiatric nurse: A psychiatric nurse may have an associate arts, bachelor's, or master's degree in nursing. Much of the psychiatric nurse's specialty training takes place in a hospital inpatient service. Among the services the psychiatric nurse is trained to provide (at the order of a medical doctor) are various patient care services, administration of medication, and other duties commonly performed by nurses, such as immunizations and skin tests.

What are the most common treatments psychiatrists use?

Psychiatrists use a wide range of treatments-including various forms of psychotherapy, medications and hospitalization-according to the needs of each patient.

Psychotherapy is a systematic treatment method in which, during regularly scheduled meetings, the psychiatrist and patient discuss troubling problems and feelings. The physician helps patients understand the basis of these problems and find solutions. Depending on the extent of the problem, treatment may take just a few sessions over one or two weeks, or many sessions over several years.

Psychiatrists use many forms of psychotherapy. These are psychotherapies that help patients change behaviors or thought patterns, psychotherapies that help patients explore the effect of past relationships and experiences on present behaviors, psychotherapies that treat troubled couples or families together, and more treatments that are tailored to help solve other problems in specific ways.

Psychoanalysis is an intensive form of individual psychotherapy which requires frequent sessions over several years. The psychiatrist, who must have additional years of training in psychoanalysis, helps the patient to recall and examine events, memories and feelings from the past, many of them long forgotten, as a means of helping the patient understand present feelings and behavior and make changes as necessary.

♣ **It's A Fact!!**
When do psychiatrists use medications?

In the same way that your family doctor can prescribe medications to help patients with high blood pressure or thyroid problems, psychiatrists can prescribe a number of medications that are effective against mental illnesses such as depression, manic-depression, panic disorder, anxiety disorders, obsessive-compulsive disorder, and schizophrenia. Psychiatrists use medications when thorough evaluation of a patient suggests that medication may correct imbalances in brain chemistry that are thought to be involved in some mental disorders. Psychiatrists usually use medications in combination with psychotherapy.

Chapter 33

Going To A Therapist

Eric went to therapy two years ago when his parents were getting divorced. Although he no longer goes, he feels the two months he spent in therapy really helped him get through the tough times as his parents worked out their differences. Melody began seeing her therapist a year ago when she was being bullied at school. She still goes every two weeks because she feels her therapy is really helping to build her self-esteem. And Britt just joined a therapy group for eating disorders led by her school's psychologist.

When our parents were in school, very few kids went to therapy. Now it's much more accepted and lots of teens wonder if therapy could help them, too.

What are some reasons that teens go to therapists?

Sometimes people who are trying as hard as they can to get through a rough time, such as family troubles or problems in school, find that they just can't cope by themselves. They may be feeling sad, angry, or overwhelmed by what's been happening—and need help sorting out their feelings, finding solutions to their problems, or just feeling better. That's when therapy can help.

About This Chapter: This information was provided by TeensHealth, one of the largest resources online for medically reviewed health information written for parents, kids, and teens. For more articles like this one, visit www.TeensHealth.org, or www.KidsHealth.org. © 2004 The Nemours Center for Children's Health Media, a division of The Nemours Foundation.

Here are just a few examples of situations in which therapy can help people work through their problems:

- Working with a therapist can help someone overcome depression, anxiety, painful shyness, or an eating disorder.

- Working with a therapist can help a person who cuts or self-injures.

- Psychotherapy can help someone manage an attention problem or a learning problem.

- People in therapy can learn to deal with the emotional side of a weight problem or a chronic illness.

- Psychotherapy can help someone whose parents are going through a separation or divorce to sort through the many feelings these changes bring.

- Therapy can help someone who has experienced a trauma, a difficult loss, or the death of someone close.

- Working with a therapist can help a family that is troubled by too much fighting or anger or a family struggling with alcoholism or other addiction problem.

- Therapy can help teens sort out common problems such as peer pressure, and it can help people build self-confidence and develop friendship skills.

- Therapy can offer a person support to get through a difficult time. Some people go to therapy to get help with managing their anger or to learn to get along better with others.

Making the decision to seek help for a problem can be hard at first. It may be your idea to go to therapy because of a problem you're having that you want to get help with. Other times, parents or teachers might bring up the idea first because they have noticed that someone they care about is dealing with a difficult situation, is losing weight, or seems unusually sad, worried, angry, or upset. Some people in this situation might welcome the idea or even feel relieved. Others might feel criticized or might not be sure about getting help at first.

Sometimes people are told by teachers or parents that they have to go see a therapist—because they have been behaving in ways that are unacceptable, self-destructive, dangerous, or worrisome. When therapy is someone else's idea at first, a person may feel like resisting the whole idea. But learning a bit more about what therapy involves and what to expect can help make it seem like a good thing after all.

What is therapy?

Therapy is the treatment of a disorder or illness. Therapy isn't just for mental health, of course—you've probably heard people discussing other types of medical therapy, such as physical therapy or chemotherapy. But the word "therapy" is most often used to mean psychotherapy (sometimes called "talk therapy")—the psychological treatment of emotional and behavioral problems.

Psychotherapy is a process that's a lot like learning. Through therapy, people learn about themselves. They discover ways to overcome troubling feelings or behaviors, develop inner strengths or skills, or make changes in themselves or their situations.

A psychotherapist (therapist for short) is a person who has been professionally trained to help people with their emotional and behavioral problems. Psychiatrists, psychologists, social workers, counselors, and school psychologists are the titles of some of the licensed professionals who work as therapists. The letters following a therapist's name (for example, MD, PhD, EdD, MA, LCSW, LPC) refer to the particular education and degree that therapist has received.

Some therapists specialize in working with a certain age group or on a particular type of problem. Other therapists treat a mix of ages and issues. Some therapists work in hospitals, clinics, or counseling centers. Others work in schools or in psychotherapy offices.

What do therapists do?

Most therapy is a combination of talking and listening, building trust, and receiving support and guidance.

Through talking, listening, and observing, a therapist is able to evaluate the problem situation that needs attention and care. In doing so, the therapist can help a person figure out what's been making him or her so unhappy and how to get things going on a better track again.

It might take a few meetings with a therapist before a person decides to talk openly. Trust is the most important ingredient in therapy—after all, therapy involves being open and honest with someone and talking about sensitive topics like feelings, ideas, relationships, problems, disappointments, and hopes. A therapist is trained to be patient with people who need to take their own time talking about themselves and their situation.

Most of the time, a person meets with a therapist one on one, which is known as individual therapy. Sometimes, though, a therapist might work with a family (called family therapy) or a group of people who all are dealing with similar issues (called group therapy or a support group). Family therapy gives family members a chance to talk together with a therapist about problems that involve them all. Group therapy and support groups help people give and receive support and learn from each other and their therapist by discussing the issues they have in common.

What happens during therapy?

If you see a therapist, he or she will talk with you about your feelings, thoughts, relationships, and important values. At the beginning, therapy sessions are focused on discussing what you'd like to work on and setting goals. Some of the goals people in therapy may set include things like:

- improving self-esteem and gaining confidence;

- feeling less depressed or less anxious;

- doing better with friends or schoolwork;

- learning to relate without arguing and managing anger;

- making healthier choices (for example, about relationships or eating) and ending self-defeating behaviors.

✔ Quick Tip
Coping With The Stigma Of Mental Illness

Even though society has become more accepting and understanding of mental illness in recent years, there is still a stigma attached to mental illness.

Families of people with mental illness can take certain steps to help cope with stigma. These steps include the following:

- Remembering that you and your loved ones have choices: You can decide who to tell about the mental illness and what to tell them.

- Remembering that you are not alone: Many other people cope with similar situations. People commonly struggle with depression, anxiety, substance abuse, and other mental illnesses.

- Keeping hope and remembering that treatment works: Safe and effective medications and psychosocial treatments are available, and newer treatments are being developed. As a result, many individuals with mental illness enjoy productive lives.

- Praising your loved one for seeking help: Mental health treatment can be difficult, as people often need to be patient in trying new medications, coping with side effects, and learning new behaviors. Helping your loved one to feel good about him/herself is important.

- Remaining active and surrounding yourself with supportive people: Social isolation can be a negative side effect of the stigma linked to mental illness. Isolating and discontinuing enjoyable activities put you at high risk for depression and burnout. Take a risk and try new activities in your community. You may want to investigate the local chapter of NAMI (National Alliance for the Mentally Ill) or a volunteer organization.

Source: "Coping with the Stigma of Mental Illness," © 2005 The Cleveland Clinic Foundation, 9500 Euclid Avenue, Cleveland, OH 44195, www.clevelandclinic.org. Additional information is available from the Cleveland Clinic Health Information Center, 216-444-3771, toll-free 800-223-2273 extension 43771, or at http://www.clevelandclinic.org/health.

During the first visit, your therapist will probably ask you to talk a bit about yourself. This helps the therapist understand you better. The therapist will ask about the problems, concerns, and symptoms that you're having.

After one or two sessions, the therapist will probably explain his or her understanding of your situation, how therapy could help, and what the process will involve. Together, you and your therapist will decide on the goals for therapy and how frequently to meet. This may be once a week, every other week, or once a month.

Once the therapist has a full understanding of your situation, he or she might teach you new skills or help you to think about a situation in a new way. For example, therapists can help people develop better relationship skills or coping skills, including ways to build confidence, express feelings, or manage anger.

Sticking to the schedule you agree on with your therapist and going to your appointments will ensure you have enough time with your therapist to work out your concerns. If your therapist suggests a schedule that you don't think you'll be able to keep, be up front about it so you can work out an alternative.

How private is it?

Therapists respect the privacy of their clients, and they keep things they're told confidential. A therapist won't tell anyone else—including parents—about what a person discusses in his or her sessions unless that person gives permission. The only exception is if therapists believe their clients may harm themselves or others. If the issue of privacy and confidentiality worries you, be sure to ask your therapist about it during your first meeting. It's important to feel comfortable with your therapist so you can talk openly about your situation.

Does it mean I'm crazy (or a freak)?

No, in fact, many people in your class have probably seen a therapist at some point—just like students often see tutors or coaches for extra help with schoolwork or sports. Getting help with an emotional problem is the same as getting help with a medical problem like asthma or diabetes.

There's nothing wrong with asking for help when you're faced with problems you can't solve alone. In fact, it's just the opposite. It takes a lot of courage and maturity to look for solutions to problems instead of ignoring or hiding them and allowing them to become worse. If you think that therapy could help you with a problem, ask an adult you trust—like a parent, school counselor, or doctor—to assist you in finding a therapist.

A few adults still resist the idea of therapy because they don't fully understand it, or they have outdated ideas about it. A couple of generations ago, people didn't know as much about the mind or the mind-body connection as they do today, and people were left to struggle with their problems on their own. It used to be that therapy was only available to people with the most serious mental health problems, but that's no longer the case.

Therapy is helpful to people of all ages and with problems that range from mild to much more serious. Some people still hold onto old beliefs about therapy, such as thinking that teens "will grow out of" their problems. If the adults in your life don't seem open to talking about therapy, mention your concerns to a school counselor, coach, or doctor.

You don't have to hide the fact that you're going to a therapist, but you also don't have to tell anyone if you'd prefer not to. Some people find that talking to a few close friends about their therapy helps them to work out their problems and feel like they're not alone. Other people choose not to tell anyone, especially if they feel that others won't understand. Either way, it's a personal decision.

What can a person get out of therapy?

What someone gets out of therapy depends on why that person is there. For example, some people go to therapy to solve a specific problem, others want to begin making better choices, and others want to start to heal from a loss or a difficult life situation.

Therapy can help people discover more about themselves. People who work with therapists might learn about motivations that lead them to behave in certain ways or about inner strengths they have. Maybe you'll learn new coping skills, develop more patience, or learn to like yourself better.

Maybe you'll learn new ways to handle problems that come up or new ways to handle yourself in tough situations.

People who work with therapists often find that they learn a lot about themselves and that therapy can help them grow and mature. Lots of people discover that the tools they learn in therapy when they're young help them cope with all kinds of difficult situations when they're older.

Chapter 34

Types Of Psychotherapy

Individual Therapy

Individual therapy is frequently done in combination with family or group therapy, and, when needed, psychopharmacology. It may take the actual form of play therapy, art therapy, or several other applicable forms depending on the child's age, development and diagnosis.

There are four theories on which individual therapy for children and adolescents are based.

Psychoanalytic: In this theory, a therapist tries to reverse the course of an emotional disturbance by reenacting and desensitizing a traumatic experience. This is accomplished through free expression in an interview or play format. The goal is to help the child understand his or her subconscious feelings and fears. While many practitioners use this form of therapy, there is in fact still very little evidence available to demonstrate that "it works."

About This Chapter: This chapter includes text from "Individual Therapy," "Cognitive Therapy," "Behavioral Therapy," "Cognitive-Behavioral Therapy," and "Family Therapy," reprinted with permission of the Center for the Advancement of Children's Mental Health, © 2003. All rights reserved. For additional information, contact The Center for the Advancement of Children's Mental Health at Columbia University, New York State Psychiatric Institute, 1051 Riverside Drive, Unit #78 New York, NY 10032, www.kidsmentalhealth.org.

Behavioral: The therapist intervenes in helping the child (and/or parent through parental management training) to either learn appropriate behavior that was never learned or in unlearning inappropriate behavior, regardless of how the behavior was or was not originally adopted.

Family Systems: The basis of this theory is for the therapist to understand the role each person, and particularly the patient, has developed within the family, and how that role or roles is reflected in the child's disorder. Like psychoanalytically based play therapy, very few studies have been conducted to show that this form of therapy "works," even though for some children it may in fact be effective.

Developmental Theories: This theory involves the knowledge and understanding of children's age-appropriate behavior and skills (social, motor, emotional, intellectual, etc.)

With individual therapy, parental involvement beyond the initial information gathering varies from an active role in therapy (such as parental management training) to merely providing transportation and bill paying.

Cognitive Therapy

Cognitive therapy as it is practiced today was developed by Aaron Beck in the 1970s, and was based on underlying theoretical assumption that a person's feelings and behavior are shaped by the way that he or she thinks about the world. According to this theory, the structure of a person's world is based on insights or reasonings, known as cognitions developed from previous experiences. Disorders in which cognitions may play a great role include obsessive-compulsive disorder, paranoid personality disorder, major depressive disorder, and somatoform disorders.

Usually, cognitive therapy is a short-term therapy, lasting up to twenty-five weeks. Maintenance may be carried out for years to follow. It is a structured therapy in which there is an active collaboration between the patient and the therapist, usually on an individual basis (although it can be carried out in a group environment).

There are three elements in cognitive therapy:

* the educational aspect;

* the cognitive aspect; and

* the behavioral aspect.

Initially, the therapist meets with the entire family in order to learn the environment in which the symptoms occur and to facilitate family involvement in the treatment.

In the educational component, the patient and therapist formulate a hypothesis together, which is thought to explain the relationship between the person's emotional difficulties (such as depression) and their thinking and behavior. This hypothesis is tested throughout the treatment process.

Once a hypothesis has been formulated, the relationship between an event or action and the patient's emotional reaction (so-called "automatic thoughts") must be identified. After identification, the youngster and therapist test whether the automatic thoughts actually make sense, in order to reject the wrong or exaggerated automatic thoughts. In this way, it becomes possible to identify patterns of overgeneralizations ("If anyone doesn't like me, no one likes me.") that have guided the youth's thinking and behavior.

Lastly, and the overall purpose of cognitive therapy, is for the patient to understand the inaccuracy of cognitive assumptions and to learn new ways of dealing with issues.

Behavioral Therapy

Basic concepts of behavioral therapy were first used in the 1920s. It was in the 1950s and 60s, however, that a systematic and comprehensive form of behavioral therapy emerged: with Joseph Wolpe in South Africa, Hans Jurgen Eyseneck and M.B. Shapiro in Great Britain, and B.F. Skinner in the United States.

Behavioral therapy, which generally is of shorter duration and less expensive to administer than most other therapies, tries to change behavior without worrying about a person's inner conflicts; it strives to unlearn problem behaviors and teach new, more adaptive behaviors. This therapy is usually used as a treatment for phobias, separation anxiety, obsessive-compulsive disorder, alcohol dependence, eating disorders (for example, anorexia nervosa or bulimia nervosa), hyperventilation, attention deficit hyperactivity disorder, and conduct problems.

When using behavioral therapy, the therapist, child, and child's family must answer the following questions:

- What are the problems and goals for the therapy?

- How will progress be measured or monitored?

- What outside influences are enabling the problem to continue?

- Which interventions will be most effective?

Types Of Interventions

Systematic Desensitization (usually progresses in three steps):

1. Relaxation Training: Relaxation will inhibit anxiety. Relaxation is usually achieved through training the person in progressive relaxation, hypnosis, or thinking of pleasant or relaxing mental images.

2. Hierarchy Construction: Determine the conditions that cause the anxiety; then create a list of such scenes in order of increasing anxiety.

3. Desensitization of Stimulus: Over time and while relaxed, the person is exposed to the anxiety invoking scenes they listed while in deeply relaxed state until "exposure" (visualization) no longer causes undue anxiety.

Graded Exposure: This intervention is similar to the systematic desensitization described above, but uses exposure of the person to the real-life feared situations (as opposed to imagery) and no relaxation.

Exposure and Response Prevention: The child/adolescent deliberately and voluntarily confronts the feared object or idea, either directly or by imagination. At the same time, he or she is strongly encouraged to refrain from doing any symptom-like habits, compulsions or rituals, with support and structure provided by the therapist.

Flooding: This technique is based on the theory that escaping an anxiety-evoking situation reinforces the anxiety. Therefore, the child is directed to confront their fear directly and remain in the situation until the fear subsides.

Participant Modeling: The child learns new behavior (new ways to deal with a situation) by watching someone else approach the feared object or situation and by observing how that person interacts or reacts with the anxiety-inducing object/situation.

Positive Reinforcement: The child is given a reward when he or she does the desired behavior (for example, attending to a task, facing a fear), or refrains from showing an undesirable behavior (for example, aggression, temper outbursts, etc.).

Response Cost: The child is penalized by removing points or some other type of positive item if he or she shows an undesirable behavior. Commonly, the response cost technique may be combined with a positive reinforcement system, so that appropriate behaviors are "rewarded," while negative behaviors are penalized, all using the same system. When the rewards and "punishments" are put into a common system of points (or stickers, stars, smiley faces, etc.), such a system is called a "token economy."

Cognitive—Behavioral Therapy

Cognitive-behavioral therapy combines many aspects of both cognitive therapy and behavioral therapy. It teaches children to react differently to the situations and bodily sensations that trigger panic attacks and other anxiety symptoms, depression, or obsessive-compulsive. In addition, children also learn to understand how their thinking patterns contribute to their symptoms and how to change their thoughts so that symptoms are less likely to occur. This awareness of thinking patterns is combined with exposure and other behavioral techniques to help people confront their feared situations.

Family Therapy

Family therapy is mainly used when a problem involves some form of family conflict. This form of therapy is often augmented with individual therapy. When family therapy is used, it is often understood at the outset that a child will blame the parents for the problems.

All families typically have an established, often implicit/unconscious, structure and set of roles for each individual. The therapist helps the family to understand these roles and patterns and how they contribute to the child's problem(s) and behavior. The theory underlying family therapy is that the child will not change unless the whole system fosters change and itself changes the behaviors/roles which are reinforcing the child's misbehavior.

Chapter 35

Medications Commonly Used To Treat Mental Illnesses

Special Message

The text in this chapter is designed to help mental health patients and their families understand how and why medications can be used as part of the treatment of mental health problems.

It is important for you to be well informed about medications you may need. You should know what medications you take and the dosage, and learn everything you can about them. Many medications now come with patient package inserts, describing the medication, how it should be taken, and side effects to look for. When you go to a new doctor, always take with you a list of all of the prescribed medications (including dosage), over-the-counter medications, and vitamin, mineral, and herbal supplements you take. The list should include herbal teas and supplements such as St. John's wort, echinacea, ginkgo, ephedra, and ginseng. Almost any substance that can change behavior can cause harm if used in the wrong amount or frequency of dosing, or in a bad combination. Drugs differ in the speed, duration of action, and in their margin for error.

About This Chapter: This chapter includes excerpts from "Medications," National Institute of Mental Health (NIMH), 2002. The full text of this document, including references and an index of medications, can be found online at http://www.nimh.nih.gov/publicat/medicate.cfm.

This information is intended to inform you, but it is not a "do-it-yourself" manual. Leave it to the doctor, working closely with you, to diagnose mental illness, interpret signs and symptoms of the illness, prescribe and manage medication, and explain any side effects. This will help you ensure that you use medication most effectively and with minimum risk of side effects or complications.

> ✔ **Quick Tip**
>
> If you are taking more than one medication, and at different times of the day, it is essential that you take the correct dosage of each medication. An easy way to make sure you do this is to use a 7-day pillbox, available in any pharmacy, and to fill the box with the proper medication at the beginning of each week. Many pharmacies also have pillboxes with sections for medications that must be taken more than once a day.
>
> Source: NIMH, 2002.

Medications For Mental Illness

In this chapter, medications are described by their generic (chemical) names and in *italics* by their trade names (brand names used by pharmaceutical companies). They are divided into four large categories—antidepressant, antianxiety, antimanic, and antipsychotic medications.

Antidepressant Medications

Antidepressants are used most often for serious depressions, but they can also be helpful for some milder depressions. Antidepressants are not "uppers" or stimulants, but rather take away or reduce the symptoms of depression and help depressed people feel the way they did before they became depressed.

The doctor chooses an antidepressant based on the individual's symptoms. Some people notice improvement in the first couple of weeks; but usually the medication must be taken regularly for at least 6 weeks and, in some cases, as many as 8 weeks before the full therapeutic effect occurs. If there is little or no change in symptoms after 6 or 8 weeks, the doctor may prescribe a different medication or add a second medication such as lithium, to augment the action of the original antidepressant. Because there is no way

♣ It's A Fact!!

FDA Warns About Suicidality In Adolescents Being Treated With Antidepressant Medications

In October 2004, the Food and Drug Administration (FDA) directed manufacturers of all antidepressant drugs to revise the labeling for their products to include a boxed warning and expanded warning statements that alert health care providers to an increased risk of suicidality (suicidal thinking and behavior) in children and adolescents being treated with these agents, and to include additional information about the results of pediatric studies.

FDA has determined that the following points are appropriate for inclusion in the boxed warning:

- Antidepressants increase the risk of suicidal thinking and behavior (suicidality) in children and adolescents with major depressive disorder and other psychiatric disorders.

- Anyone considering the use of an antidepressant in a child or adolescent for any clinical use must balance the risk of increased suicidality with the clinical need.

- Patients who are started on therapy should be observed closely for clinical worsening, suicidality, or unusual changes in behavior.

- Families and caregivers should be advised to closely observe the patient and to communicate with the prescriber.

- A statement regarding whether the particular drug is approved for any pediatric indication(s) and, if so, which one(s).

Among the antidepressants, only *Prozac* is approved for use in treating major depressive disorder in pediatric patients. *Prozac*, *Zoloft*, *Luvox*, and *Anafranil* are approved for OCD in pediatric patients. None of the drugs is approved for other psychiatric indications in children.

Source: Excerpted from "Suicidality in Children and Adolescents Being Treated with Antidepressant Medications," U.S. Food and Drug Administration, October 15, 2004. The full text of this document is available online at http://www.fda.gov/cder/drug/antidepressants/SSRIPHA200410.htm.

of knowing beforehand which medication will be effective, the doctor may have to prescribe first one and then another. To give a medication time to be effective and to prevent a relapse of the depression once the patient is responding to an antidepressant, the medication should be continued for 6 to 12 months, or in some cases longer, carefully following the doctor's instructions. When a patient and the doctor feel that medication can be discontinued, withdrawal should be discussed as to how best to taper off the medication gradually. Never discontinue medication without talking to the doctor about it. For those who have had several bouts of depression, long-term treatment with medication is the most effective means of preventing more episodes.

Dosage of antidepressants varies, depending on the type of drug and the person's body chemistry, age, and, sometimes, body weight. Traditionally, antidepressant dosages are started low and raised gradually over time until the desired effect is reached without the appearance of troublesome side effects. Newer antidepressants may be started at or near therapeutic doses.

Early Antidepressants: From the 1960s through the 1980s, tricyclic antidepressants (named for their chemical structure) were the first line of treatment for major depression. Most of these medications affected two chemical neurotransmitters, norepinephrine and serotonin. Though the tricyclics are as effective in treating depression as the newer antidepressants, their side effects are usually more unpleasant. Other antidepressants introduced during this period were monoamine oxidase inhibitors (MAOIs). MAOIs are effective for some people with major depression who do not respond to other antidepressants. They are also effective for the treatment of panic disorder and bipolar depression. MAOIs approved for the treatment of depression are phenelzine (*Nardil*), tranylcypromine (*Parnate*), and isocarboxazid (*Marplan*). Because substances in certain foods, beverages, and medications can cause dangerous interactions when combined with MAOIs, people on these agents must adhere to dietary restrictions.

The past decades have seen the introduction of many new antidepressants that work as well as the older ones but have fewer side effects. Some of these medications primarily affect one neurotransmitter, serotonin, and are called selective serotonin reuptake inhibitors (SSRIs). These include fluoxetine (*Prozac*), sertraline (*Zoloft*), fluvoxamine (*Luvox*), paroxetine (*Paxil*), and citalopram (*Celexa*).

The late 1990s ushered in new medications that, like the tricyclics, affect both norepinephrine and serotonin but have fewer side effects. These new medications include venlafaxine (*Effexor*) and nefazodone (*Serzone*).

Cases of life-threatening hepatic (liver) failure have been reported in patients treated with nefazodone (*Serzone*). Patients should call the doctor if the following symptoms of liver dysfunction occur—yellowing of the skin or white of eyes, unusually dark urine, loss of appetite that lasts for several days, nausea, or abdominal pain.

Other newer medications chemically unrelated to the other antidepressants are the sedating mirtazapine (*Remeron*) and the more activating bupropion (*Wellbutrin*). *Wellbutrin* has not been associated with weight gain or sexual dysfunction but is not used for people with, or at risk for, a seizure disorder.

Each antidepressant differs in its side effects and in its effectiveness in treating an individual person, but the majority of people with depression can be treated effectively by one of these antidepressants.

Side Effects Of Antidepressant Medications: Antidepressants may cause mild, and often temporary, side effects (sometimes referred to as adverse effects) in some people. Typically, these are not serious. However, any reactions or side effects that are unusual, annoying, or that interfere with functioning should be reported to the doctor immediately. The most common side effects of tricyclic antidepressants, and ways to deal with them, are as follows:

- **Dry Mouth:** It is helpful to drink sips of water; chew sugarless gum; brush teeth daily.

- **Constipation:** Bran cereals, prunes, fruit, and vegetables should be in the diet.

♣ **It's A Fact!!**

Antidepressant Medications For Children And Adolescents?

Research has shown that, as in adults, depression in children and adolescents can be treated. In particular, antidepressant medications—called selective serotonin reuptake inhibitors (SSRIs) because they specifically target the neurotransmitter serotonin—have been shown to be of benefit to children and adolescents with major depressive disorder. Certain types of psychological therapies have also been shown to be beneficial. In those with moderate to severe depression they are especially useful when combined with medication. Our knowledge of antidepressant treatments in youth, though growing substantially, remains limited when compared with what we know about treatment of depression in adults.

Concerns have been raised that the use of antidepressant medications themselves may induce suicidal behavior in youths. In fact, following a thorough and comprehensive review of all the available published and unpublished controlled clinical trials of antidepressants in children and adolescents, the U.S. Food and Drug Administration (FDA) has warned the public about an increased risk of suicidal thoughts or behavior ("suicidality") in children and adolescents treated with SSRI antidepressant medications.

Studies show, however, that there are substantial benefits from medication treatment for adolescents with moderate and severe depression, including many with suicidal ideation.

What Remains Unknown: Currently, there is no way of telling who may be sensitive to an SSRI's positive or adverse effects. Results thus far are based on populations—some individuals may show marked improvement, some may see no change, and some may be vulnerable to adverse effects. The response to medication of an individual patient cannot be predicted with certainty from the kind of studies that have been done so far.

It is extremely difficult to determine whether SSRI medications do or do not increase the risk of completed suicide, especially since depression itself increases the risk for suicide and because completed suicide is a rare event. Controlled trials typically include only hundreds of patients, not the thousands needed to detect effects for rare events. In addition, controlled trials typically exclude patients considered at high risk for suicide, such as those with a history of suicide attempts.

Source: Excerpted from "Antidepressant Medications for Children and Adolescents: Information for Parents and Caregivers," National Institute of Mental Health, 2005. The full text of this document is available online at http://www.nimh.nih.gov/healthinformation/antidepressant_child.cfm.

- **Bladder Problems:** Emptying the bladder completely may be difficult, and the urine stream may not be as strong as usual. Older men with enlarged prostate conditions may be at particular risk for this problem. The doctor should be notified if there is any pain.

- **Sexual Problems:** Sexual functioning may be impaired; if this is worrisome, it should be discussed with the doctor.

- **Blurred Vision:** This is usually temporary and will not necessitate new glasses. Glaucoma patients should report any change in vision to the doctor.

- **Dizziness:** Rising from the bed or chair slowly is helpful.

- **Drowsiness As A Daytime Problem:** This usually passes soon. A person who feels drowsy or sedated should not drive or operate heavy equipment. The more sedating antidepressants are generally taken at bedtime to help sleep and to minimize daytime drowsiness.

- **Increased Heart Rate:** Pulse rate is often elevated. Older patients should have an electrocardiogram (EKG) before beginning tricyclic treatment.

The newer antidepressants, including SSRIs, have different types of side effects, as follows:

- **Sexual Problems:** Fairly common, but reversible, in both men and women. The doctor should be consulted if the problem is persistent or worrisome.

- **Headache:** This will usually go away after a short time.

- **Nausea:** May occur after a dose, but it will disappear quickly.

- **Nervousness And Insomnia** (trouble falling asleep or waking often during the night): These may occur during the first few weeks; dosage reductions or time will usually resolve them.

- **Agitation** (feeling jittery): If this happens for the first time after the drug is taken and is more than temporary, the doctor should be notified.

Any of these side effects may be amplified when an SSRI is combined with other medications that affect serotonin. In the most extreme cases, such a combination of medications (for example, an SSRI and an MAOI) may result in a potentially serious or even fatal "serotonin syndrome," characterized by fever, confusion, muscle rigidity, and cardiac, liver, or kidney problems.

♣ It's A Fact!!
Combination Treatment Most Effective In Adolescents With Depression

A clinical trial of 439 adolescents with major depression has found a combination of medication and psychotherapy to be the most effective treatment. Funded by the National Institutes of Health (NIH)'s National Institute of Mental Health (NIMH), the study compared cognitive-behavioral therapy (CBT) with fluoxetine, currently the only antidepressant approved by the U.S. Food and Drug Administration for use in children and adolescents. John March, M.D., Duke University, and colleagues, report on findings of the multi-site trial in the August 18, 2004, *Journal of the American Medical Association* (*JAMA*).

Clinically significant suicidal thinking, which was present in 29 percent of the volunteers at the beginning of the study, improved significantly in all four treatment groups, with those receiving medication and therapy showing the greatest reduction.

Source: Excerpted from a National Institutes of Health press release dated August 17, 2004. The full text of this press release is available online at http://www.nih.gov/news/pr/aug2004/nimh-17.htm.

> ### 🖅 Remember!!
>
> Medications of any kind—prescribed, over-the-counter, or herbal supplements—should never be mixed without consulting the doctor; nor should medications ever be borrowed from another person. Other health professionals who may prescribe a drug—such as a dentist or other medical specialist—should be told about any medications you are taking.
>
> Source: NIMH, 2002.

The small number of people for whom MAOIs are the best treatment need to avoid taking decongestants and consuming certain foods that contain high levels of tyramine, such as many cheeses, wines, and pickles. The interaction of tyramine with MAOIs can bring on a sharp increase in blood pressure that can lead to a stroke. The doctor should furnish a complete list of prohibited foods that the individual should carry at all times. Other forms of antidepressants require no food restrictions. MAOIs also should not be combined with other antidepressants, especially SSRIs, due to the risk of serotonin syndrome.

Antianxiety Medications

Both antidepressants and antianxiety medications are used to treat anxiety disorders. The first medication specifically approved for use in the treatment of OCD was the tricyclic antidepressant clomipramine (*Anafranil*). The SSRIs, fluoxetine (*Prozac*), fluvoxamine (*Luvox*), paroxetine (*Paxil*), and sertraline (*Zoloft*) have now been approved for use with OCD. Paroxetine has also been approved for social anxiety disorder (social phobia), GAD, and panic disorder; and sertraline is approved for panic disorder and PTSD. Venlafaxine (*Effexor*) has been approved for GAD.

Antianxiety medications include the benzodiazepines, which can relieve symptoms within a short time. They have relatively few side effects: drowsiness and loss of coordination are most common; fatigue and mental slowing or confusion can also occur. These effects make it dangerous for people taking benzodiazepines to drive or operate some machinery. Other side effects are rare. Commonly used benzodiazepines include clonazepam (*Klonopin*), alprazolam (*Xanax*), diazepam (*Valium*), and lorazepam (*Ativan*).

Benzodiazepines vary in duration of action in different people; they may be taken two or three times a day, sometimes only once a day, or just on an "as-needed" basis. Dosage is generally started at a low level and gradually raised until symptoms are diminished or removed. The dosage will vary a great deal depending on the symptoms and the individual's body chemistry.

♣ **It's A Fact!!**

The interaction between benzodiazepines and alcohol can lead to serious and possibly life-threatening complications.

Source: NIMH, 2002.

People taking benzodiazepines for weeks or months may develop tolerance for and dependence on these drugs. Abuse and withdrawal reactions are also possible. For these reasons, the medications are generally prescribed for brief periods of time—days or weeks—and sometimes just for stressful situations or anxiety attacks. However, some patients may need long-term treatment.

The only medication specifically for anxiety disorders other than the benzodiazepines is buspirone (*BuSpar*). Unlike the benzodiazepines, buspirone must be taken consistently for at least 2 weeks to achieve an antianxiety effect and therefore cannot be used on an "as-needed" basis.

Beta blockers, medications often used to treat heart conditions and high blood pressure, are sometimes used to control "performance anxiety" when the individual must face a specific stressful situation—a speech, a presentation in class, or an important meeting. Propranolol (*Inderal, Inderide*) is a commonly used beta blocker.

Antimanic Medications

The medication used most often to treat bipolar disorder is lithium. Lithium evens out mood swings in both directions—from mania to depression, and depression to mania—so it is used not just for manic attacks or flare-ups of the illness but also as an ongoing maintenance treatment for bipolar disorder.

Although lithium will reduce severe manic symptoms in about 5 to 14 days, it may be weeks to several months before the condition is fully controlled. Antipsychotic medications are sometimes used in the first several days of treatment to control manic symptoms until the lithium begins to take effect. Antidepressants may also be added to lithium during the depressive phase of bipolar disorder. If given in the absence of lithium or another mood stabilizer, antidepressants may provoke a switch into mania in people with bipolar disorder.

Regular blood tests are an important part of treatment with lithium. If too little is taken, lithium will not be effective. If too much is taken, a variety of side effects may occur. The range between an effective dose and a toxic one is small. Blood lithium levels are checked at the beginning of treatment to determine the best lithium dosage. Once a person is stable and on a maintenance dosage, the lithium level should be checked every few months. How much lithium people need to take may vary over time, depending on how ill they are, their body chemistry, and their physical condition.

Side Effects Of Lithium: When people first take lithium, they may experience side effects such as drowsiness, weakness, nausea, fatigue, hand tremor, or increased thirst and urination. Some may disappear or decrease quickly, although hand tremor may persist. Weight gain may also occur. Dieting will help, but crash diets should be avoided because they may raise or lower the lithium level. Drinking low-calorie or no-calorie beverages, especially water, will help keep weight down. Kidney changes—increased urination and, in children, enuresis (bed wetting)—may develop during treatment. These changes are generally manageable and are reduced by lowering the dosage. Because lithium may cause the thyroid gland to become underactive (hypothyroidism) or sometimes enlarged (goiter), thyroid function monitoring is a part of the therapy. To restore normal thyroid function, thyroid hormone may be given along with lithium.

Lithium, when combined with certain other medications, can have unwanted effects. Some diuretics—substances that remove water from the body—increase the level of lithium and can cause toxicity. Other diuretics, like coffee and tea, can lower the level of lithium. Signs of lithium toxicity may include nausea, vomiting, drowsiness, mental dullness, slurred speech, blurred vision, confusion, dizziness, muscle twitching, irregular heartbeat, and, ultimately, seizures. A lithium overdose can be life-threatening. People who are taking lithium should tell every doctor who is treating them, including dentists, about all medications they are taking.

Anticonvulsants: Some people with symptoms of mania who do not benefit from or would prefer to avoid lithium have been found to respond to anticonvulsant medications commonly prescribed to treat seizures. The anticonvulsant valproic acid (*Depakote, Divalproex sodium*) is the main alternative therapy for bipolar disorder. It is as effective in non-rapid-cycling bipolar disorder as lithium and appears to be superior to lithium in rapid-cycling bipolar disorder. Although valproic acid can cause gastrointestinal side effects, the incidence is low. Other adverse effects occasionally reported are headache, double vision, dizziness, anxiety, or confusion. Because in some cases valproic acid has caused liver dysfunction, liver function tests should be performed before therapy and at frequent intervals thereafter, particularly during the first 6 months of therapy.

Other anticonvulsants used for bipolar disorder include carbamazepine (*Tegretol*), lamotrigine (*Lamictal*), gabapentin (*Neurontin*), and topiramate (*Topamax*). The evidence for anticonvulsant effectiveness is stronger for acute mania than for long-term maintenance of bipolar disorder. Some studies suggest particular efficacy of lamotrigine in bipolar depression. At present, the lack of formal approval from the U.S. Food and Drug Administration (FDA) of anticonvulsants other than valproic acid for bipolar disorder may limit insurance coverage for these medications.

♣
It's A Fact!!
Studies conducted in Finland in patients with epilepsy have shown that valproic acid may increase testosterone levels in teenage girls and produce polycystic ovary syndrome (POS) in women who began taking the medication before age 20. POS can cause obesity, hirsutism (body hair), and amenorrhea. Therefore, young female patients should be monitored carefully by a doctor.

Source: NIMH, 2002.

Most people who have bipolar disorder take more than one medication. Along with the mood stabilizer—lithium and/or an anticonvulsant—they may take a medication for accompanying agitation, anxiety, insomnia, or depression. It is important to continue taking the mood stabilizer when taking an antidepressant because research has shown that treatment with an antidepressant alone increases the risk that the patient will switch to mania or hypomania, or develop rapid cycling. Sometimes, when a bipolar patient is not responsive to other medications, an atypical antipsychotic medication is prescribed. Finding the best possible medication, or combination of medications, is of utmost importance to the patient and requires close monitoring by a doctor and strict adherence to the recommended treatment regimen.

Antipsychotic Medications

The first antipsychotic (neuroleptic) medications were introduced in the 1950s. Antipsychotic medications have helped many patients with psychosis lead more normal and fulfilling lives by alleviating such symptoms as hallucinations (both visual and auditory) and paranoid thoughts. However, the early antipsychotic medications often have unpleasant side effects, such as muscle stiffness, tremor, and abnormal movements, leading researchers to continue their search for better drugs.

The 1990s saw the development of several new drugs for schizophrenia, called "atypical antipsychotics." Because they have fewer side effects than the older drugs, today they are often used as a first-line treatment. The first atypical antipsychotic, clozapine (*Clozaril*), was introduced in the United States in 1990. In clinical trials, this medication was found to be more effective than conventional or "typical" antipsychotic medications in individuals with treatment-resistant schizophrenia (schizophrenia that has not responded to other drugs), and the risk of tardive dyskinesia (a movement disorder) was lower. However, because of the potential side effect of a serious blood disorder—agranulocytosis (loss of the white blood cells that fight infection)—patients who are on clozapine must have a blood test every 1 or 2 weeks. The inconvenience and cost of blood tests and the medication itself have made maintenance on clozapine difficult for many people. Clozapine, however, continues to be the drug of choice for treatment-resistant schizophrenia patients.

Several other atypical antipsychotics have been developed since clozapine was introduced. The first was risperidone (*Risperdal*), followed by olanzapine (*Zyprexa*), quetiapine (*Seroquel*), and ziprasidone (*Geodon*). Each has a unique side effect profile, but in general, these medications are better tolerated than the earlier drugs.

Tardive Dyskinesia: Long-term treatment of schizophrenia with one of the older, or "conventional," antipsychotics may cause a person to develop tardive dyskinesia (TD). Tardive dyskinesia is a condition characterized by involuntary movements, most often around the mouth. It may range from mild to severe. In some people, it cannot be reversed, while others recover partially or completely. Tardive dyskinesia is sometimes seen in people with schizophrenia who have never been treated with an antipsychotic medication; this is called "spontaneous dyskinesia." However, it is most often seen after long-term treatment with older antipsychotic medications. The risk

---

♣ It's A Fact!!

What difference does it make if a medication is specifically approved for use in children or not?

Approval of a medication by the U.S. Food and Drug Administration (FDA) means that adequate data have been provided to the FDA by the drug manufacturer to show safety and efficacy for a particular therapy in a particular population. Based on the data, a label indication for the drug is established that includes proper dosage, potential side effects, and approved age. Doctors prescribe medications as they feel appropriate even if those uses are not included in the labeling. Although in some cases there is extensive clinical experience in using medications for children or adolescents, in many cases there is not. Everyone agrees that more studies in children are needed if we are to know the appropriate dosages, how a drug works in children, and what effects there are on learning and development.

Source: Excerpted from "Treatment of Children with Mental Disorders," National Institute of Mental Health, 2004. The full text of this document, including references, can be found online at http://www.nimh.nih.gov/publicat/childqa.cfm.

has been reduced with the newer "atypical" medications. There is a higher incidence in women, and the risk rises with age. The possible risks of long-term treatment with an antipsychotic medication must be weighed against the benefits in each case. The risk for TD is 5 percent per year with older medications; it is less with the newer medications.

Medications For Children And Teens

Based on clinical experience and medication knowledge, a physician may prescribe to young children a medication that has been approved by the FDA for use in adults or older children. This use of the medication is called "off-label." Most medications prescribed for childhood mental disorders, including many of the newer medications that are proving helpful, are prescribed off-label because only a few of them have been systematically studied for safety and efficacy in children. Medications that have not undergone such testing are dispensed with the statement that "safety and efficacy have not been established in pediatric patients." The FDA has been urging that products be appropriately studied in children and has offered incentives to drug manufacturers to carry out such testing. The National Institutes of Health and the FDA are examining the issue of medication research in children and are developing new research approaches.

Chapter 36

Electroconvulsive Therapy

Treating Depression

Electroconvulsive therapy, or ECT, is the fastest and surest way to relieve depression. When other treatments have failed, when a patient is too suicidal for anything less effective, when depression is too severe to wait for drugs to work, electroconvulsive therapy is the treatment of choice. Compared to drugs, though, it is expensive, often requires hospitalization, and demands a greater commitment from patients. For these reasons it is reserved for more serious and unresponsive depressions.

A treatment consists of a medically controlled seizure initiated by passing an electric current between two scalp electrodes. If the seizure were unmodified it would look like a typical epileptic convulsion lasting 20 seconds to a minute and causing the muscles of the body to contract rhythmically.

The term "medically controlled seizure" refers to a number of treatment modifications. Before the treatment, patients receive a short-acting anesthetic in a vein so they are anesthetized throughout the procedure. Once anesthetized, they receive a drug to relax the muscles to prevent the hard muscle contractions that are associated with epileptic seizures. Since the seizure and the muscle relaxant can both interfere with breathing, an

About This Chapter: © 2004 Raymond Crowe, MD. Dr. Crowe is a Professor in the Department of Psychiatry at the University of Iowa College of Medicine.

anesthesiologist provides oxygen through a facemask. Next, the treating physician passes an electric current of several seconds duration to start the seizure. After the seizure ends and the anesthetic has worn off, the next step is a short stay in the recovery room. ECT causes mental confusion that is most marked during the hour after treatment and close observation needs to be provided during this time. Once the confusion has cleared substantially patients are discharged from the treatment suite.

Risks And Side Effects

ECT is a safe medical procedure. It has been given safely in all nine months of pregnancy, in advanced age, and in a wide variety of medical conditions. The benefits must be weighed against the risks of worsening the medical illness, though, particularly in the face of a recent heart attack, heart failure, unstable angina, respiratory failure, recent blood clots, or any condition causing pressure on the brain.

♣ **It's A Fact!!**
ECT is given as a series of 8 to 12 individual treatments three days a week, so a series of treatments requires three to four weeks to complete. Improvement often begins after a week but the treatment is continued until the depression has cleared. An antidepressant medication is started toward the end of the treatment series to provide further protection against a recurrence of the illness.

The side effects of ECT are usually not serious though they can be bothersome. Headache and nausea on awakening from the treatment are a common complaint. This can be treated with medicine for pain and nausea and prevented by giving these drugs before the anesthesia wears off.

The most publicized effect of ECT is its effect on memory. In order to remember an experience the brain must record the event and then store it in long-term memory for recall hours, days or even years later. ECT interferes with this storage. Thus, events that occur during the course of treatment may be forgotten, but events that have already been stored remain intact. After the treatments are over the ability to store new memories returns to normal. (One exception to this rule is that some memory loss occurs in a retrograde fashion; memories formed shortly before starting treatments are affected the most, though treatments can affect memories for as far back as a year.) The net effect is that memory for many events during and shortly before the treatment course can be lost permanently, but the ability to retain and recollect new memories returns to normal after the treatments are over.

Memory loss can be minimized by stimulating only one side of the head. The left side of the brain is usually dominant, so stimulating on the right side typically causes less memory loss than stimulating both sides. This benefit has to be balanced against the observation that stimulating on one side is sometimes less effective so that more treatments are needed to recover. However, in recent years the effectiveness of unilateral treatments has improved considerably.

Effectiveness

How effective is ECT for depression? Most studies find that approximately 80% of patients recover or are much improved. The rate of recovery can be as important as effectiveness. Recovery usually begins after a week whereas drugs require at least two weeks and sometimes take as long as six. ECT also remains quite effective in patients who have not responded to one or more trials of antidepressant drug therapy.

ECT is an effective treatment for mania, although it is rarely used for this now because the illness responds so well to drugs. ECT is reserved for the unusual circumstance when manic excitement and psychosis cannot be controlled with antipsychotic and mood stabilizing medications.

✦ It's A Fact!!

A question often asked about ECT is whether it causes permanent brain damage. Because an electric current is passed through the brain and memory is altered, many people have been concerned that the treatment may injure the brain. Medical research has addressed this question by carefully testing a wide variety of mental abilities in persons who have had ECT and the results are reassuring. No evidence of permanent brain damage has ever been uncovered.

In the past ECT was used extensively to treat schizophrenia but this is rarely necessary now because most schizophrenic episodes can be controlled with antipsychotic medication. With an expanding armamentarium of new antipsychotic drugs to treat schizophrenia, ECT will probably be needed less and less. When it is needed, it is effective against psychotic symptoms, such as delusions and hallucinations, and complicating depression. It is not an effective treatment for the emotional and social withdrawal of schizophrenia unless these behaviors are caused by psychotic symptoms.

ECT is very effective in catatonia. This severe abnormality of movement usually presents with profound withdrawal and absence of spontaneous movements or responses to other people. Bizarre movements such as unusual postures can be seen as well. It usually appears as a complication of schizophrenia or manic-depressive illness, but it also can complicate underlying medical illness. Catatonia is so responsive to ECT that patients often improve noticeably after a single treatment. Although it is rare it is an important use of ECT because it responds poorly to medications.

Recent changes in our health care system have changed the way ECT is given as well. Until recently, ECT has been a treatment for hospitalized patients, but today many patients are receiving part or all of their treatments as outpatients. A common practice is to begin the treatments in the hospital and complete them at home once the depression has lifted enough to return home safely. Another group of patients who benefit from outpatient ECT are those who have not responded to other treatments and need maintenance ECT to remain well. Not everyone can be treated as an outpatient, however, because it requires someone to transport the patient to and from treatments and remain with them on the day of the treatment. Even with these restrictions, some people suffering from depression now receive all of their treatments without entering a hospital.

Chapter 37

Psychiatric Hospitalization

Hospitalization for psychiatric illness has undergone revolutionary changes in the last three decades. At mid-century, there were two basic sources of care for people with mental illnesses: a psychiatrist's private office, or a mental hospital. Those who went to the hospital often stayed for many months, even years. The hospital, frequently operated by the state, offered protection from the stresses of living which could be overwhelming for those with severe illness. It also offered protection from self-inflicted harm. But it offered little in the way of treatment. The use of medication as a mainstay of rehabilitative treatment had just begun.

Today people with a mental illness have many treatment options depending upon medical need: 24-hour inpatient care in general hospital psychiatric units, private psychiatric hospitals, state and federal public psychiatric hospitals and Veterans Administration (VA) hospitals; partial hospitalization or day care; residential care; community mental health centers; care in the offices of psychiatrists and other mental health practitioners, and support groups.

In all these settings, health care professionals work very hard to provide care according to a treatment plan developed by each patient's psychiatrist. The goal is to restore maximum independent living as rapidly as possible, using the appropriate level of care for the appropriate illness. Frequently, the family is involved as part of the treatment team.

About This Chapter: © 2006 American Psychiatric Association; reprinted with permission from www.healthyminds.org and American Psychiatric Association.

Today, people turn to psychiatric hospitals for help with a wide range of mental illnesses: families coping with the ravages of addiction; a young mother or a grandfather fighting depression; a girl whose eating disorder has put her life in danger; a young executive who cannot shake compulsions that threaten to take over his life; a once-prominent attorney who is nearly a prisoner in her own home because of phobias and anxiety; a veteran of the Vietnam war who can't seem to get over the pain of his past; a youngster whose uncontrollable and destructive behavior threatens to tear her family apart; a college freshman who is frightened and confused by strange voices and delusions.

When Hospitalization Is Needed

A psychiatrist's decision to admit a patient to the hospital depends primarily on the severity of the patient's illness. No one is sent to the hospital who can better be treated in the psychiatrist's office or in another less restrictive setting. The presence or absence of social support—family members or other caretakers—can also figure in the psychiatrist's decision to hospitalize a patient. With sufficient social support, a person who might otherwise require hospitalization can often be cared for at home.

In much the same way a physician decides to hospitalize a person for other medical illnesses, the psychiatrist—who is a medical doctor—evaluates the symptoms to determine a treatment plan and the most appropriate treatment setting.

♣ It's A Fact!!

The procedure for hospital admission for a psychiatric illness resembles that for other illnesses. Often, that means a person's health insurance company may require a pre-admission certification before agreeing to pay for a hospitalization. Working with the psychiatrist, insurance company staff will review a patient's case and decide if it is serious enough to require inpatient care. If so, they will approve admission for a limited hospital stay, then periodically review the patient's progress to determine whether the stay should be extended. If care is denied, the psychiatrist and patient may appeal.

What To Expect In The Hospital

Many psychiatric hospitals and mental health units of general hospitals provide the full range of care, from psychotherapy to medication, from vocational training to social services.

Hospitalization reduces the stresses of responsibility for the patient for a brief time and allows the person to concentrate on recovery. As the crisis · lessens and the person is better able to assume the challenge, the mental health care team can help him or her to plan for discharge and the community-based services that will help him or her to continue recuperating while living at home.

People in the hospital receive treatment that follows a plan developed by the psychiatrist. The therapies outlined in that plan may involve a variety of mental health professionals: the psychiatrist, a clinical psychologist, nurses, social workers, activity and rehabilitation therapists and, when necessary, an addiction counselor.

Before psychiatric treatment in any hospital begins, a patient undergoes a complete physical examination to determine the overall state of his or her health. Generally, once treatment begins, patients in the hospital receive individual therapy with a primary therapist, group therapy with peers, and family therapy with spouse, children, parents or other significant people. At the same time, patients often receive one or more psychiatric medicines. During therapy sessions, a patient can develop insights into his or her emotional and mental functioning, learn about his or her illness and its effect on relationships and daily living, and establish healthy ways of responding to the illness and daily stresses that can affect mental health. In addition, patients can receive occupational therapy to develop skills for daily living, activity therapy to learn how to develop healthy social relationships in the community, and drug and alcohol evaluation. Throughout the hospital stay, each patient works with his or her treatment team to put together a plan for continued care after the hospital stay is over.

Residential treatment programs are categorized as either medically based or socially based. In medically based programs patients receive very structured care, including such services as medically necessary supervision and psychotherapy. In socially based programs patients receive psychotherapy, but also learn how to take advantage of community support systems and increase their independence. For example, under a socially based program, patients learn how to apply for government medical assistance that will enable them to get psychiatric and medical services in the community rather than relying on hospitalization for help.

Residential care can also help patients to learn how to maintain a household, cooperate with other residents and work with social and health agencies to get the services they need. This, in turn, improves their self-esteem and confidence.

Hospital personnel pay careful attention to the physical well being of patients. Hospital physicians and nurses monitor the patient's medications, and, with those patients whose severe illnesses may make them a danger to themselves or other patients, take steps to protect them from injury. This can sometimes mean use of restraints or isolation from other patients, measures that are used to protect, not to punish, and only for very brief periods of time. Hospital personnel also work to be sure each patient understands the importance of good nutrition and knows the dietary restrictions that may be necessary because of his or her medications.

♣ It's A Fact!!
Length Of Stay

Today the average length of stay for adults in a psychiatric facility is 12 days. The mental health care team and patient begin planning for discharge on the first day of admission. Because medical research has produced highly effective treatments, people who suffer from mental illness today recover from severe episodes much more quickly than in the past.

Likewise, people who suffer from alcohol and substance abuse no longer routinely stay in residential treatment centers for prolonged periods of time. Most recover with short-term stays that average ten days, followed by partial hospitalization, outpatient and support group services.

Other Hospitalization Options

Once psychiatric treatment stabilizes a patient's condition, he or she may progress to a less-intensive treatment setting. The psychiatrist may recommend partial hospitalization. This option isn't limited to people who are ending a hospital stay; it also meets the needs of people who live in the community and need a higher level of care without the services of overnight, 24-hour nursing.

Partial hospitalization provides individual and group psychotherapy, social and vocational rehabilitation, occupational therapy, assistance with educational needs, and other services to help patients maintain their abilities to function at home, at work and in social circles. However, because their treatment setting helps them to develop a support network of friends and family that can help monitor their conditions when they are not in the hospital, they can return home at night and on weekends. Partial hospitalization or day treatment works best for people whose symptoms are under control. They enter care directly from the community or after being discharged from 24-hour care.

Partial hospitalization is most effective for patients who are ready for therapy and rehabilitation that can move them comfortably back into the community.

When Children Need Hospital Care

Children and teenagers can have mental illnesses. Some of these illnesses—such as conduct disorder and attention deficit/hyperactivity disorder—usually emerge during these early years. Youngsters also can suffer with illnesses most people would associate first with adults, such as depression or schizophrenia. And like those of adults, children's illnesses can go into remission or worsen from time to time.

When a child's symptoms become severe, a psychiatrist may recommend hospitalization. The physician will consider several factors in making the recommendation including the following:

- Whether the child poses an actual or imminent danger to him or herself or others

- Whether the child's behavior is bizarre and destructive to the community

- Whether the child requires medication that must be closely monitored

- Whether the child needs 24-hour care in order to become stabilized

- Whether the child has failed to improve in other, less restrictive environments

As with adults, children receiving inpatient care will have a treatment plan that identifies the therapies and goals unique to each child. The treatment team will work with each child in individual, group and family therapy as well as occupational therapy. Youngsters are also often involved in activity therapy, which teaches social skills, and drug and alcohol evaluation and treatment. In addition, the hospital will provide an academic program.

Because the family is integral to a child's recuperation, the treatment team will work closely with parents or guardians to ensure good communication and understanding about the illness, treatment process and recovery prognosis. Families will learn how to work with their children and cope with the stresses that can develop with a serious or chronic illness.

Involuntary Treatment

The National Association of Psychiatric Health Systems reports that about 88 percent of adults treated in its members' hospitals are admitted voluntarily. In many states, people so disabled by their illnesses that they don't fully recognize the need for 24-hour inpatient care and who refuse hospital treatment may be involuntarily admitted to the hospital, but only with the knowledge of the court system and following an examination by a physician.

Commitment procedures vary from state to state. There has been some attempt made to shield mentally ill people from the stigma of public court appearances, and sometimes patients can be too ill to attend a hearing. For these reasons, a mentally ill person may, in some states, be admitted on the advice of one or two physicians who act within a very strict set of procedures to insure full protection of the patient's legal rights. Most states allow a physician to prescribe that a person be admitted involuntarily to a hospital for a brief evaluation period, usually three-days.

♣ It's A Fact!!

Involuntary treatment is sometimes necessary, but is used only in unusual circumstances and is always subject to a review which protects the civil liberties of patients.

During the evaluation period, a team of psychiatrists and mental health professionals can learn whether the person's illness requires longer hospital care or can be managed effectively with less intensive treatment, such as partial hospitalization.

If the evaluation team thinks a patient requires inpatient care past the three-day period, it can request longer admission—a request that, it should be emphasized, is subject to a hearing. At this hearing, the patient or his or her representative must be present. No decisions regarding a patient's hospitalization and subsequent treatment can be made without the presence of the patient or this representative. If involuntary admission is recommended, the court can issue an order for only a specific period of time. At the end of that period, the question of hospitalization must again go to a court hearing.

There If You Need It

If your physician prescribes hospitalization, you, a member of your family, a friend or other advocate should tour the recommended facility and learn about its admissions procedure, daily schedules and the mental health care team with whom you or your family member will be working. Learn how treatment progress will be communicated and what your role will be. This may help you to feel more comfortable about complying with your physician's recommendation. And that comfort can only contribute to the progress you or your loved one will make during hospital care.

Regardless of the illness, it's good to know that a range of health care services are available for patients and their families. Certainly outpatient care is the most common treatment setting. But when an illness becomes severe, effective hospital services are there to meet the need.

Chapter 38

Alternative Approaches To Mental Health Care

An alternative approach to mental health care is one that emphasizes the interrelationship between mind, body, and spirit. Although some alternative approaches have a long history, many remain controversial. The National Center for Complementary and Alternative Medicine at the National Institutes of Health was created in 1992 to help evaluate alternative methods of treatment and to integrate those that are effective into mainstream health care practice. It is crucial, however, to consult with your health care providers about the approaches you are using to achieve mental wellness.

Self-Help

Many people with mental illnesses find that self-help groups are an invaluable resource for recovery and for empowerment. Self-help generally refers to groups or meetings that include the following:

- involve people who have similar needs;

- are facilitated by a consumer, survivor, or other layperson;

About This Chapter: This chapter begins with "Alternative Approaches to Mental Health Care," Substance Abuse and Mental Health Service Administration (SAMHSA), April 2003. "St. John's Wort and the Treatment of Depression," is from a fact sheet produced by the National Center for Complementary and Alternative Medicine (NCCAM), March 2004.

- assist people to deal with a "life-disrupting" event, such as a death, abuse, serious accident, addiction, or diagnosis of a physical, emotional, or mental disability, for oneself or a relative;

- are operated on an informal, free-of-charge, and nonprofit basis;

- provide support and education;

- are voluntary, anonymous, and confidential.

Diet And Nutrition

Adjusting both diet and nutrition may help some people with mental illnesses manage their symptoms and promote recovery. For example, research suggests that eliminating milk and wheat products can reduce the severity of symptoms for some people who have schizophrenia and some children with autism. Similarly, some holistic/natural physicians use herbal treatments, B-complex vitamins, riboflavin, magnesium, and thiamine to treat anxiety, autism, depression, drug-induced psychoses, and hyperactivity.

Pastoral Counseling

Some people prefer to seek help for mental health problems from their pastor, rabbi, or priest, rather than from therapists who are not affiliated with a religious community. Counselors working within traditional faith communities increasingly are recognizing the need to incorporate psychotherapy and/or medication, along with prayer and spirituality, to effectively help some people with mental disorders.

Animal Assisted Therapies

Working with an animal (or animals) under the guidance of a health care professional may benefit some people with mental illness by facilitating positive changes, such as increased empathy and enhanced socialization skills. Animals can be used as part of group therapy programs to encourage communication and increase the ability to focus. Developing self-esteem and reducing loneliness and anxiety are just some potential benefits of individual-animal therapy (Delta Society, 2002).

Expressive Therapies

Art Therapy: Drawing, painting, and sculpting help many people to reconcile inner conflicts, release deeply repressed emotions, and foster self-awareness, as well as personal growth. Some mental health providers use art therapy as both a diagnostic tool and as a way to help treat disorders such as depression, abuse-related trauma, and schizophrenia. You may be able to find a therapist in your area who has received special training and certification in art therapy.

Dance/Movement Therapy: Some people find that their spirits soar when they let their feet fly. Others—particularly those who prefer more structure or who feel they have "two left feet"—gain the same sense of release and inner peace from the Eastern martial arts, such as Aikido and Tai Chi. Those who are recovering from physical, sexual, or emotional abuse may find these techniques especially helpful for gaining a sense of ease with their own bodies. The underlying premise to dance/movement therapy is that it can help a person integrate the emotional, physical, and cognitive facets of "self."

Music/Sound Therapy: It is no coincidence that many people turn on soothing music to relax or snazzy tunes to help feel upbeat. Research suggests that music stimulates the body's natural "feel good" chemicals (opiates and endorphins). This stimulation results in improved blood flow, blood pressure, pulse rate, breathing, and posture changes. Music or sound therapy has been used to treat disorders such as stress, grief, depression, schizophrenia, and autism in children, and to diagnose mental health needs.

Culturally Based Healing Arts

Traditional Oriental medicine (such as acupuncture, shiatsu, and Reiki), Indian systems of health care (such as Ayurveda and yoga), and Native American healing practices (such as the Sweat Lodge and Talking Circles) all incorporate the following beliefs:

- Wellness is a state of balance between the spiritual, physical, and mental/emotional "selves."

- An imbalance of forces within the body is the cause of illness.

- Herbal/natural remedies, combined with sound nutrition, exercise, and meditation/prayer, will correct this imbalance.

Acupuncture: The Chinese practice of inserting needles into the body at specific points manipulates the body's flow of energy to balance the endocrine system. This manipulation regulates functions such as heart rate, body temperature, and respiration, as well as sleep patterns and emotional changes. Acupuncture has been used in clinics to assist people with substance abuse disorders through detoxification; to relieve stress and anxiety; to treat attention deficit and hyperactivity disorder in children; to reduce symptoms of depression; and to help people with physical ailments.

Ayurveda: Ayurvedic medicine is described as "knowledge of how to live." It incorporates an individualized regimen—such as diet, meditation, herbal preparations, or other techniques—to treat a variety of conditions, including depression, to facilitate lifestyle changes, and to teach people how to release stress and tension through yoga or transcendental meditation.

Yoga/meditation: Practitioners of this ancient Indian system of health care use breathing exercises, posture, stretches, and meditation to balance the body's energy centers. Yoga is used in combination with other treatment for depression, anxiety, and stress-related disorders.

Native American traditional practices: Ceremonial dances, chants, and cleansing rituals are part of Indian Health Service programs to heal depression, stress, trauma (including those related to physical and sexual abuse), and substance abuse.

Cuentos: Based on folktales, this form of therapy originated in Puerto Rico. The stories used contain healing themes and models of behavior such as self-transformation and endurance through adversity. Cuentos is used primarily to help Hispanic children recover from depression and other mental health problems related to leaving one's homeland and living in a foreign culture.

Relaxation And Stress Reduction Techniques

Biofeedback: Learning to control muscle tension and "involuntary" body functioning, such as heart rate and skin temperature, can be a path to mastering one's fears. It is used in combination with, or as an alternative to, medication to treat disorders such as anxiety, panic, and phobias. For example, a person can learn to "retrain" his or her breathing habits in stressful situations to induce relaxation and decrease hyperventilation. Some preliminary research indicates it may offer an additional tool for treating schizophrenia and depression.

Guided imagery or visualization: This process involves going into a state of deep relaxation and creating a mental image of recovery and wellness. Physicians, nurses, and mental health providers occasionally use this approach to treat alcohol and drug addictions, depression, panic disorders, phobias, and stress.

Massage therapy: The underlying principle of this approach is that rubbing, kneading, brushing, and tapping a person's muscles can help release tension and pent emotions. It has been used to treat trauma-related depression and stress. A highly unregulated industry, certification for massage therapy varies widely from state to state. Some states have strict guidelines, while others have none.

Technology-Based Applications

The boom in electronic tools at home and in the office makes access to mental health information just a telephone call or a "mouse click" away. Technology is also making treatment more widely available in once-isolated areas.

Telemedicine: Plugging into video and computer technology is a relatively new innovation in health care. It allows both consumers and providers in remote or rural areas to gain access to mental health or specialty expertise. Telemedicine can enable consulting providers to speak to and observe patients directly. It also can be used in education and training programs for generalist clinicians.

Telephone counseling: Active listening skills are a hallmark of telephone counselors. These also provide information and referral to interested callers. For many people telephone counseling often is a first step to receiving in-depth mental health care. Research shows that such counseling from specially trained mental health providers reaches many people who otherwise might not get the help they need. Before calling, be sure to check the telephone number for service fees; a 900 area code means you will be billed for the call, an 800 or 888 area code means the call is toll-free.

Electronic communications: Technologies such as the internet, bulletin boards, and electronic mail lists provide access directly to consumers and the public on a wide range of information. On-line consumer groups can exchange information, experiences, and views on mental health, treatment systems, alternative medicine, and other related topics.

Radio psychiatry: Another relative newcomer to therapy, radio psychiatry was first introduced in the United States in 1976. Radio psychiatrists and psychologists provide advice, information, and referrals in response to a variety of mental health questions from callers. The American Psychiatric Association and the American Psychological Association have issued ethical guidelines for the role of psychiatrists and psychologists on radio shows.

St. John's Wort And The Treatment Of Depression

What is St. John's wort?

St. John's wort (*Hypericum perforatum* in Latin) is a long-living plant with yellow flowers. It contains many chemical compounds. Some are believed to be the active ingredients that produce the herb's effects, including the compounds hypericin and hyperforin.

How these compounds actually work in the body is not yet known, but several theories have been suggested. Preliminary studies suggest that St. John's wort might work by preventing nerve cells in the brain from reabsorbing the chemical messenger serotonin, or by reducing levels of a protein involved in the body's immune system functioning.

For what medicinal purposes has St. John's wort been used?

St. John's wort has been used for centuries to treat mental disorders as well as nerve pain. In ancient times, doctors and herbalists (specialists in herbs) wrote about its use as a sedative and treatment for malaria as well as a balm for wounds, burns, and insect bites. Today, St. John's wort is used by some people to treat mild to moderate depression, anxiety, or sleep disorders.

📎 What's It Mean?

Complementary and alternative medicine (CAM): A group of diverse medical and health care systems, practices, and products that are not presently considered an integral part of conventional medicine. Complementary medicine is used together with conventional medicine, and alternative medicine is used in place of conventional medicine. Some health care providers practice both CAM and conventional medicine.

Conventional medicine: A whole medical system practiced by holders of M.D. (medical doctor) or D.O. (doctor of osteopathy) degrees and by their allied health professionals, such as physical therapists, psychologists, and registered nurses. Other terms for conventional medicine include allopathy; Western, mainstream, and orthodox medicine; and biomedicine.

Source: Excerpted from "Acupuncture," National Center for Complementary and Alternative Medicine, December 2004.

What is depression?

Depression is a medical condition that affects nearly 19 million Americans each year. A person's mood, thoughts, physical health, and behavior all may be affected. Symptoms commonly include:

- Ongoing sad mood

- Loss of interest or pleasure in activities that the person once enjoyed

- Significant change in appetite or weight

- Oversleeping or difficulty sleeping

- Agitation or unusual slowness

- Loss of energy

- Feelings of worthlessness or guilt

- Difficulty "thinking," such as concentrating or making decisions

- Recurrent thoughts of death or suicide

Depressive illness comes in different forms. The three major forms are described below. Each can vary from person to person in terms of symptoms experienced and the severity of depression.

- In major depression, people experience a sad mood or loss of interest or pleasure in activities for at least two weeks. In addition, they have at least four other symptoms of depression. Major depression can be mild, moderate, or severe. If it is not treated, it can last for six months or more.

> ♣ **It's A Fact!!**
> St. John's wort is an herb that has been used for centuries for medicinal purposes, including to treat depression.
>
> Source: NCCAM, 2004.

- In minor depression, people experience the same symptoms as major depression, but they are fewer in number and are less disabling. Symptoms last at least six months but less than two years continuously.

- In dysthymia, a milder, but more chronic form of depression, people experience a depressed mood for at least two years (one year for children) accompanied by at least two other symptoms of depression.

- In bipolar disorder, also called manic depression, a person has periods of depressive symptoms that alternate with periods of mania. Symptoms of mania include an abnormally high level of excitement and energy, racing thoughts, and behavior that is impulsive and inappropriate.

Some people still hold outdated beliefs about depression—for example, that the emotional symptoms caused by depression are "not real" and that a person can merely "will" himself out of it. Depression is a real medical condition. It can be treated effectively with conventional medicine, including by antidepressant drugs and certain types of psychotherapy (talk therapy).

Why is St. John's wort used as an alternative therapy for depression?

Some patients who take antidepressant drugs do not experience relief from their depression. Other patients have reported unpleasant side effects from their prescription medication, such as a dry mouth, nausea, headache, or effects on sexual function or sleep.

Sometimes people turn to herbal preparations like St. John's wort because they believe "natural" products are better for them than prescription medications, or that natural products are always safe. Neither of these statements is true.

Finally, cost can be a reason. St. John's wort costs less than many antidepressant medications, and it is sold without a prescription (over the counter).

How widely is St. John's wort used for treating depression?

In Europe, St. John's wort is widely prescribed for depression. In the United States, St. John's wort is not a prescription medication, but there is considerable public interest in it. St. John's wort remains among the top-selling herbal products in the United States.

How is St. John's wort sold?

St. John's wort products are sold in the following forms:

• Capsules

• Teas—the dried herb is added to boiling water and steeped for a period of time.

♣ It's A Fact!!

The composition of St. John's wort and how it might work are not well understood.

Source: NCCAM, 2004.

• Extracts—specific types of chemicals are removed from the herb, leaving the desired chemicals in a concentrated form.

Does St. John's wort work as a treatment for depression?

There has been scientific research to try to answer this question.

In Europe, results from a number of scientific studies have supported the effectiveness of certain St. John's wort extracts for depression. An overview of 23 clinical studies found that the herb might be useful in cases of mild to moderate depression. The studies, which included 1,757 outpatients, reported that St. John's wort was more effective than a placebo (here, a "dummy" pill designed to have no effect) and appeared to produce fewer side effects than some standard antidepressants (Linde et al. British Medical Journal, 1996).

Other studies conducted recently have found no benefit from the use of St. John's wort for certain types of depression. For example, the results of a study funded by Pfizer Inc., a pharmaceutical company, found that St. John's wort, when compared with placebo, was not effective for treating major depression (Shelton et al. *JAMA*, 2001).

In addition, several components of the National Institutes of Health (NIH)—NCCAM, the Office of Dietary Supplements (ODS), and the National Institute of Mental Health (NIMH)—funded a large, carefully designed research study to find out whether St. John's wort extract benefits people with major depression of moderate severity. This clinical trial (a research study in people) found that St. John's wort was no more effective for treating major depression of moderate severity than placebo (Hypericum Depression Trial Study Group. *JAMA*, 2002; for further information, view the press release online at nccam.nih.gov/news/2002 or contact the NCCAM Clearinghouse).

> **♣ It's A Fact!!**
>
> There is some scientific evidence that St. John's wort is useful for treating mild to moderate depression. However, recent studies suggest that St. John's wort is of no benefit in treating major depression of moderate severity. More research is required to help us know whether St. John's wort has value in treating other forms of depression.
>
> Source: NCCAM, 2004.

Are there any risks to taking St. John's wort for depression?

Yes, there are risks in taking St. John's wort for depression.

Many so-called "natural" substances can have harmful effects—especially if they are taken in too large a quantity or if they interact with something else the person is taking.

Research from NIH has shown that St. John's wort interacts with some drugs—including certain drugs used to control HIV infection (such as indinavir). Other research shows that St. John's wort can interact with chemotherapeutic, or anticancer, drugs (such as irinotecan). The herb may also interact with drugs that help prevent the body from rejecting transplanted organs (such as cyclosporine). Using St. John's wort limits these drugs' effectiveness.

Also, St. John's wort is not a proven therapy for depression. If depression is not adequately treated, it can become severe and, in some cases, may be associated with suicide. Consult a health care practitioner if you or someone you care about may be experiencing depression.

People can experience side effects from taking St. John's wort. The most common side effects include dry mouth, dizziness, diarrhea, nausea, increased sensitivity to sunlight, and fatigue.

What are some other possible problems with using St. John's wort?

Herbal products such as St. John's wort are classified as dietary supplements by the U.S. Food and Drug Administration (FDA), a regulatory agency of the Federal Government. The FDA's requirements for testing and obtaining approval to sell dietary supplements are less strict than its requirements for drugs. Unlike drugs, herbal products can be sold without requiring studies on dosage, safety, or effectiveness.

✔ Quick Tip

St. John's wort interacts with certain drugs, and these interactions can be dangerous.

Source: NCCAM, 2004.

The strength and quality of herbal products are often unpredictable. Products can differ in content not only from brand to brand, but from batch to batch. Information on labels may be misleading or inaccurate.

Is NCCAM funding research on St. John's wort, including for depression and other mental illnesses?

Yes. For example, recent projects supported by NCCAM include the following:

• Safety and effectiveness of St. John's wort for the treatment of minor depression

• Safety of St. John's wort for the treatment of social phobia

• Effectiveness of St. John's wort for the treatment of obsessive compulsive disorder

- Effects of St. John's wort on how well birth control pills work

- Possible adverse interactions of St. John's wort and narcotic pain medications

✔ **Quick Tip**

It is important to inform all of your health care providers about any therapy that you are currently using or considering, including any dietary supplements. This is to help ensure a safe and coordinated course of care.

Source: NCCAM, 2004.

Part Five

Other Issues Related To Mental Wellness In Teens

Chapter 39

Learning Disabilities

LD At A Glance

Learning disabilities are real. A person can be of average or above-average intelligence, not have any major sensory problems (like blindness or hearing impairment), and yet struggle to keep up with people of the same age in learning and regular functioning.

What is a learning disability?

A learning disability (LD) is a neurological disorder that affects the brain's ability to receive, process, store and respond to information. The term learning disability is used to describe the seeming unexplained difficulty a person of at least average intelligence has in acquiring basic academic skills. These skills are essential for success at school and work, and for coping with life in general. LD is not a single disorder. It is a term that refers to a group of disorders.

How can one tell if a person has a learning disability?

Learning disabilities can affect a person's ability in the areas of:

- Listening
- Speaking
- Reading
- Writing
- Mathematics

Other features of a learning disability are:

- A distinct gap between the level of achievement that is expected and what is actually being achieved;

- Difficulties that can become apparent in different ways with different people;

- Difficulties that manifest themselves differently throughout development;

- Difficulties with socio-emotional skills and behavior.

A learning disability is not a disease, so there is no cure, but there are ways to overcome the challenges it poses through identification and accommodation.

> **♣ It's A Fact!!**
> **Are learning disabilities common?**
>
> Currently, almost 2.9 million school-aged children in the US are classified as having specific learning disabilities (SLD) and receive some kind of special education support. They are approximately 5% of all school-aged children in public schools. These numbers do not include children in private and religious schools or home-schooled children.
>
> Studies show that learning disabilities do not fall evenly across racial and ethnic groups. For instance, in 2001, 1% of white children and 2.6% of non-Hispanic black children were receiving LD-related special education services (Executive Summary, National Research Council, 2001). The same studies suggest that this has to do with economic status and not ethnic background. LD is not caused by economic disadvantage, but the increased risk of exposure to harmful toxins (lead, tobacco, alcohol, etc.) at early stages of development are prevalent in low-income communities.

Identification: If there is reason to think a person might have LD, it is important to collect observations by parents, teachers, doctors and others regularly in contact with that person. If there does seem to be a pattern of trouble that is more than just an isolated case of difficulty, the next step is to seek help from school or consult a learning specialist for an evaluation.

Accommodation and Modification: Depending on the type of learning disability and its severity, as well as the person's age, different kinds of assistance can be provided. Under the Individuals with Disabilities Education Act (IDEA) of 1997 and Americans with Disabilities Act (ADA) of 1990 people of all ages with LD are protected against discrimination and have a right to different forms of assistance in the classroom and workplace.

What causes learning disabilities?

Experts aren't exactly sure what causes learning disabilities. LD may be due to:

- **Heredity:** often learning disabilities run in the family, so it's not uncommon to find that people with LD have parents or other relatives with similar difficulties.

- **Problems during pregnancy and birth:** LD may be caused by illness or injury during or before birth. It may also be caused by drug and alcohol use during pregnancy, low birth weight, lack of oxygen and premature or prolonged labor.

- **Incidents after birth:** Head injuries, nutritional deprivation and exposure to toxic substances (for example lead) can contribute to LD.

Learning disabilities are NOT caused by economic disadvantage, environmental factors or cultural differences. In fact, there is frequently no apparent cause for LD.

Each type of strategy should be considered when planning instruction and support. A person with dysgraphia will benefit from help from both specialists and those who are closest to the person. Finding the most beneficial type of support is a process of trying different ideas and openly exchanging thoughts on what works best.

What can one do about learning disabilities?

Learning disabilities are lifelong, and although they won't go away, they don't have to stop a person from achieving goals. Help is available if they are identified. Learning disabilities affect every person differently, and the disorder can range from mild to severe. Sometimes people have more than one learning disability. In addition, approximately one third of people with LD also have attention deficit hyperactivity disorder (AD/HD), which makes it difficult for them to concentrate, stay focused or manage their attention to specific tasks.

LD And Children: Early identification is vital in helping a child to succeed academically, as well as socially. If you think your child is displaying signs of a learning disability, share them with classroom teachers and others who come in contact with your child. Observe the way your child develops the language, motor coordination and social skills and behaviors important for success in school. And remember-early is better-even preschoolers can show signs of risk for LD.

Don't panic. Not all children who are slow to develop skills have LD. If your child does have a learning disability, early intervention with specialized teaching strategies can help to overcome difficulties. As a parent, it is important to learn as much as you can and to help your child understand that he or she is not alone: other children struggle too, and adults are there to help.

LD And Adulthood: It is never too late to get help for a learning disability. Finding out about a learning disability can be a great relief to adults who could not explain the reason for their struggles in the past. Testing specialists are available for people of all ages, and assistance is available for every stage of life. Taking the initiative to seek out support and services than can provide help is the first step to overcoming a learning disability.

Many adults (some of whom are unaware of their LD) have developed ways to cope with their difficulties and are able to lead successful, functioning lives. LD shouldn't hinder a person from attaining goals. Regardless of the situation, understanding the specific challenges and learning strategies to deal with LD directly at every stage can alleviate a lot of frustration and make successful living much easier.

Self-Advocacy For Teens And Adults

Having learning disabilities often means having special needs. It's up to you to make sure your rights are being respected and that the accommodations you need are available to you. Whether at school or at work, being an advocate for yourself means understanding your rights, understanding how you work best and working with others to ensure that your special needs are met.

LD.org has a section called Living with LD that has details about dealing with the different aspects of learning disabilities (LD) that you may face as a teenager and as an adult. Here, we'll focus on how to be your own best spokesperson at school and at work.

Being Your Own Advocate In High School

- Attend all your IEP (Individualized Education Plan) meetings. You have a right to be there and should take an active part in the meetings. It's a great opportunity to talk to teachers, administrators and others that are involved with your education (including your parents or guardians) about how you learn and what kinds of services and supports you need to do well in school. Make sure the specific accommodations you need are outlined in your IEP.

- Set goals for yourself and think realistically about reaching them. Part of your IEP process calls for establishing a transition plan as early as possible, outlining your path to graduation, what you want to do after high school and the accommodations you might need after you leave. If you hope to go to college, what subjects do you want to study? What college are you interested in? Will that college permit you to substitute requirements or have them waived? To get into that school, what grades will you need to get and which classes should you take? Don't feel like once you decide on something that it's set in stone - adjusting your goals is an important part of realizing what you want and what it will take to achieve success.

- Be aware of what you're good at, what you struggle with, what activities you have a passion for and what your ideal job or project would be—being able to share this kind of information with others is a valuable part of representing yourself.

- Learn as much as you can about your LD. The more you know about your specific learning disability, the easier it will be for you to figure out how you learn best and the accommodations you will need to be successful.

- Meet with your teachers and counselors outside of the IEP meeting to talk about your classes, about the accommodations you may have (extra time on tests or a note-taking buddy, for example) and other helpful strategies, as well as what you're interested in pursuing next.

- Request that your school update your LD documentation before you leave high school.

Being Your Own Advocate In College

Once you graduate from high school, responsibility for attending to your special needs moves away from the educational system and onto your shoulders. It's up to you to make your college career successful. Here are some tips:

- Make sure you arrive on campus able to provide current documentation of your disability.

- Know your rights. You have a right to participate in educational programs without discrimination and to receive reasonable accommodations in courses and exams.

- Meet with your advisors to talk about what you want to learn; discuss what challenges you may encounter and how you can accommodate for them. If you need specific support and services, you must disclose your learning disability to your instructors and others who can help you.

Chapter 40

Attention Deficit Hyperactivity Disorder

Attention deficit hyperactivity disorder (ADHD) was first described in 1845 by Dr. Heinrich Hoffman, a physician who wrote books on medicine and psychiatry. Yet it was not until 1902 that Sir George F. Still published a series of lectures to the Royal College of Physicians in England in which he described a group of impulsive children with significant behavioral problems, caused by a genetic dysfunction and not by poor child rearing—children who today would be easily recognized as having ADHD. Since then, several thousand scientific papers on the disorder have been published, providing information on its nature, course, causes, impairments, and treatments.

Symptoms

The principal characteristics of ADHD are inattention, hyperactivity, and impulsivity. These symptoms appear early in a child's life. Because many normal children may have these symptoms, but at a low level, or the symptoms may be caused by another disorder, it is important that the child receive a thorough examination and appropriate diagnosis by a well-qualified professional.

About This Chapter: Text in this chapter is excerpted from "Attention Deficit Hyperactivity Disorder," National Institute on Mental Health (NIMH), 2003. The complete text of this booklet, including references, is available online at http://www.nimh.gov/publicat/adhd.cfm.

Symptoms of ADHD will appear over the course of many months, often with the symptoms of impulsiveness and hyperactivity preceding those of inattention, which may not emerge for a year or more. Different symptoms may appear in different settings, depending on the demands the situation may pose for the child's self-control. A child who "can't sit still" or is otherwise disruptive will be noticeable in school, but the inattentive daydreamer may be overlooked. The

♣ It's A Fact!!

It is estimated that between 3 and 5 percent of children have ADHD, or approximately 2 million children in the United States. This means that in a classroom of 25 to 30 children, it is likely that at least one will have ADHD.

Source: NIMH, 2003.

impulsive child who acts before thinking may be considered just a "discipline problem," while the child who is passive or sluggish may be viewed as merely unmotivated. Yet both may have different types of ADHD. All children are sometimes restless, sometimes act without thinking, sometimes daydream the time away. When the child's hyperactivity, distractibility, poor concentration, or impulsivity begin to affect performance in school, social relationships with other children, or behavior at home, ADHD may be suspected. But because the symptoms vary so much across settings, ADHD is not easy to diagnose. This is especially true when inattentiveness is the primary symptom.

♣ It's A Fact!!

According to the most recent version of the *Diagnostic and Statistical Manual of Mental Disorders* (*DSM-IV-TR*), there are three patterns of behavior that indicate ADHD:

- predominantly hyperactive-impulsive type (that does not show significant inattention)

- predominantly inattentive type (that does not show significant hyperactive-impulsive behavior)

- combined type (that displays both inattentive and hyperactive-impulsive symptoms)

Source: NIMH, 2003.

Hyperactivity, Impulsivity, And Inattention

Hyperactive children always seem to be "on the go" or constantly in motion. They dash around touching or playing with whatever is in sight, or talk incessantly. Sitting still at dinner or during a school lesson or story can be a difficult task. They squirm and fidget in their seats or roam around the room. Or they may wiggle their feet, touch everything, or noisily tap their pencil. Hyperactive teenagers or adults may feel internally restless. They often report needing to stay busy and may try to do several things at once.

Impulsive children seem unable to curb their immediate reactions or think before they act. They will often blurt out inappropriate comments, display their emotions without restraint, and act without regard for the later consequences of their conduct. Their impulsivity may make it hard for them to wait for things they want or to take their turn in games. They may grab a toy from another child or hit when they're upset. Even as teenagers or adults, they may impulsively choose to do things that have an immediate but small payoff rather than engage in activities that may take more effort yet provide much greater but delayed rewards.

Children who are inattentive have a hard time keeping their minds on any one thing and may get bored with a task after only a few minutes. If they are doing something they really enjoy, they have no trouble paying attention. But focusing deliberate, conscious attention to organizing and completing a task or learning something new is difficult. Homework is particularly hard for these children. They will forget to write down an assignment, or leave it at school. They will forget to bring a book home, or bring the wrong one. The homework, if finally finished, is full of errors and erasures. Homework is often accompanied by frustration for both parent and child.

Professionals Who Make The Diagnosis

Ideally, a diagnosis of ADHD should be made by a professional in your area with training in ADHD or in the diagnosis of mental disorders. Child psychiatrists and psychologists, developmental/behavioral pediatricians, or behavioral neurologists are those most often trained in differential diagnosis. Clinical social workers may also have such training.

A family can start by talking with a child's pediatrician or family doctor. Some pediatricians may do the assessment themselves, but often they refer the family to an appropriate mental health specialist they know and trust. In addition, state and local agencies that serve families and children, as well as some of the volunteer organizations listed at the end of this document, can help identify appropriate specialists.

☞ **Remember!!**

Not everyone who is overly hyperactive, inattentive, or impulsive has ADHD. Because everyone shows some of these behaviors at times, the diagnosis requires that such behavior be demonstrated to a degree that is inappropriate for the person's age. The behaviors must create a real handicap in at least two areas of a person's life such as in the schoolroom, on the playground, at home, in the community, or in social settings.

Source: NIMH, 2003.

Knowing the differences in qualifications and services can help a family choose someone who can best meet their needs. There are several types of specialists qualified to diagnose and treat ADHD. Child psychiatrists are doctors who specialize in diagnosing and treating childhood mental and behavioral disorders. A psychiatrist can provide therapy and prescribe any needed medications. Child psychologists are also qualified to diagnose and treat ADHD. They can provide therapy for the child and help the family develop ways to deal with the disorder. But psychologists are not medical doctors and must rely on the child's physician to do medical exams and prescribe medication. Neurologists, doctors who work with disorders of the brain and nervous system, can also diagnose ADHD and prescribe medicines. But unlike psychiatrists and psychologists, neurologists usually do not provide therapy for the emotional aspects of the disorder.

Within each specialty, individual doctors and mental health professionals differ in their experiences with ADHD. So in selecting a specialist, it's important to find someone with specific training and experience in diagnosing and treating the disorder.

Whatever the specialist's expertise, his or her first task is to gather information that will rule out other possible reasons for the child's behavior. Among possible causes of ADHD-like behavior are the following:

- A sudden change in the child's life—the death of a parent or grandparent; parents' divorce; a parent's job loss

- Undetected seizures, such as in petit mal or temporal lobe seizures

- A middle ear infection that causes intermittent hearing problems

- Medical disorders that may affect brain functioning

- Underachievement caused by learning disability

- Anxiety or depression

What Causes ADHD?

There is little compelling evidence at this time that ADHD can arise purely from social factors or child-rearing methods. Most substantiated causes appear to fall in the realm of neurobiology and genetics. This is not to say that environmental factors may not influence the severity of the disorder, and especially the degree of impairment and suffering the child may experience, but that such factors do not seem to give rise to the condition by themselves.

Table 40.1. Who Treats Attention Deficit Hyperactivity Disorder?

Specialty	Can Diagnose ADHD	Can prescribe medication, if needed	Provides counseling or training
Psychiatrists	yes	yes	yes
Psychologists	yes	no	yes
Pediatricians or Family Physicians	yes	yes	no
Neurologists	yes	yes	no
Clinical Social Workers	yes	no	yes

Environmental agents: Studies have shown a possible correlation between the use of cigarettes and alcohol during pregnancy and risk for ADHD in the offspring of that pregnancy. As a precaution, it is best during pregnancy to refrain from both cigarette and alcohol use.

Another environmental agent that may be associated with a higher risk of ADHD is high levels of lead in the bodies of young preschool children. Since lead is no longer allowed in paint and is usually found only in older buildings, exposure to toxic levels is not as prevalent as it once was. Children who live in old buildings may be at risk.

Brain injury: One early theory was that attention disorders were caused by brain injury. Some children who have suffered accidents leading to brain injury may show some signs of behavior similar to that of ADHD, but only a small percentage of children with ADHD have been found to have suffered a traumatic brain injury.

Food additives and sugar: It has been suggested that attention disorders are caused by refined sugar or food additives, or that symptoms of ADHD are exacerbated by sugar or food additives. In 1982, the National Institutes of Health held a scientific consensus conference to discuss this issue. It was found that diet restrictions helped about 5 percent of children with ADHD, mostly young children who had food allergies. A more recent study on the effect of sugar on children, using sugar one day and a sugar substitute on alternate days, without parents, staff, or children knowing which substance was being used, showed no significant effects of the sugar on behavior or learning.

Genetics: Attention disorders often run in families, so there are likely to be genetic influences. Studies indicate that 25 percent of the close relatives in the families of ADHD children also have ADHD, whereas the rate is about 5 percent in the general population. Many studies of twins now show that a strong genetic influence exists in the disorder.

Brain anatomy: Research scientists searching for a physical basis for attention deficit hyperactivity disorder have focused on in their search is the frontal lobes of the cerebrum. The frontal lobes allow us to solve problems, plan ahead, understand the behavior of others, and restrain our impulses.

The two frontal lobes, the right and the left, communicate with each other through the corpus callosum, (nerve fibers that connect the right and left frontal lobes). The basal ganglia are the interconnected gray masses deep in the cerebral hemisphere that serve as the connection between the cerebrum and the cerebellum and, with the cerebellum, are responsible for motor coordination. The cerebellum is divided into three parts. The middle part is called the vermis.

In one study, as a group, ADHD children showed 3–4 percent smaller brain volumes in all regions—the frontal lobes, temporal gray matter, caudate nucleus, and cerebellum. The study also showed that the ADHD children who were on medication had a white matter volume that did not differ from that of controls. Those never-medicated patients had an abnormally small volume of white matter. The white matter consists of fibers that establish long-distance connections between brain regions. It normally thickens as a child grows older and the brain matures.

Disorders That Sometimes Accompany ADHD

Learning disabilities: Many children with ADHD—approximately 20 to 30 percent—also have a specific learning disability (LD). In preschool years, these disabilities include difficulty in understanding certain sounds or words and/or difficulty in expressing oneself in words. In school age children, reading or spelling disabilities, writing disorders, and arithmetic disorders may appear. A type of reading disorder, dyslexia, is quite widespread. Reading disabilities affect up to 8 percent of elementary school children.

Tourette syndrome: A very small proportion of people with ADHD have a neurological disorder called Tourette syndrome. People with Tourette syndrome have various nervous tics and repetitive mannerisms, such as eye blinks, facial twitches, or grimacing. Others may clear their throats frequently, snort, sniff, or bark out words. These behaviors can be controlled with medication. While very few children have this syndrome, many of the cases of Tourette syndrome have associated ADHD. In such cases, both disorders often require treatment that may include medications.

Oppositional defiant disorder: As many as one-third to one-half of all children with ADHD—mostly boys—have another condition, known as oppositional defiant disorder (ODD). These children are often defiant, stubborn, non-compliant, have outbursts of temper, or become belligerent. They argue with adults and refuse to obey.

Conduct disorder: About 20 to 40 percent of ADHD children may eventually develop conduct disorder (CD), a more serious pattern of antisocial behavior. These children frequently lie or steal, fight with, or bully others, and are at a real risk of getting into trouble at school or with the police. They violate the basic rights of other people, are aggressive toward people and/or animals, destroy property, break into people's homes, commit thefts, carry or use weapons, or engage in vandalism. These children or teens are at greater risk for substance use experimentation, and later dependence and abuse. They need immediate help.

Anxiety and depression: Some children with ADHD often have co-occurring anxiety or depression. If the anxiety or depression is recognized and treated, the child will be better able to handle the problems that accompany ADHD. Conversely, effective treatment of ADHD can have a positive impact on anxiety as the child is better able to master academic tasks.

♣ It's A Fact!!

On April 6, 2006 the U.S. Food and Drug Administration approved Daytrana, the first transdermal (skin) patch, for treating attention deficit hyperactivity disorder in children six to 12 years of age. Daytrana is a once daily treatment containing the drug methylphenidate, a central nervous system stimulant. Daytrana is applied each morning to the alternating hip and worn for nine hours, although the prescriber may change the amount of time the patch is worn to help manage how long the medication works each day.

Source: Excerpted from "FDA Approves Methylphenidate Patch to Treat Attention Deficit Hyperactivity Disorder in Children," U.S. Food and Drug Administration, press release dated April 10, 2006.

Bipolar disorder: There are no accurate statistics on how many children with ADHD also have bipolar disorder. Differentiating between ADHD and bipolar disorder in childhood can be difficult. In its classic form, bipolar disorder is characterized by mood cycling between periods of intense highs and lows. But in children, bipolar disorder often seems to be a rather chronic mood dysregulation with a mixture of elation, depression, and irritability. Furthermore, there are some symptoms that can be present both in ADHD and bipolar disorder, such as a high level of energy and a reduced need for sleep. Of the symptoms differentiating children with ADHD from those with bipolar disorder, elated mood and grandiosity of the bipolar child are distinguishing characteristics.

Treatment Of ADHD

For children with ADHD, no single treatment is the answer for every child. A child may sometimes have undesirable side effects to a medication that would make that particular treatment unacceptable. And if a child with ADHD also has anxiety or depression, a treatment combining medication and behavioral therapy might be best. Each child's needs and personal history must be carefully considered.

Medications

For decades, medications have been used to treat the symptoms of ADHD. The medications that seem to be the most effective are a class of drugs known as stimulants. Table 40.2 presents a list of the stimulants, their trade (or brand) names, and their generic names. "Approved age" means that the drug has been tested and found safe and effective in children of that age.

The U.S. Food and Drug Administration (FDA) recently approved a medication for ADHD that is not a stimulant. The medication, Strattera®, or atomoxetine, works on the neurotransmitter norepinephrine, whereas the stimulants primarily work on dopamine. Both of theses neurotransmitters are believed to play a role in ADHD. More studies will need to be done to contrast Strattera with the medications already available, but the evidence to date indicates that over 70 percent of children with ADHD given Strattera manifest significant improvement in their symptoms.

Table 40.2. Stimulants Used To Treat ADHD

Trade Name	Generic Name	Approved Age
Adderall	amphetamine	3 and older
Concerta	methylphenidate (long acting)	6 and older
Cylert*	pemoline	6 and older
Dexedrine	dextroamphetamine	3 and older
Dextrostat	dextroamphetamine	3 and older
Focalin	dexmethylphenidate 6 and older	
Metadate ER	methylphenidate (extended release)	6 and older
Metadate CD	methylphenidate (extended release)	6 and older
Ritalin	methylphenidate	6 and older
Ritalin SR	methylphenidate (extended release)	6 and older
Ritalin LA	methylphenidate (long acting)	6 and older

*Because of its potential for serious side effects affecting the liver, Cylert should not ordinarily be considered as first-line drug therapy for ADHD.

Some people get better results from one medication, some from another. It is important to work with the prescribing physician to find the right medication and the right dosage. For many people, the stimulants dramatically reduce their hyperactivity and impulsivity and improve their ability to focus, work, and learn. The medications may also improve physical coordination, such as that needed in handwriting and in sports.

Most side effects of the stimulant medications are minor and are usually related to the dosage of the medication being taken. Higher doses produce more side effects. The most common side effects are decreased appetite, insomnia, increased anxiety, and/or irritability. Some children report mild stomach aches or headaches.

Behavioral therapy, emotional counseling, and practical support will help ADHD children cope with everyday problems and feel better about themselves.

The Family And The ADHD Child

Although medication can help the ADHD child in everyday life, it takes time to undo the frustration, blame, and anger that may have gone on. Both parents and children may need special help to develop techniques for managing the patterns of behavior. In such cases, mental health professionals can counsel the child and the family, helping them to develop new skills, attitudes, and ways of relating to each other. In individual counseling, the therapist helps children with ADHD learn to feel better about themselves. The therapist can also help them to identify and build on their strengths, cope with daily problems, and control their attention and aggression. Sometimes only the child with ADHD needs counseling support. But in many cases, because the problem affects the family as a whole, the entire family may need help. The therapist assists the family in finding better ways to handle the disruptive behaviors and promote change.

Remember!!

Facts About Medication for ADHD

Medications for ADHD help many children focus and be more successful at school, home, and play. Avoiding negative experiences now may actually help prevent addictions and other emotional problems later.

About 80 percent of children who need medication for ADHD still need it as teenagers. Over 50 percent need medication as adults.

Source: NIMH, 2003.

Several intervention approaches are available. Knowing something about the various types of interventions makes it easier for families to choose a therapist that is right for their needs.

Psychotherapy works to help people with ADHD to like and accept themselves despite their disorder. It does not address the symptoms or underlying causes of the disorder. In psychotherapy, patients talk with the therapist about upsetting thoughts and feelings, explore self-defeating patterns of behavior, and learn alternative ways to handle their emotions. As they talk, the therapist tries to help them understand how they can change or better cope with their disorder.

Behavioral therapy (BT) helps people develop more effective ways to work on immediate issues. Rather than helping the child understand his or her feelings and actions, it helps directly in changing their thinking and coping and thus may lead to changes in behavior. The support might be practical assistance, like help in organizing tasks or schoolwork or dealing with emotionally charged events. Or the support might be in self-monitoring one's own behavior and giving self-praise or rewards for acting in a desired way such as controlling anger or thinking before acting.

Social skills training can also help children learn new behaviors. In social skills training, the therapist discusses and models appropriate behaviors important in developing and maintaining social relationships, like waiting for a turn, sharing, asking for help, or responding to teasing, then gives children a chance to practice. For example, a child might learn to "read" other people's facial expression and tone of voice in order to respond appropriately. Social skills training helps the child to develop better ways to play and work with other children.

Support groups help parents connect with other people who have similar problems and concerns with their ADHD children. Members of support groups often meet on a regular basis (such as monthly) to hear lectures from experts on ADHD, share frustrations and successes, and obtain referrals to qualified specialists and information about what works. There is strength in numbers, and sharing experiences with others who have similar problems helps people know that they aren't alone. National organizations are listed at the end of this document.

Parenting skills training, offered by therapists or in special classes, gives parents tools and techniques for managing their child's behavior. One such technique is the use of token or point systems for immediately rewarding good behavior or work. Another is the use of "time-out" or isolation to a chair or bedroom when the child becomes too unruly or out of control. Parents may also be taught to give the child "quality time" each day, in which they share a pleasurable or relaxing activity. During this time together, the parent looks for opportunities to notice and point out what the child does well, and praise his or her strengths and abilities.

Teenagers With ADHD

The teen years are challenging for most children; for the child with ADHD these years are doubly hard. All the adolescent problems—peer pressure, the fear of failure in both school and socially, low self-esteem—are harder for the ADHD child to handle. The desire to be independent, to try new and forbidden things—alcohol, drugs, and sexual activity—can lead to unforeseen consequences. The rules that once were, for the most part, followed, are often now flaunted. Parents may not agree with each other on how the teenager's behavior should be handled.

Now, more than ever, rules should be straightforward and easy to understand. Communication between the adolescent and parents can help the teenager to know the reasons for each rule. When a rule is set, it should be clear why the rule is set. Sometimes it helps to have a chart, posted usually in the kitchen, that lists all household rules and all rules for outside the home (social and school). Another chart could list household chores with space to check off a chore once it is done.

When rules are broken, parents should respond to inappropriate behavior as calmly and matter-of-factly as possible. Punishment should be used sparingly. Even with teens, a time-out can work. Impulsivity and hot temper often accompany ADHD. A short time alone can help.

✔ Quick Tip

People with ADHD may need help in organizing.

- **Schedule:** Have the same routine every day, from wake-up time to bedtime. The schedule should include homework time and playtime (including outdoor recreation and indoor activities such as computer games). Have the schedule on the refrigerator or a bulletin board in the kitchen. If a schedule change must be made, make it as far in advance as possible.

- **Organization:** Organize needed everyday items. Have a place for everything and keep everything in its place. This includes clothing, backpacks, and school supplies. Use homework and notebook organizers. Stress the importance of writing down assignments and bringing home needed books.

- **Rules:** Children with ADHD need consistent rules that they can understand and follow.

Source: NIMH, 2003.

ADHD And Driving

Teenagers begin talking about driving by the time they are 15. In some states, a learner's permit is available at 15 and a driver's license at 16. Statistics show that 16-year-old drivers have more accidents per driving mile than any other age. In the year 2000, 18 percent of those who died in speed-related crashes were youth ages 15 to 19. Sixty-six percent of these youth were not wearing safety belts. In their first 2 to 5 years of driving, youth with ADHD have nearly four times as many automobile accidents, are more likely to cause bodily injury in accidents, and have three times as many citations for speeding as the young drivers without ADHD.

Most states, after looking at the statistics for automobile accidents involving teenage drivers, have begun to use a graduated driver licensing system (GDL). This system eases young drivers onto the roads by a slow progression of exposure to more difficult driving experiences. The program, as developed by the National Highway Traffic Safety Administration and the American Association of Motor Vehicle Administrators, consists of three stages: learner's permit, intermediate (provisional) license, and full licensure. Drivers must demonstrate responsible driving behavior at each stage before advancing to the next level. During the learner's permit stage, a licensed adult must be in the car at all times. This period of time will give the learner a chance to practice, practice, practice. The more a child drives, the more efficient he or she will become. The sense of accomplishment the teenager with ADHD will feel when the coveted license is finally in his or her hands will make all the time and effort involved worthwhile.

Chapter 41

Tourette Syndrome

What is Tourette syndrome?

Tourette syndrome (TS) is a neurological disorder characterized by repetitive, stereotyped, involuntary movements and vocalizations called tics. The disorder is named for Dr. Georges Gilles de la Tourette, the pioneering French neurologist who in 1885 first described the condition in an 86-year-old French noblewoman.

The early symptoms of TS are almost always noticed first in childhood, with the average onset between the ages of seven and ten years. TS occurs in people from all ethnic groups; males are affected about three to four times more often than females. It is estimated that 200,000 Americans have the most severe form of TS, and as many as one in 100 exhibit milder and less complex symptoms such as chronic motor or vocal tics or transient tics of childhood. Although TS can be a chronic condition with symptoms lasting a lifetime, most people with the condition experience their worst symptoms in their early teens, with improvement occurring in the late teens and continuing into adulthood.

About This Chapter: "Tourette Syndrome Fact Sheet," National Institute of Neurological Disorders and Stroke, April 2005.

What are the symptoms?

Tics are classified as either simple or complex. Simple motor tics are sudden, brief, repetitive movements that involve a limited number of muscle groups. Some of the more common simple tics include eye blinking and other vision irregularities, facial grimacing, shoulder shrugging, and head or shoulder jerking. Simple vocalizations might include repetitive throat-clearing, sniffing, or grunting sounds. Complex tics are distinct, coordinated patterns of movements involving several muscle groups. Complex motor tics might include facial grimacing combined with a head twist and a shoulder shrug. Other complex motor tics may actually appear purposeful, including sniffing or touching objects, hopping, jumping, bending, or twisting. Simple vocal tics may include throat-clearing, sniffing/snorting, grunting, or barking. More complex vocal tics include words or phrases. Perhaps the most dramatic and disabling tics include motor movements that result in self-harm such as punching oneself in the face or vocal tics including coprolalia (uttering swear words) or echolalia (repeating the words or phrases of others). Some tics are preceded by an urge or sensation in the affected muscle group, commonly called a premonitory urge. Some with TS will describe a need to complete a tic in a certain way or a certain number of times in order to relieve the urge or decrease the sensation.

What is the course of TS?

Tics come and go over time, varying in type, frequency, location, and severity. The first symptoms usually occur in the head and neck area and may progress to include muscles of the trunk and extremities. Motor tics generally precede the development of vocal tics and simple tics often precede complex tics. Most patients experience peak tic severity before the mid-teen years

♣ It's A Fact!!

Tics are often worse with excitement or anxiety and better during calm, focused activities. Certain physical experiences can trigger or worsen tics, for example tight collars may trigger neck tics, or hearing another person sniff or throat-clear may trigger similar sounds. Tics do not go away during sleep but are often significantly diminished.

Source: National Institute of Neurological Disorders and Stroke, April 2005.

with improvement for the majority of patients in the late teen years and early adulthood. Approximately 10 percent of those affected have a progressive or disabling course that lasts into adulthood.

Can people with TS control their tics?

Although the symptoms of TS are involuntary, some people can sometimes suppress, camouflage, or otherwise manage their tics in an effort to minimize their impact on functioning. However, people with TS often report a substantial buildup in tension when suppressing their tics to the point where they feel that the tic must be expressed. Tics in response to an environmental trigger can appear to be voluntary or purposeful but are not.

What causes TS?

Although the cause of TS is unknown, current research points to abnormalities in certain brain regions (including the basal ganglia, frontal lobes, and cortex), the circuits that interconnect these regions, and the neurotransmitters (dopamine, serotonin, and norepinephrine) responsible for communication among nerve cells. Given the often complex presentation of TS, the cause of the disorder is likely to be equally complex.

What disorders are associated with TS?

Many with TS experience additional neurobehavioral problems including inattention; hyperactivity and impulsivity (attention deficit hyperactivity disorder—ADHD) and related problems with reading, writing, and arithmetic; and obsessive-compulsive symptoms such as intrusive thoughts/worries and repetitive behaviors. For example, worries about dirt and germs may be associated with repetitive hand-washing, and concerns about bad things happening may be associated with ritualistic behaviors such as counting, repeating, or ordering and arranging. People with TS have also reported problems with depression or anxiety disorders, as well as other difficulties with living, that may or may not be directly related to TS. Given the range of potential complications, people with TS are best served by receiving medical care that provides a comprehensive treatment plan.

How is TS diagnosed?

TS is a diagnosis that doctors make after verifying that the patient has had both motor and vocal tics for at least one year. The existence of other neurological or psychiatric conditions (these include childhood-onset involuntary movement disorders such as dystonia, or psychiatric disorders characterized by repetitive behaviors/movements; for example, stereotypic behaviors in autism and compulsive behaviors in obsessive-compulsive disorder—OCD) can also help doctors arrive at a diagnosis. Common tics are not often misdiagnosed by knowledgeable clinicians. But atypical symptoms or atypical presentation (for example, onset of symptoms in adulthood) may require specific specialty expertise for diagnosis. There are no blood or laboratory tests needed for diagnosis, but neuroimaging studies, such as magnetic resonance imaging (MRI), computerized tomography (CT), and electroencephalogram (EEG) scans, or certain blood tests may be used to rule out other conditions that might be confused with TS.

It is not uncommon for patients to obtain a formal diagnosis of TS only after symptoms have been present for some time. There are many reasons for this. For families and physicians unfamiliar with TS, mild and even moderate tic symptoms may be considered inconsequential, part of a developmental phase, or the result of another condition. For example, parents may think that eye blinking is related to vision problems or that sniffing is related to seasonal allergies. Many patients are self-diagnosed after they, their parents, other relatives, or friends read or hear about TS from others.

How is TS treated?

Because tic symptoms do not often cause impairment, the majority of people with TS require no medication for tic suppression. However, effective medications are available for those whose symptoms interfere with functioning. Neuroleptics are the most consistently useful medications for tic suppression; a number are available but some are more effective than others (for example, haloperidol and pimozide). Unfortunately, there is no one medication that is helpful to all people with TS, nor does any medication completely eliminate symptoms. In addition, all medications have side effects. Most neuroleptic side effects can be managed by initiating treatment slowly and reducing the dose when side effects occur. The most common side effects of neuroleptics include sedation, weight gain, and cognitive dulling. Neurological side effects such as tremor, dystonic reactions (twisting movements or postures), parkinsonian-like symptoms, and other dyskinetic (involuntary) movements are less common and are readily managed with dose reduction. Discontinuing neuroleptics after long-term use must be done slowly to avoid rebound increases in tics and withdrawal dyskinesias. One form of withdrawal dyskinesia called tardive dyskinesia is a movement disorder distinct from TS that may result from the chronic use of neuroleptics. The risk of this side effect can be reduced by using lower doses of neuroleptics for shorter periods of time.

♣ It's A Fact!!
Scientists Discover First Gene For Tourette Syndrome

A team of scientists has discovered the first gene mutation that may cause some cases of Tourette syndrome (TS), an inherited neuropsychiatric disorder known for involuntary muscle and vocal tics.

The gene, named *SLITRK1*, was found through genetic analysis of a boy with TS who was previously identified as having an "inversion" on chromosome 13—a portion of the chromosome had an orientation opposite that of the normal chromosome. He was the only family member with TS and the inversion, suggesting that these two events were related.

The team then screened *SLITRK1* (found near where the boy's chromosome was abnormal) in 174 patients with TS and discovered an abnormality in the coding sequence of the gene in one family. The researchers also identified a separate mutated gene sequence in two unrelated individuals with the disorder. None of these mutations were identified among several thousand unaffected control individuals. Additional testing in cell cultures showed changes in protein expression or function, confirming the finding of the mutated gene.

The normal *SLITRK1* gene is involved with the growth of nerve cells and how they connect with other neurons. The mutated gene was found in regions of the brain (basal ganglia, cortex, and frontal lobes) previously identified as being associated with TS.

Source: Excerpted from a National Institute of Neurological Disorders and Stroke press release, December 15, 2005.

Other medications may also be useful for reducing tic severity, but most have not been as extensively studied or shown to be as consistently useful as neuroleptics. Additional medications with demonstrated efficacy include alpha-adrenergic agonists such as clonidine and guanfacine. These medications are used primarily for hypertension but are also used in the treatment of tics. The most common side effect from these medications that precludes their use is sedation.

Effective medications are also available to treat some of the associated neurobehavioral disorders that can occur in patients with TS. Recent research shows that stimulant medications such as methylphenidate and dextroamphetamine can lessen ADHD symptoms in people with TS without causing tics to become more severe. However, the product labeling for stimulants currently contraindicates the use of these drugs in children with tics/TS and those with a family history of tics. Scientists hope that future studies will include a thorough discussion of the risks and benefits of stimulants in those with TS or a family history of TS and will clarify this issue. For obsessive-compulsive symptoms that significantly disrupt daily functioning, the serotonin reuptake inhibitors (clomipramine, fluoxetine, fluvoxamine, paroxetine, and sertraline) have been proven effective in some patients.

Psychotherapy may also be helpful. Although psychological problems do not cause TS, such problems may result from TS. Psychotherapy can help the person with TS better cope with the disorder and deal with the secondary social and emotional problems that sometimes occur. More recently, specific behavioral treatments that include awareness training and competing response training, such as voluntarily moving in response to a premonitory urge, have shown effectiveness in small controlled trials. Larger and more definitive NIH-funded studies are underway.

Is TS inherited?

Evidence from twin and family studies suggests that TS is an inherited disorder. Although early family studies suggested an autosomal dominant mode of inheritance (an autosomal dominant disorder is one in which only one copy of the defective gene, inherited from one parent, is necessary to produce the disorder), more recent studies suggest that the pattern of inheritance is much more complex. Although there may be a few genes with substantial effects, it is also possible that many genes with smaller effects and environmental factors may play a role in the development of TS. Genetic studies also suggest that some forms of ADHD and OCD are genetically related to TS, but there is less evidence for a genetic relationship between TS and other neurobehavioral problems that commonly co-occur with TS. It is important for families to understand that genetic predisposition may not necessarily result in full-blown TS; instead, it may express itself as a milder tic disorder or as obsessive-compulsive behaviors. It is also possible that the gene-carrying offspring will not develop any TS symptoms.

The sex of the person also plays an important role in TS gene expression. At-risk males are more likely to have tics and at-risk females are more likely to have obsessive-compulsive symptoms.

What is the prognosis?

Although there is no cure for TS, the condition in many individuals improves in the late teens and early 20s. As a result, some may actually become symptom-free or no longer need medication for tic suppression. Although the disorder is generally lifelong and chronic, it is not a degenerative condition. Individuals with TS have a normal life expectancy. TS does not impair intelligence. Although tic symptoms tend to decrease with age, it is possible that neurobehavioral disorders such as depression, panic attacks, mood swings, and antisocial behaviors can persist and cause impairment in adult life.

What is the best educational setting for children with TS?

Although students with TS often function well in the regular classroom, ADHD, learning disabilities, obsessive-compulsive symptoms, and frequent tics can greatly interfere with academic performance or social adjustment.

After a comprehensive assessment, students should be placed in an educational setting that meets their individual needs. Students may require tutoring, smaller or special classes, and in some cases special schools.

All students with TS need a tolerant and compassionate setting that both encourages them to work to their full potential and is flexible enough to accommodate their special needs. This setting may include a private study area, exams outside the regular classroom, or even oral exams when the child's symptoms interfere with his or her ability to write. Untimed testing reduces stress for students with TS.

What research is being done?

Within the Federal government, the leading supporter of research on TS and other neurological disorders is the National Institute of Neurological Disorders and Stroke (NINDS). The NINDS, a part of the National Institutes of Health (NIH), is responsible for supporting and conducting research on the brain and central nervous system.

NINDS sponsors research on TS both in its laboratories at the NIH and through grants to major medical institutions across the country. The National Institute of Mental Health, the National Center for Research Resources, the National Institute of Child Health and Human Development, the National Institute on Drug Abuse, and the National Institute on Deafness and Other Communication Disorders also support research of relevance to TS. And another component of the Department of Health and Human Services, the Centers for Disease Control and Prevention, funds professional education programs as well as TS research.

Knowledge about TS comes from studies across a number of medical and scientific disciplines, including genetics, neuroimaging, neuropathology, clinical trials (medication and non-medication), epidemiology, neurophysiology, neuroimmunology, and descriptive/diagnostic clinical science.

Genetic studies: Currently, NIH-funded investigators are conducting a variety of large-scale genetic studies. Rapid advances in the technology of gene finding will allow for genome-wide screening approaches in TS, and finding a gene or genes for TS would be a major step toward understanding genetic risk factors. In addition, understanding the genetics of TS genes will strengthen clinical diagnosis, improve genetic counseling, lead to the clarification of pathophysiology, and provide clues for more effective therapies.

Neuroimaging studies: Within the past five years, advances in imaging technology and an increase in trained investigators have led to an increasing use of novel and powerful techniques to identify brain regions, circuitry, and neurochemical factors important in TS and related conditions.

Neuropathology: Within the past five years, there has been an increase in the number and quality of donated postmortem brains from TS patients available for research purposes. This increase, coupled with advances in neuropathological techniques, has led to initial findings with implications for neuroimaging studies and animal models of TS.

Clinical trials: A number of clinical trials in TS have recently been completed or are currently underway. These include studies of stimulant treatment of ADHD in TS and behavioral treatments for reducing tic severity in children and adults. Smaller trials of novel approaches to treatment such as dopamine agonist and GABAergic medications also show promise.

Epidemiology and clinical science: Careful epidemiological studies now estimate the prevalence of TS to be substantially higher than previously thought with a wider range of clinical severity. Furthermore, clinical studies are providing new findings regarding TS and co-existing conditions. These include subtyping studies of TS and OCD, an examination of the link between ADHD and learning problems in children with TS, a new appreciation of sensory tics, and the role of co-existing disorders in rage attacks. One of the most important and controversial areas of TS science involves the relationship between TS and autoimmune brain injury associated with group A beta-hemolytic streptococcal infections or other infectious processes. There are a number of epidemiological and clinical investigations currently underway in this intriguing area.

Chapter 42

Bullying

A lot of young people have a good idea of what bullying is because they see it every day. Bullying happens when someone hurts or scares another person on purpose and the person being bullied has a hard time defending himself or herself. Usually, bullying happens over and over:

- Punching, shoving, and other acts that hurt people physically

- Spreading bad rumors about people

- Keeping certain people out of a "group"

- Teasing people in a mean way

- Getting certain people to "gang up" on others

Bullying also can happen on-line or electronically. Cyberbullying is when children or teens bully each other using the internet, mobile phones, or other cyber technology. This can include the following:

- Sending mean text, e-mail, or instant messages

- Posting nasty pictures or messages about others in blogs or on websites

About This Chapter: Information in this chapter is from "Stop Bullying Now!" Health Resources and Services Administration (http://stopbullyingnow.hrsa.gov), March 2004.

- Using someone else's user name to spread rumors or lies about someone

There are many ways that young people bully each other, even if they don't realize it at the time.

What are the effects of bullying?

If you've ever heard an adult—or anyone else—say that bullying is "just a fact of life" or "no big deal," you're not alone. Too often, people just don't take bullying seriously—or until the sad and sometimes scary stories are revealed.

- **It happens a lot more than some people think:** Studies show that between 15–25% of U.S. students are bullied with some frequency, while 15–20% report they bully others with some frequency (Melton et al, 1988; Nansel et al, 2001).

- **It can mess up a kid's future:** Young people who bully are more likely than those who don't bully to skip school and drop out of school. They are also more likely to smoke, drink alcohol, and get into fights (Nansel et al, 2003; Olweus, 1993).

> ### ♣ It's A Fact!!
>
> These three conditions create a bullying situation:
>
> - Negative or malicious behavior.
>
> - Behavior repeated over a period of time.
>
> - A relationship in which there is an imbalance in strength or power between the parties involved.
>
> Source: Excerpted from "Some Facts about Bullying among Children and Young People," from *Bullying is Not a Fact of Life*, Substance Abuse and Mental Health Services Administration, SVP-0052, Printed 2003.

- **It scares some people so much that they skip school:** As many as 160,000 students may stay home on any given day because they're afraid of being bullied (Pollack, 1998).

- **It can lead to huge problems later in life:** Children who bully are more likely to get into fights, vandalize property, and drop out of school. And 60% of boys who were bullies in middle school had at least one criminal conviction by the age of 24 (Olweus, 1993).

🖋 What's It Mean?

Potential victims of bullying can be divided into two main groups:

The passive or submissive victim: Most children in this category are not aggressive or teasing in their manner and usually do not actively provoke others in their surroundings. However, passive victims of bullying generally signal, through their behavior and attitudes, that they are a bit anxious and unsure of themselves. These students are usually quiet, careful, sensitive, and may start crying easily. They are unsure of themselves and have poor self-confidence (negative self-image). The boys in this group do not like to fight, and they are often physically weaker than their classmates, especially the bullies. They have few or no friends.

The provocative victim: This category is less common and accounts for only about 10 to 20 percent of the victims. They can be quick tempered and may try to retaliate if they are attacked or harassed, but often without much success. They are often restless, clumsy, immature, unable to concentrate, and generally considered difficult. Some may be characterized as hyperactive (unsettled and restless because of concentration difficulties) and often have reading/ writing problems. They may also be disliked by adults— their teacher, for example— because of their irritating behavior. They may themselves try to bully weaker students.

Source: Excerpted from "Some Facts about Bullying among Children and Young People," from *Bullying is Not a Fact of Life*, Substance Abuse and Mental Health Services Administration, SVP-0052, Printed 2003.

Why do kids bully?

There are all kinds of reasons why young people bully others, either occasionally or often. Do any of these sound familiar to you?

- Because I see others doing it

- Because it's what you do if you want to hang out with the right crowd

- Because it makes me feel, stronger, smarter, or better than the person I'm bullying

- Because it's one of the best ways to keep others from bullying me

Whatever the reason, bullying is something we all need to think about. Whether we've done it ourselves, or whether friends or other people we know are doing it, we all need to recognize that bullying has a terrible effect on the lives of young people.

Are you being bullied?

So you're being bullied, huh? That can feel pretty awful. But, no matter how bad it makes you feel sometimes, you should know you're not alone. That's right, there are plenty of kids all over the world who go through the same things you do every day. And, even though you may feel helpless sometimes, there are a lot of things you and others can do to help stop the bullying. Give these tips a try:

Always tell an adult. It's hard to talk about serious things with adults sometimes, but they can help put a stop to bullying. Tell an adult that you trust and can talk to—your parents, your teacher, your school counselor, your coach, or your neighbor. If you've told a grown-up before and they haven't done anything about it, tell someone else. And if you're afraid to tell an adult that you have been bullied, get another person—like a friend or a sister or brother—to go with you. Having someone else there to support you can make it a lot less scary. Tell the adults exactly what has happened—who did the bullying, where and when it happened, how long it's been happening to you, and how it's making you feel. If you talk with an adult at your school, ask them what they will do to help stop the bullying. It is their job to help keep you safe. Most adults really care about bullying and will do everything they can to help you.

Stay in a group. Kids who bully like to pick on kids who are by themselves a lot— it's easier and they're more likely to get away with their bad behavior. If you spend more time with other kids, you may not be an easy target, and you'll have others around to help you if you get into a difficult situation.

If it feels safe, try to stand up to the person who is bullying you. If the person who is bullying you thinks you won't do anything about it, they are more likely to keep picking on you. This doesn't mean you should fight back or bully them back. Instead, tell the person bullying you that you don't like it and that they should stop. Keep it simple. You might just say, "Cut it out, Miranda!", and then walk away. If possible, try to talk to them in a calm voice. Kids who bully often like to see that they can make you upset. If you're afraid to talk to the person who is bullying you by yourself, then you might want to ask someone else to be there with you. Kids who bully are more likely to listen, and less likely to bully you, when you're with someone and not alone. If you're not comfortable standing up to someone who has bullied you, that's definitely OK. Just walk away. But be sure to tell an adult.

♣ It's A Fact!!

Research shows that two to three times as many students are bullied at school compared to those who are bullied on the way to school. Approximately 40 to 75 percent of bullying takes place during breaks—in the schoolyard, in the corridors, at recess, or in more secluded places, like bathrooms. It can also take place during classes unless the teacher is attentive and cracks down on any tendencies toward bullying. Without a doubt, school is the place where most bullying occurs.

Source: Excerpted from "Some Facts about Bullying among Children and Young People," from *Bullying is Not a Fact of Life*, Substance Abuse and Mental Health Services Administration, SVP-0052, Printed 2003.

If you are being bullied on-line, don't reply. This may actually make the bullying worse. Instead, be sure to tell a family member or another adult you trust. If possible, block any more communications from this person. (For example, it might be a good idea only to accept messages from people you know.) Save evidence of the bullying. If you get a nasty e-mail, print it out or save it so that you can show it to an adult.

Join clubs or take part in activities where you'll meet other kids. Sometimes, it can help to join clubs or take part in activities that interest you. Think about joining a sports team, taking an art class, or joining a scouting group, for example. You can meet other kids who share your interests and you might make some good friends.

What NOT to do if you are bullied. Don't do the following:

- think it's your fault. Nobody deserves to be bullied

- fight back or bully a person back. This probably won't make things any better and it might get you into big trouble. Besides, you should try to act better than the person who bullies you.

- keep it to yourself and just hope the bullying will "go away." It's normal to want to try to ignore bullying and hope that it will stop—or hope that the person will start to pick on someone else. But, often, bullying won't stop until adults and other kids get involved. So, be sure to report the bullying.

- skip school or avoid clubs or sports because you're afraid of being bullied. Missing out on school or activities that you enjoy isn't the answer. You have a right to be there.

- think that you're a "tattle tale" if you tell an adult that you've been bullied. Telling is NOT tattling. It's the right thing to do.

- hurt yourself. Some kids who are bullied get so sad and depressed that they may try to hurt themselves because they think there is nothing else they can do. This definitely isn't the answer. Talk with an adult immediately and tell them how you are feeling. They can help stop the bullying.

Are you a bystander?

So, you aren't someone who bullies others, and you haven't been bullied yourself. But if you see it happening to others, you can help put a stop to it. In order to stop bullying, everyone needs to lend a hand and get involved. Even though it might be easier to stand by and watch (or try to ignore the bullying), just remember, we all need a little help from time to time. Think about how you might feel if the bullying was happening to you. There are all kinds of great things you can do to help. So the next time you see someone being bullied, try one (or more) of these ideas and make a real difference.

Report the bullying to an adult. Many kids who are bullied are scared to tell an adult about it (especially a teacher or principal), because they are afraid the person bullying them will find out and the bullying will just get worse. That's where you come in. Even if it's a little scary for you to tell an adult about bullying that you see, it's the right thing to do. It's not tattling—you're helping someone out. Who should you tell? You could tell your teacher, school counselor, school nurse, parents, coach, or any adult you feel comfortable talking with. It might be a little less scary if you ask a friend to go along with you. Be sure to tell the adult exactly what happened—who was bullied, who did the bullying, and where and when it happened. If you're not sure if another kid is being bullied but you think they probably are—it's good to report that, too. Most adults really care about bullying and will be very glad that you told them about it. If you told an adult and you don't think they did anything about the bullying (or if it isn't getting any better), find another adult to tell.

Support someone who is being bullied. Sometimes the best thing you can do for a person who is being bullied is just to be there for him or her and be a friend. Whether this means agreeing to walk home with him or her after school, sitting with him or her on the bus or at lunch, trying to include him or her in your school or social activities, or just spending some time with him or her and trying to understand what he or she is going through, it will make a huge difference. Although these may seem like small things to you, they will show a kid who is being bullied that you care about him or her and the problems he or she is facing, and that can be a big help.

Stand up to the person doing the bullying. If you feel safe doing this, tell a person who is bullying that what he or she is doing is wrong and that he or she should stop. Keep it simple. You could just say, "Ben, cut it out. Nobody thinks that's funny." If you can, get some friends to join you. When kids who bully see that other kids don't think it's cool, they are more likely to stop. Just be sure you don't bully them back. It's not easy to stand up to kids who may be bigger and stronger than you or really popular, so if you're not comfortable doing this, that's ok. (But be sure to tell an adult.)

Do you bully others?

Hey—let's face it, hurting and making others feel bad is never cool. Just admitting that you are doing things to harm others takes some guts. But that's not enough. Trying to find out what you should do to change the way you're acting, now that's a step in the right direction. So check out these tips, they'll help you to start treating others with the respect they deserve.

♣ It's A Fact!!

Bullying may be a group phenomenon with particular characteristics. This means that there are a number of children and young people who may at times be involved in bullying, but who would not usually take the initiative themselves.

Some of the mechanisms that may be active in group bullying are as follows:

Social contagion: Some students may be influenced to take part in bullying if the student leading the bullying is someone they admire. Children or young people who are themselves somewhat insecure and who want to assert themselves are mostly the ones who join in.

Weakening of normal controls: If neither the teachers nor the other students try to stop bullying, the bully or bullies are rewarded through their "victory" over their victim. This can contribute to weakening the controls against the aggressive tendencies of neutral students and may contribute to their participation in bullying.

Decreased sense of individual responsibility: Social psychology notes that a person's sense of individual responsibility for a negative action such as bullying may be considerably reduced when several people participate. In this way, students who are usually nice, but easily influenced, can at times take part in bullying without particular misgivings.

Gradual changes in the perception of the victim of bullying: As a result of repeated attacks and degrading comments, the victim will gradually be perceived as a fairly worthless person who almost "begs to be beaten up." This also results in lesser feelings of guilt in those who are taking part in the bullying and may be part of the explanation of why other students do not try to stop the harassment of the victim.

Source: Excerpted from "Some Facts about Bullying among Children and Young People," from *Bullying is Not a Fact of Life*, Substance Abuse and Mental Health Services Administration, SVP-0052, Printed 2003.

know how it feels—awful. So the next time you are about to bully someone do the following:

- put yourself in their shoes

- think about how it must make them feel

- and just don't do it

Talk to an adult. Making other people feel badly should never make you feel good. If it does, or if you're not really sure why you bully other kids, you need to talk to an adult about it. Even though you might think an adult won't understand, or that you'll get yourself into trouble, they can help. Whether it is your parent, a teacher or another trusted grown-up, you should tell an adult how you've been acting so that they help you deal with it. School counselors are also great people to talk to about how you feel and how to change the way you treat others.

Okay, time for the truth. Or at least time to consider if you have a confession to make. Think about the following to find out if you've ever bullied someone.

- There's a boy or a girl (or maybe more than one) whom you've repeatedly shoved, or punched or physically pushed around in a mean way just because you felt like it.

- You had someone else hurt someone you don't like.

- You've spread a nasty rumor about someone, in conversation, in a note, or through e-mail or instant messaging.

- You and your friends have regularly kept one or more kids from hanging out or playing with you. Examples: at your lunch table at school, during sports or other activities, or activities that are a part of a club or other kind of group activity.

- You've teased people in a mean way, calling them names, making fun of their appearance, or the way they talk or dress or act.

- You've been part of a group that did any of these things—even if you only wanted to be part of the crowd.

If any of these statements are true, you're not alone. All over the country, in all types of neighborhoods and schools, there are all types of young people who bully others. Bullying is serious business. It causes young people a lot of pain, and it can affect their ability to do well in school and their general happiness.

But it doesn't have to be that way. You can learn about better ways to treat your friends and acquaintances, as well as become part of the solution to this serious problem.

Chapter 43

Dating Violence

What is teen dating violence?

Dating violence (or relationship abuse) is a pattern of violent behavior that someone uses against a girlfriend or boyfriend. Dating violence can take many forms, including psychological and emotional abuse, physical abuse, and sexual abuse. So, you may experience dating violence even if you are not being physically abused. It can occur in both casual dating situations and serious, long-term relationships.

Is teen dating violence similar to adult domestic violence?

Teen dating violence is similar to adult domestic violence in several ways:

- Both teen dating violence and adult domestic violence effect people from all socioeconomic, racial, and ethnic, and religious groups

- Both occur in heterosexual, gay, and lesbian relationships

- Both tend to show patterns of repeated violence which escalate over time

About This Chapter: This chapter begins with text excerpted from "General Information on Teen Dating Violence," © 2004 WomensLaw.org. Reprinted with permission. "Teens And Domestic Violence Restraining/Protective Orders" is reprinted with permission from Break the Cycle, a nonprofit organization whose mission is to work with youth to end dating and domestic violence. © 2006 Break the Cycle. All rights reserved. For additional information, visit www.breakthecycle.org or call 1-888-988-TEEN.

- Both tend to display violent and abusive behavior interchanged with apologies and promises to change

- Both tend to show increased danger for the victim when she is trying to terminate the abusive relationship

How is teen dating violence different from adult domestic violence?

There are several things that make teenage dating violence different from adult domestic violence. Usually, when a teen is abused, she becomes isolated from her peers because of the controlling behavior of her abusive partner.

The isolation teens face in abusive dating situations often:

- makes it hard to develop new and mature relationships with peers of both sexes.

- makes it hard to feel emotionally independent.

- makes it hard to develop personal values and beliefs.

- makes it hard to stay focused on school and get good grades.

What might happen to me if I'm in an abusive relationship?

Possible effects of being in an abusive relationship include the following:

- loss of appetite

- headaches

- nervousness

- weight loss

- bruises or broken bones

- sadness

- self-blame

- confusion

- anxiety

- guilt

- shame

✦ **It's A Fact!!**
Roughly 85% of all people who are the victims in an abusive relationship are women. (Bureau of Justice Statistics Special Report, Intimate Partner Violence and Age of Victim, 1993-99, Oct 2001).

Source: © 2004 WomensLaw.org. Reprinted with permission.

♣ It's A Fact!! Reality Check

Nothing is quite as exciting as a first love. It's the stuff of Romeo and Juliet—passion that sweeps you off your feet. What could be wrong with that? Usually, nothing. But sometimes what can seem like intense love and devotion at first, can really be signs of jealousy, possessiveness, and control—characteristics that can be early red flags for relationship abuse.

What do we mean when we talk about dating violence? Dating violence isn't an argument every once in a while or a bad mood after a bad day. Dating violence (or relationship abuse) is a pattern of violent behavior that someone uses against a girlfriend or boyfriend. Abuse can cause injury and even death, but it doesn't have to be physical. It can include verbal and emotional abuse—constant insults, isolation from friends and family, name calling, controlling what someone wears—and it can also include sexual abuse. It can happen to anyone, at any age, no matter what race or religion they are, no matter what their level of education or economic background. Dating violence also occurs in same-sex relationships.

Source: Excerpted from "What You Need to Know about Dating Violence: A Teen's Handbook," reprinted with permission from Love is not Abuse, http://www.loveisnotabuse.com. © 2006 Liz Claiborne, Inc. All rights reserved.

- mistrust of self
- mistrust of others
- depression
- fear
- feelings of worthlessness
- terror
- permanent injury
- death
- suicide

How can I tell if my friend is in an abusive relationship?

Answer the questions below. If you answer "yes" to two or more of them, your friend might be in an abusive relationship.

- Does your friend show physical signs of injury?

- Is she doing worse in school, or has dropped out completely?

- Has she changed her clothing or makeup style?

- Has she lost confidence and does she have difficulty making decisions?

- Has she quit her normal after-school activities?

- Has she started using drugs or alcohol?

- Does she have mood swings or emotional outbursts?

- Has she isolated herself from friends and family?

- Has she become pregnant?

- Does she apologize for her boyfriend's abusive behavior?

- Does she seem overly worried about upsetting or angering her boyfriend?

How can I find help on talking to my friend who may be in an abusive relationship?

If you suspect a friend is in an abusive relationship, you might want to try talking to them to find out for sure. The Love Is Not Abuse website (www.loveisnotabuse.com) has a list of Do's and Don'ts to keep in mind when you're talking to a friend who may be experiencing dating violence. You might want to check out that site before talking to your friend.

How do I find help on talking to my friend who may be the abuser in a relationship?

It's hard to know how to talk to a friend when you think his behavior is out of control. For ideas on how to talk to your friend about his behavior go

---

✔ Quick Tip

If You're Afraid Or In Danger

Are you afraid to disagree with your partner? Does his temper scare you? Is he very jealous? Does he call you names or yell at you? Does he try to control the way you dress or who you see? Has he threatened to harm you or commit suicide if you leave? Does he throw or break things in anger? Does he hit, shove, slap, or kick you, or force you to have sex when you don't want to?

No one deserves to be abused. If you are being hurt in your relationship, or are afraid that you might be at risk, call the National Domestic Violence Hotline at 1-800-799-SAFE for confidential advice and referrals. There are people nearby who can help you.

Source: Excerpted from "What You Need to Know about Dating Violence: A Teen's Handbook," reprinted with permission from Love is not Abuse, http://www.loveisnotabuse.com. © 2006 Liz Claiborne, Inc. All rights reserved.

to the Love Is Not Abuse website. Scroll down to the bottom of the page—they have a list of Dos and Don'ts to keep in mind when you're talking to a friend who may be the abuser in a dating relationship.

How can I find help on when I should talk to an adult?

Talking about relationships problems is never easy, especially when you're talking to an adult. It's normal to want to solve your problems on your own. It's normal not to want to get anyone in trouble, or betray a friend's confidence.

Sometimes, however, there are problems too big to handle without help, and it can be a big relief to involve a trusted adult. The Love Is Not Abuse website has ideas on how to figure out when you should talk to an adult, who you should talk to, and what to say.

What should I do when an abusive relationship ends?

Unfortunately, just because a violent relationship is over, doesn't mean the risk of violence is over. You might want to check out the Love Is Not Abuse website (www.loveisnotabuse.com). It has tips for how you can stay safe after ending an abusive relationship.

Teens And Domestic Violence Restraining/Protective Orders

Although many do not realize it, teens and young adults are among the most likely to experience dating and domestic violence in their relationships. Going to court and getting a restraining order against your abuser is not just for adults or people who are married. Many states understand that young people are a large portion of victims of domestic violence, and have made sure that their laws allow teens and young adults to be protected.

Do I qualify for a restraining order?

In general, to qualify for a domestic violence restraining order or protective order, you must have a relationship with the abuser and some abuse must have occurred. While what qualifies as a "relationship" is different in every state, almost all states allow you to get an order against someone you are related to, someone you are living with, or someone you have a child with. Many also allow you to get one if you are dating the abuser.

Can I get a restraining order even if I am under 18?

In most states, you can apply to get an order even if you are under 18, but you must have an adult's name on the court papers, and that adult must ask for the order on your behalf. The adult can be one of your parents or your legal guardian. But, if you don't want (or are scared) to tell your parents what is happening, you may still have some options.

You may be able to have another adult (for example, a relative, friend, or teacher) go to court with you instead of your parents. In some states a judge must approve of the adult who you choose (called a guardian *ad litem*). For this to happen, you must fill out paperwork asking for the adult to be your guardian *ad litem*, and a judge must approve the request. In other states, you still have to have an adult appear with you in court, but there's no additional paperwork to fill out, and the judge doesn't have to approve of who you choose.

Several states will allow you to go to court to get a domestic violence restraining order alone, without involving your parents or any adults. Most states that allow minors to apply for restraining orders on their own require that you are at least 16 years old. A few, however, let minors of any age, or minors 12 or older, go to court without an adult.

Depending on the laws in your state, there are very big differences in what protection is available to you. If you are thinking about getting a restraining order, you need to find out what specific requirements your state has.

Who can help me?

Break the Cycle can help. For more information visit www.breakthecycle.org or contact:

Break the Cycle
P.O. Box 64996
Los Angeles, CA 90064
Toll-Free: 888-988-TEEN
Phone: 310-286-3366

Chapter 44

Child Abuse

Child abuse is both shocking and commonplace. Child abusers inflict physical, sexual, and emotional trauma on defenseless children every day. The scars can be deep and long-lasting. Unfortunately, the more subtle forms of child abuse such as neglect and emotional abuse can be just as traumatizing as violent physical abuse. Focused support can help both the victims of child abuse and the child abusers themselves.

What is the definition of child abuse?

Child abuse consists of any act or failure to act that endangers a child's physical or emotional health and development. A person caring for a child is abusive if he or she fails to nurture the child, physically injures the child, or relates sexually to the child.

What are the types of child abuse?

The four major types of child abuse are:

- Physical abuse
- Sexual abuse
- Emotional abuse
- Neglect

Another type of abuse is child exploitation (distinct from sexual exploitation). This is the use of a child in work or other activities for the benefit of others. Child labor is an example of child exploitation for commercial reasons. Using a child in this way detracts from their own physical, mental, and social development.

What is physical abuse?

Physical abuse is any non-accidental physical injury to a child. Even if the parent or caretaker who inflicts the injury might not have intended to hurt the child, the injury is not considered an accident if the caretaker's actions were intentional. This injury may be the result of any assault on a child's body, such as the following:

✔ **Quick Tip**
To report abuse, call the National Child Abuse Hotline:

1-800-4-A-CHILD
(1-800-422-4453)

If the abuse is a life-threatening emergency, call 911.

Source: © 2006 Helpguide.org.

- beating, whipping, paddling, punching, slapping, or hitting

- pushing, shoving, shaking, kicking or throwing

- pinching, biting, choking, or hair-pulling

- burning with cigarettes, scalding water, or other hot objects

- severe physical punishment that is inappropriate to child's age

Corporal (physical) punishment is distinguished from physical abuse in that physical punishment is the use of physical force with the intent of inflicting bodily pain, but not injury, for the purpose of correction or control. Physical abuse is an injury that results from physical aggression. However, physical punishment easily gets out of control and can become physical abuse. Corporal punishment is against the law in schools in some states, but not in others. In many families, physical punishment is the norm.

Hundreds of thousands of children are physically abused each year by someone close to them, and thousands of children die from the injuries. For those who survive, the emotional scars are deeper than the physical scars.

♣ It's A Fact!!

- The leading cause of death in children ages four and younger is child abuse or neglect.

- Most child fatalities from physical abuse are by fathers or other male caretakers. Mothers are considered to be responsible for most child fatalities caused by neglect.

- Most children are abused by people they know.

- Many people are afraid of reporting child abuse.

- Most sexual abuse is probably never reported to authorities.

- Possibly one in three cases of child sexual abuse is not remembered by the adults who experienced the abuse. The younger the child was at the time of the abuse, and the closer the relationship to the abuser, the less likely the adult will remember.

- Other children are often the perpetrators of child abuse.

- Shaken baby syndrome is the leading cause of death from child abuse in the United States.

Source: © 2006 Helpguide.org.

What is sexual abuse?

Sexual abuse of a child is any sexual act between an adult and a child. This includes the following:

- fondling, touching, or kissing a child's genitals

- making the child fondle the adult's genitals

- penetration, intercourse, incest, rape, oral sex or sodomy

- exposing the child to adult sexuality in other forms (showing sex organs to a child, forced observation of sexual acts, showing pornographic material, telling "dirty" stories, group sex including a child)

- other privacy violations (forcing the child to undress, spying on a child in the bathroom or bedroom)

- sexual exploitation

- enticing children to pornographic sites or material on the internet

- luring children through the internet to meet for sexual liaisons

- exposing children to pornographic movies or magazines

- child prostitution

- using a child in the production of pornography, such as a film or magazine

The above acts are considered child abuse when they are committed by a relative or by a caretaker, such as a parent, babysitter, or daycare provider, whether inside the home or apart from the home. (If a stranger commits the act, it is called sexual assault.)

The legal age of consent for two people to have sexual relations ranges from twelve to twenty-one, and varies by state within the United States and by country. In most states, having sex with a person younger than the legal age of consent is against the law. Even if the two parties agree to the sexual relationship, it is still against the law. Each state is very specific as to its laws about sex with minors.

Sexual abuse is especially complicated because of the power differential between the adult and child, because of the negotiations that must occur between adult and child, and because the child has no way to assimilate the experience into a mature understanding of intimacy. Regardless of the child's

✎ What's It Mean?

Physical Abuse is physical injury (ranging from minor bruises to severe fractures or death) as a result of punching, beating, kicking, biting, shaking, throwing, stabbing, choking, hitting (with a hand, stick, strap, or other object), burning, or otherwise harming a child. Such injury is considered abuse regardless of whether the caretaker intended to hurt the child.

Sexual Abuse includes activities by a parent or caretaker such as fondling a child's genitals, penetration, incest, rape, sodomy, indecent exposure, and exploitation through prostitution or the production of pornographic materials.

Emotional Abuse is a pattern of behavior that impairs a child's emotional development or sense of self-worth. This may include constant criticism, threats, or rejection, as well as withholding love, support, or guidance. Emotional abuse is often difficult to prove and, therefore, CPS may not be able to intervene without evidence of harm to the child. Emotional abuse is almost always present when other forms are identified.

behavior or reactions, it is the responsibility of the adult not to engage in sexual acts with children. Sexual abuse is never the child's fault.

Sexual abusers can be any of the following:

- parents, siblings, or other relatives
- childcare professionals
- clergy, teachers, or athletic coaches
- neighbors or friends
- strangers

What is emotional abuse?

Emotional abuse is any attitude, behavior, or failure to act on the part of the caregiver that interferes with a child's mental health or social development.

Other names for emotional abuse include the following:

- verbal abuse
- mental abuse
- psychological maltreatment or abuse

Emotional abuse can range from a simple verbal insult to an extreme form of punishment. The following are examples of emotional abuse:

- ignoring, withdrawal of attention, or rejection
- lack of physical affection such as hugs
- lack of praise, positive reinforcement, or saying "I love you"
- yelling or screaming
- threatening or frightening
- negative comparisons to others
- belittling; telling the child he or she is "no good," "worthless," "bad," or "a mistake"
- using derogatory terms to describe the child, name-calling

- shaming or humiliating

- habitual scapegoating or blaming

- using extreme or bizarre forms of punishment, such as confinement to a closet or dark room, tying to a chair for long periods of time, or terrorizing a child

- parental child abduction

Emotional abuse is almost always present when another form of abuse is found. Some overlap exists between the definitions of emotional abuse and emotional neglect; regardless, they are both child abuse.

Emotional abuse of children can come from adults or from other children:

- parents or caregivers

- teachers or athletic coaches

- siblings

- bullies at school

- middle- and high-school girls in social cliques

What is neglect?

Neglect is a failure to provide for the child's basic needs. The types of neglect are as follows:

- physical

- educational

- emotional

Physical Neglect

Physical neglect is not providing for a child's physical needs, including the following:

- inadequate provision of food, housing, or clothing appropriate for season or weather

- lack of supervision

- expulsion from the home or refusal to allow a runaway to return home

- abandonment

- denial or delay of medical care

- inadequate hygiene

Educational Neglect

Educational neglect is the failure to enroll a child of mandatory school age in school or to provide necessary special education. This includes allowing excessive truancies from school.

Emotional (Psychological) Neglect

Emotional neglect is a lack of emotional support and love, such as the following:

- not attending to the child's needs, including need for affection

- failure to provide necessary psychological care

- domestic violence in the child's presence, such as spousal or partner abuse

- drug and alcohol abuse in the presence of the child, or allowing the child to participate in drug and alcohol use

When authorities examine emotional neglect, they take into consideration cultural values and standards of care, as well as the level of family income, which may interfere with proper care.

Some overlap exists between the definitions of emotional abuse and emotional neglect; regardless, they are both child abuse.

What are the signs and symptoms of child abuse?

If you suspect child abuse, but aren't sure, look for clusters of the following physical and behavioral signs.

Some Signs Of Physical Abuse

- Unexplained burns, cuts, bruises, or welts in the shape of an object

- Bite marks

- Anti-social behavior

- Problems in school
- Fear of adults
- Drug or alcohol abuse
- Self-destructive or suicidal behavior
- Depression or poor self-image

Some Signs Of Emotional Abuse

- Apathy
- Hostility
- Eating disorders
- Depression
- Lack of concentration

Some Signs Of Sexual Abuse

- Inappropriate interest in or knowledge of sexual acts
- Seductiveness
- Avoidance of things related to sexuality, or rejection of own genitals or bodies
- Nightmares and bed wetting
- Drastic changes in appetite
- Over-compliance or excessive aggression
- Fear of a particular person or family member
- Withdrawal, secretiveness, or depression
- Suicidal behavior
- Eating disorders
- Self-injury

Sometimes there are no obvious physical signs of sexual abuse, and a physician must examine the child to confirm the abuse.

Some Signs Of Neglect

- Unsuitable clothing for weather
- Being dirty or unbathed

- Extreme hunger

- Apparent lack of supervision

What are the causes of child abuse?

Why would someone abuse a child? What kind of person abuses a child? Not all abuse is deliberate or intended. Several factors in a person's life may combine to move them toward abusing a child:

- general stress

- the stress of having children in the family, when one didn't have children before

- dealing with a child who has a disability or difficult behaviors

- the stress of caring for someone besides oneself

- a personal history of being abused (childhood trauma)

- alcohol or drug use

- marital conflict

- unemployment

No one has been able to predict which of these factors will cause someone to abuse a child. A significant factor is that abuse tends to be intergenerational— those who were abused as children are more likely to repeat the act when they become parents or caretakers.

In addition, many forms of abuse arise from ignorance, isolation, or benign neglect. Sometimes a cultural tradition leads to abuse, for example, such beliefs as the following:

- children are property

- parents (especially males) have the right to control their children in any way they wish

- children need to be toughened up to face the hardships of life

- girls need to be genitally mutilated to assure virginity and later marriage

What are the results of child abuse?

Child abuse can have the following dire consequences:

- The child may become someone who lies, resents, fears, and retaliates, rather than loves, trusts, and listens.

- The child may become reclusive, and alienated from you and from the rest of your family.

- The child will have low self-esteem, and is likely to engage in self-destructive behaviors.

- The child's psychological development and social behavior will be impaired.

- For the adult, the child may abuse his or her own children, who would be the adult's grandchildren.

- For the adult, the child may exclude them, including from celebrations and family gatherings. The adult may not be permitted to spend time with their grandchildren.

♣ It's A Fact!!

Much research has been done about the possible consequences of child abuse and neglect. The effects vary depending on the circumstances of the abuse or neglect, personal characteristics of the child, and the child's environment. Consequences may be mild or severe; disappear after a short period or last a lifetime; and affect the child physically, psychologically, behaviorally, or in some combination of all three ways. Ultimately, due to related costs to public entities such as the health care, human services, and educational systems, abuse and neglect impact not just the child and family, but society as a whole.

Source: Excerpted from "Long-term Consequences of Child Abuse and Neglect," National Clearinghouse on Child Abuse and Neglect Information, 2005.

The results of being abused as a child vary according to the severity of the abuse and the surrounding environment of the child. If the social environment of the family or school is nurturing and supportive, the child will probably have a better outcome.

Results Of Physical Abuse

Physical abuse may result in the following:

- difficulty establishing intimate personal relationships
- difficulty in adulthood with physical closeness, touching, intimacy, or trust
- high levels of anxiety, depression, substance abuse, medical illness, or problems at school or work
- becoming an abusive parent or caregiver

Results Of Emotional Abuse

Emotional abuse can result in serious behavioral, cognitive, emotional, or mental disorders.

Results Of Sexual Abuse

Some results of prolonged sexual abuse are the following:

- low self-esteem
- a feeling of worthlessness
- an abnormal or distorted view of sex
- personality disorders
- difficulty relating to others except on sexual terms
- tendency to become child abusers or prostitutes
- other serious problems in adulthood

How can I get help if I am a child or teen who is being abused?

Call the National Child Abuse Hotline: 1-800-4-A-CHILD (1-800-422-4453).

Some kids are afraid to report the abuse because they fear punishment, loss of love, or family dishonor for telling a secret.

The hotline will make sure you are protected from further abuse. They will help you to report the abuse to an agency that will make sure you are safe. The hotline staff members will call Child Protective Services or the police and stay on the line in a three-way call to help you talk to the agency. Even if you have told the person who is abusing you that you will keep a secret about the things you do together, it is okay to call the hotline and get help for yourself.

The hotline can help you find ongoing support from caring adults. It is not your fault that you are being abused, and you need help from other adults to protect your safety. If the abuse is within your own family, you need protection while your family learns new ways to act with each other.

You may wish to learn to protect yourself against someone who may try to abuse you. Several organizations can teach you to say "No" with words and by your actions.

How do I report suspected child abuse?

Many people don't know where to report suspected child abuse. Also, some people are afraid of reporting child abuse because of possible repercussions to the children or to themselves. In many states, it is required by law for all citizens to report suspected abuse. Each state has a different procedure for reporting abuse.

From any state, to get immediate guidance and help when you suspect child abuse, call the Childhelp USA National Child Abuse Hotline: 1-800-4-A-CHILD (1-800-422-4453).

The National Child Abuse Hotline will give you the local agency for you to call to report the incident. The abuse report must eventually go to an agency within your own state.

You probably will be relieved to know the following:

• If you report child abuse, it is unlikely that the child will be removed from their home immediately. The authorities will investigate to find out if your suspicions are correct. If child abuse is confirmed, the child would then be removed from the home and placed in safe care.

• You do not have to give your name when you report child abuse, in most states.

• The child abuser cannot find out who reported them.

• Remember that suspected abuse is sufficient reason to make a report to authorities. You do not need proof. Your call may make the difference in the very life of a child.

How do I get help if I think I may abuse a child, or if I have already abused a child?

Call the National Child Abuse Hotline: 1-800-4-A-CHILD (1-800-422-4453).

The hotline can talk you through a parenting or care-taking crisis and offer guidance about how to better handle the situation. You need help and support. The hotline can find out about parenting support groups for you to attend, or local counselors who can talk with you.

I am a child abuse survivor; where can I get help?

The National Child Abuse Hotline can lead you to a support group in your community for survivors of child abuse, or they can offer one-on-one support: 1-800-4-A-CHILD (1-800-422-4453).

Child abuse is a trauma, and you may have developed post-traumatic stress disorder (PTSD). You may find that you are more fearful than other people, as if the traumatic event were occurring in the present. You may also re-experience the trauma with flashbacks and nightmares. And you may have become unresponsive and numb to other people and events as a way of protecting yourself psychologically. Given support in a safe environment and from caring individuals, you may be able to recover psychologically.

How can child abuse be prevented? Is there hope?

Child abuse tends to be cyclical, repeated generation after generation. A child who has experienced trauma may repeat the pattern by growing into an adult who delivers trauma to the next generation. The only way to stop such a cycle is to work with parents, prospective parents, and other caregivers who seek help or who are referred for help. Mental health professionals particularly wish to help those who find themselves about to repeat the pattern of traumatizing children. The avenues that offer hope are:

- Establishing educational programs to teach caregivers good parenting and coping skills.

• Making people aware of alternatives to abusive behaviors so that they seek help for their own abusive tendencies.

• Educating the public about abuse so that people report abuse early enough for intervention.

• Establishing relationships of trust with children so that they feel comfortable disclosing abuse. Then someone can intervene early on.

Chapter 45

Substance Abuse And Addiction

Dealing With Addiction

Jason and Brent have been best friends since kindergarten. Now that they're in high school, they're drifting apart. It's not because they're in different classes, it's because Brent has noticed some changes in Jason. His grades have slipped, he's moody, he doesn't talk to his old friends, and he rarely shows up for practice. Brent is aware that Jason has been doing drugs and he's worried that Jason has become addicted.

Defining an addiction is tricky, and knowing how to handle one is even harder—keep reading to find out more about addiction.

What Are Substance Abuse And Addiction?

The difference between substance abuse and addiction is very slight. Addiction begins as abuse, or using a substance like marijuana or cocaine.

About This Chapter: This chapter begins with "Dealing with Addiction," information provided by TeensHealth, one of the largest resources online for medically reviewed health information written for parents, kids, and teens. For more articles like this one, visit www.TeensHealth.org, or www.KidsHealth.org. © 2004 The Nemours Center for Children's Health Media, a division of The Nemours Foundation. Text under the heading "Drug Abuse and Mental Illness" is from the National Drug Intelligence Center, U.S. Department of Justice No. 2004-L0559-005, 2004.

You can abuse a drug (or alcohol) without having an addiction. For example, just because Sara smoked weed a few times doesn't mean that she has an addiction, but it does mean that she's abusing a drug—and that could lead to an addiction.

People can get addicted to all sorts of substances. When we think of addiction, we usually think of alcohol or illegal drugs. But people become addicted to medications, cigarettes, even glue. And some substances are more addictive than others: Drugs like crack or heroin are so addictive that they may only be used once or twice before the user loses control.

Addiction means a person has no control over whether he or she uses a drug or drinks. A person who's addicted to cocaine has grown so used to the drug that he or she has to have it. Addiction can be physical, psychological, or both.

Physical addiction is when a person's body actually becomes dependent on a particular substance (even smoking is physically addictive). It also means that a person builds tolerance to that substance, so that person needs a larger dose than ever before to get the same effects. When a person who is physically addicted stops using a substance like drugs, alcohol, or cigarettes, he or she may experience withdrawal symptoms. Withdrawal can be like having the flu—common symptoms are diarrhea, shaking, and generally feeling awful.

Psychological addiction happens when the cravings for a drug are psychological or emotional. People who are psychologically addicted feel overcome by the desire to have a drug. They may lie or steal to get it.

A person crosses the line between abuse and addiction when he or she is no longer trying the drug to have fun or get high, but because he or she has come to depend on it. His or her whole life centers around the need for the drug. An addicted person—whether it's a physical or psychological addiction or both—no longer has a choice in taking a substance.

Signs Of Addiction

The most obvious sign of an addiction is the need to have a particular drug or substance. However, there are many other signs that can suggest a possible addiction, such as changes in mood or weight loss or gain. (These are also signs of other conditions, too, though, such as depression or eating disorders.)

Signs that you or someone you know may have a drug or alcohol addiction include:

♣ **It's A Fact!!**
Mental Or Emotional Problems

Teenagers who suffer from anxiety and depression disorders are much more likely to abuse or be dependent on alcohol. Sometimes problems with alcohol can lead to depression and anxiety, but more frequently, teens with depression and anxiety disorders seek out alcohol and other drugs to avoid dealing with the pain caused by these illnesses. Teens with conduct disorders or certain types of attention-deficit disorders are also more likely to have problems with alcohol.

Source: Excerpted from "Teens and Alcohol," National Youth Violence Prevention Resource Center (www.safeyouth.org), 2002.

Psychological Signals

• use of drugs or alcohol as a way to forget problems or to relax

• withdrawal or keeping secrets from family and friends

• loss of interest in activities that used to be important

• problems with schoolwork, such as slipping grades or absences

• changes in friendships, such as hanging out only with friends who use drugs

• spending a lot of time figuring out how to get drugs

• stealing or selling belongings to be able to afford drugs

• failed attempts to stop taking drugs or drinking

• anxiety, anger, or depression

• mood swings

Physical Signals

• changes in sleeping habits

• feeling shaky or sick when trying to stop

• needing to take more of the substance to get the same effect

• changes in eating habits, including weight loss or gain

Getting Help

If you think you are addicted to drugs or alcohol, recognizing that you have a problem is the first step in getting help.

A lot of people think they can kick the problem on their own, but that doesn't work for most people. Find someone you trust to talk to. It may help to talk to a friend or someone your own age at first, but a supportive and understanding adult is your best option for getting help. If you can't talk to your parents, you may want to approach a school counselor, relative, doctor, favorite teacher, or religious leader.

Unfortunately, overcoming addiction is not easy. Quitting drugs or drinking is probably going to be the hardest thing you've ever done. It's not a sign

---

♣ It's A Fact!!
How Nicotine Addiction Happens

With each puff of a cigarette, a smoker pulls nicotine into his or her lungs where it is absorbed into the blood. In eight seconds, nicotine is in the brain, changing the way the brain works. This process happens so fast because nicotine is shaped like the natural brain chemical acetylcholine. Acetylcholine is one of many chemicals called neurotransmitters that carry messages between brain cells. Neurons have special spaces called receptors, into which specific neurotransmitters can fit, like a key fitting into a lock. Nicotine locks into acetylcholine receptors in different parts of the brain, rapidly causing changes in the body and brain. Nicotine raises the heart rate and respiration (breathing) rate, and causes more glucose, or blood sugar, to be released into the blood. This might be why smokers feel more alert after smoking a cigarette.

Nicotine also attaches to neurons (brain cells) that release a neurotransmitter called dopamine. Nicotine stimulates neurons to release unusually large amounts of dopamine. Dopamine stimulates the brain's pleasure and reward circuit, a group of brain structures called the limbic system involved in appetite, learning, memory, and feelings of pleasure. Normally, pleasurable feelings come from food, comfort, and the company of people you love. But smoking cigarettes causes a flood of dopamine in the smoker's brain. It's this flood of dopamine that gives the smoker intense feelings of pleasure.

of weakness if you need professional help from a trained drug counselor or therapist. Most people who try to kick a drug or alcohol program need professional assistance or treatment programs to do so.

Once you start a treatment program, try these tips to make the road to recovery less bumpy:

- **Tell your friends about your decision to stop using drugs.** Your true friends will respect your decision. This may mean that you need to find a new group of friends who will be 100% supportive. Unless everyone decides to kick their drug habit at once, you probably won't be able to hang out with the friends you did drugs with before.

Normally, neurons reabsorb neurotransmitters after they've done their job of signaling other brain cells. But cigarette smoke causes dopamine to stay in the spaces between neurons called synapses. Researchers don't yet know exactly what component of tobacco smoke blocks the reabsorption of dopamine into neurons.

In 40 minutes, half the effects of nicotine are gone. So smokers get the urge to light up for another dose of the drug. After repeated doses of nicotine, the brain changes. To adjust to too much dopamine, the brain cuts production of the neurotransmitter and reduces the number of some receptors. Now, the smoker needs nicotine just to create normal levels of dopamine in his or her brain. Without nicotine, the smoker feels irritable and depressed. The smoker has trained the limbic system to crave tobacco. Think about how you long for a cold drink on a hot day. Or how you want a sandwich when you are hungry. Craving for tobacco is much stronger.

These changes in the brain and body make nicotine highly addictive. Other addictive drugs of abuse, including heroin and cocaine, cause the same changes in the brain.

Source: Excerpted from "Nicotine," NIDA for Teens: The Science Behind Drug Abuse, National Institute on Drug Abuse (http://teens.drugabuse.gov), 2003.

♣ **It's A Fact!!**

Why does drinking alcohol increase aggressive behavior?

- There is some evidence to suggest that drinking leads to increased aggressiveness because it lowers inhibitions, including those that would normally prevent aggressive behavior.

- Alcohol also impairs judgment and may cause people to overreact to perceived threats or to fail to consider the future risks of an impulsive violent response.

- Drinking may also increase aggression because people expect it to. In studies where people were told that their beverage contained alcohol, they began to act more aggressively, regardless of whether their beverage actually did contain alcohol or not.

- In addition, it may be that some people drink when they intend to engage in violence in order to bolster their courage or in hopes of using alcohol as an excuse for the violence.

- Finally, as mentioned earlier, people who drink a lot are also likely to engage in other risky behaviors, including fighting and weapon-carrying. It may just be that violent people are more likely than non-violent people to hang out with people and choose situations that encourage heavy drinking.

Source: Excerpted from "Teens and Alcohol," National Youth Violence Prevention Resource Center (www.safeyouth.org), 2002.

- **Ask your friends or family to be available when you need them.** You may need to call someone in the middle of the night just to talk. If you're going through a tough time, don't try to handle things on your own—accept the help your family and friends offer.

- **Accept only invitations to events that you know won't involve drugs or alcohol.** Going to the movies is probably safe, but you may want to skip a Friday night party until you're feeling more secure. Plan activities that don't involve drugs. Go to the movies, try bowling, or take an art class with a friend.

- **Have a plan about what you'll do if you find yourself in a place with drugs or alcohol.** The temptation will be there sometimes, but if you know how you're going to handle it, you'll be OK. Establish a plan with your parents or siblings so that if you call home using a code, they'll know that your call is a signal you need a ride out of there.

- **Remind yourself that having an addiction doesn't make you bad or weak.** If you backslide a bit, talk to an adult as soon as possible. There's nothing to be ashamed about, but it's important to get help soon so that all of the hard work you put into your recovery is not lost.

If you're worried about a friend who has an addiction, use these tips to help him or her, too. For example, let your friend know that you are available to talk or offer your support. If you notice a friend backsliding, talk about it openly and ask what you can do to help. If your friend is going back to drugs or drinking and won't accept your help, don't be afraid to talk to a nonthreatening, understanding adult, like your parent or school counselor. It may seem like you're ratting your friend out, but it's the best support you can offer.

♣ It's A Fact!!
Nervous Or Depressed?

Scientists are learning how tobacco and nicotine affect teen smokers. Studies going on for 25 years show a link between heavy teen smoking and fear of going outside (agoraphobia). Teens who smoke were six times more likely to get agoraphobia. And, teen smokers were 15 times more likely to have panic attacks than teens who did not smoke. Scientists think the reason is that nicotine hurts blood vessels to the brain, and also blocks air from the lungs. Whatever the reason, teen smokers are more likely to have panic attacks, anxiety disorders, and depression.

Source: Excerpted from "Nicotine," NIDA for Teens: The Science Behind Drug Abuse, National Institute on Drug Abuse (http://teens.drugabuse.gov), 2003.

Above all, offer a friend who's battling an addiction lots of encouragement and praise. It may seem corny, but hearing that you care is just the kind of motivation your friend needs.

Staying Clean

Recovering from a drug or alcohol addiction doesn't end with a six-week treatment program. It's a lifelong process. Many people find that joining a support group can help them stay clean. There are support groups specifically for teens and younger people. You'll meet people who have gone through the same experiences you have, and you'll be able to participate in real-life discussions about drugs that you won't hear in your school's health class.

Table 45.1. Disorders With Increased Risk of Drug Abuse

Disorder	Risk
Antisocial personality disorder	15.5%
Manic episode	14.5%
Schizophrenia	10.1%
Panic disorder	04. 3%
Major depressive episode	04.1%
Obsessive-compulsive disorder	03.4%
Phobias	02.1%

Source: National Institute of Mental Health.

Many people find that helping others is also the best way to help themselves. Your understanding of how difficult the recovery process can be will help you to support others—both teens and adults—who are battling an addiction.

If you do have a relapse, recognizing the problem as soon as possible is critical. Get help right away so that you don't undo all the hard work you put into your initial recovery. And don't ever be afraid to ask for help.

♣ It's A Fact!!

The younger teens are when they begin to drink, the greater the risk for addiction.

People who begin drinking before the age of 15 are four times more likely to be dependent on alcohol as adults than those who wait until age 21. More than 40% of those who start drinking at age 14 or younger become dependent on alcohol as adults.

Source: Excerpted from "Teens and Alcohol," National Youth Violence Prevention Resource Center (www.safeyouth.org), 2002.

Drug Abuse And Mental Illness

What is the relationship between drug abuse and mental illness?

Many chronic drug abusers—the individuals we commonly regard as addicts—often simultaneously suffer from a serious mental disorder. Drug treatment and medical professionals call this condition a co-occurring disorder or a dual diagnosis.

What is chronic drug abuse?

Chronic drug abuse is the habitual abuse of licit or illicit drugs to the extent that the abuse substantially injures a person's health or substantially interferes with his or her social or economic functioning. Furthermore, any person who has lost the power of self-control over the use of drugs is considered a chronic drug abuser.

What are some serious mental disorders associated with chronic drug abuse?

Chronic drug abuse may occur in conjunction with any mental illness identified in the American Psychiatric Association (DSM-IV). Some common serious mental disorders associated with chronic drug abuse include schizophrenia, bipolar disorder, manic depression, attention deficit hyperactivity disorder (ADHD), generalized anxiety disorder, obsessive-compulsive disorder, post-traumatic stress disorder, panic disorder, and antisocial personality disorder. Some of these disorders carry with them an increased risk of drug abuse.

♣ **It's A Fact!!**

Teens Who Drink Are Also More Likely To Attempt Suicide

Alcohol use among teenagers has been associated with considering, planning, attempting, and completing suicide. In one study of teen suicide, drug and alcohol abuse was the most common characteristic of those who attempted suicide; 70 percent of these teenagers frequently used alcohol and/or other drugs. However, research has not proven that drinking actually causes suicidal behavior, only that the two behaviors are associated.

Source: Excerpted from "Teens and Alcohol," National Youth Violence Prevention Resource Center (www.safeyouth.org), 2002.

How prevalent are co-occurring disorders?

Co-occurring disorders are very common. In 2002 an estimated 4.0 million adults met the criteria for both serious mental illness and substance dependence or abuse in the past year.

Which occurs first—chronic drug abuse or serious mental illness?

It depends. In some cases, people suffering from serious mental disorders (often undiagnosed ones) take drugs to alleviate their symptoms—a practice known as self-medicating. According to the American Psychiatric Association, individuals with schizophrenia sometimes use substances such as marijuana to mitigate the disorder's negative symptoms (depression, apathy, and social withdrawal), to combat auditory hallucinations and paranoid delusions, or to lessen the adverse effects of their medication, which can include depression and restlessness.

♣ It's A Fact!!

Teens Often Underestimate The Risk That Drinking Can Pose

In a recent survey, only 56% of eighth graders and 43% of high-school seniors said that they thought drinking heavily once or twice a weekend was a great risk.

What are some of the real risks?

- Drinking alcohol increases the risk that a teen will commit or be a victim of a serious crime, such assault, rape, or murder.

- Drinking alcohol increases teens' risk of death from car crashes and drowning.

- Drinking alcohol increases the likelihood that a teen will engage in risky unprotected sex.

- Teens who drink are more likely than other teens to attempt suicide.

- If a teen drinks a large amount of alcohol in a short period of time, alcohol poisoning can occur, leading to coma or even death.

Source: Excerpted from "Teens and Alcohol," National Youth Violence Prevention Resource Center (www.safeyouth.org), 2002.

✤ It's A Fact!!
**Drinking Among Teenagers Is A
Serious Problem In The United States**

Alcohol is the most commonly used drug among teens.

One survey of students found the following:

- 52% of eighth graders (and 80% of high-school seniors) have used alcohol at some time

- 25% of eighth graders (and 62% of high-school seniors) have been drunk

Source: Excerpted from "Teens and Alcohol," National Youth Violence Prevention Resource Center (www.safeyouth.org), 2002.

In other cases mental disorders are caused by drug abuse. For example, MDMA (3,4-methylenedioxymethamphetamine, commonly known as ecstasy), produces long-term deficits in serotonin function in the brain, leading to mental disorders such as depression and anxiety. Chronic drug abuse by adolescents during formative years is a particular concern because it can interfere with normal socialization and cognitive development and thus frequently contributes to the development of mental disorders.

Finally, chronic substance abuse and serious mental disorders may exist completely independently of one another.

Can people with co-occurring disorders be treated effectively?

Yes, chronic drug abusers who also suffer from mental illness can be treated. Researchers currently are investigating the most effective way to treat drug abusers with mental illness, and especially whether or not treating both conditions simultaneously leads to better recovery. Currently, the two conditions often are treated separately or without regard to each other. As a result, many individuals with co-occurring disorders are sent back and forth between substance abuse and mental health treatment settings.

♣ It's A Fact!!
Teens Who Drink Are Much More Likely To Engage In Violence Against Others

Alcohol is involved in a high percentage of serious violent crimes committed by teenagers and adults.

Although estimates vary, studies have found that alcohol plays a key role in many violent crimes, including murder, assault, manslaughter, and rape.

The Link Between Alcohol And Increased Violence And Aggressiveness Is Not Entirely Clear, However

Not everyone who drinks or gets drunk becomes aggressive and violent. Alcohol appears to increase the risk of violent behavior only for certain individuals and only in some situations.

Source: Excerpted from "Teens and Alcohol," National Youth Violence Prevention Resource Center (www.safeyouth.org), 2002.

Chapter 46

Suicide

Teen suicide is becoming more common every year in the United States. In fact, only car accidents and homicides (murders) kill more people between the ages of 15 and 24, making suicide the third leading cause of death in teens and overall in youths ages 10 to 19 years old.

Read on to learn more about this serious issue—including what causes a person to consider taking their own life, what puts a teen at risk for suicide or self-harm, and warning signs that someone might be considering suicide and how they can get help to find other solutions.

Thinking About Suicide

It's common for teens to think about death to some degree. Teens' thinking capabilities have matured in a way that allows them to think more deeply—about their existence in the world, the meaning of life, and other profound questions and ideas. Unlike kids, teens realize that death is permanent. They may begin to consider spiritual or philosophical questions such as what happens after people die. To some, death, and even suicide, may seem poetic

About This Chapter: This information was provided by TeensHealth, one of the largest resources online for medically reviewed health information written for parents, kids, and teens. For more articles like this one, visit www.TeensHealth.org, or www.KidsHealth.org. © 2002 The Nemours Center for Children's Health Media, a division of The Nemours Foundation.

(consider Romeo and Juliet, for example). To others, death may seem frightening or be a source of worry. For many, death is mysterious and beyond our human experience and understanding.

Thinking about suicide goes beyond normal ideas teens may have about death and life. Wishing to be dead, thinking about suicide, or feeling helpless and hopeless about how to solve life's problems are signs that a teen may be at risk—and in need of help and support. Beyond thoughts of suicide, actually making a plan or carrying out a suicide attempt is even more serious.

What makes some teens begin to think about suicide—and even worse, to plan or do something with the intention of ending their own lives? One of the biggest factors is depression. Suicide attempts are usually made when a person is seriously depressed or upset. A teen who is feeling suicidal may see no other way out of problems, no other escape from emotional pain, or no other way to communicate their desperate unhappiness.

✔ Quick Tip
If You Are Thinking About Suicide

Talk with a trusted adult or call your local crisis intervention center immediately. You may be feeling tired, alone, depressed, scared, angry, hopeless, or unloved, and it may seem that things will never get better. However, no matter how overwhelming your problems seem, confidential help is available.

Trained, caring adults can help you to find alternatives you may not have considered and solutions to problems or situations that may seem hopeless. If you are depressed, effective treatments are available that will help to relieve your sadness, anger, and pain.

Numbers for suicide hotlines and crisis centers should be available in your local phone book or call 1-800-SUICIDE.

Source: Excerpted from "Teen Suicide," National Youth Violence Prevention Resource Center (www.safeyouth.org), 2002.

The Link Between Depression And Suicide

The majority of suicide attempts and suicide deaths happen among teens with depression. Consider these statistics about teen suicide and teen depression: about 1% of all teens attempts suicide and about 1% of those suicide attempts results in death (that means about 1 in 10,000 teens dies from suicide). But for adolescents who have depressive illnesses, the rates of suicidal thinking and behavior are much higher. Most teens who have depression think about suicide, and between 15% and 30% of teens with serious depression who think about suicide go on to make a suicide attempt.

Keep in mind that most of the time for most teens depression is a passing mood. The sadness, loneliness, grief, and disappointment we all feel at times are normal reactions to some of the struggles of life. With the right support, some resilience, an inner belief that there will be a brighter day, and decent coping skills, most teens can get through the depressed mood that happens occasionally when life throws them a curve ball.

But sometimes depression doesn't lift after a few hours or a few days. Instead it lasts, and it can seem too heavy to bear. When someone has a depressed or sad mood that is intense and lingers almost all day, almost every day for two weeks or more, it may be a sign that the person has developed major depression. Major depression, sometimes called clinical depression, is beyond a passing depressed mood—it is the term mental health professionals use for depression that has become an illness in need of treatment. Another form of serious depression is called bipolar disorder, which includes extreme low moods (major depression) as well as extreme high moods (these are called manic episodes).

Though children can experience depression, too, teens are much more vulnerable to major depression and bipolar illness. Hormones and sleep cycles, which both change dramatically during adolescence, have an effect on mood and may partly explain why teens (especially girls) are particularly prone to depression. Believe it or not, as many as 20% of all teens have had depression that's this severe at some point. The good news is that depression is treatable—most teens get better with the right help.

It's not hard to see why serious depression and suicide are connected. Serious depression (with both major depression and bipolar illness) involves a long-lasting sad mood that doesn't let up, and a loss of pleasure in things you once enjoyed. It also involves thoughts about death, negative thoughts about oneself, a sense of worthlessness, a sense of hopelessness that things could get better, low energy, and noticeable changes in appetite or sleep.

Depression also distorts a person's viewpoint, allowing them to focus only on their failures and disappointments and to exaggerate these negative things. Depressed thinking can convince someone there is nothing to live for. The loss of pleasure that is part of depression can seem like further evidence that there's nothing good about the present. The hopelessness can make it seem like there will be nothing good in the future; helplessness can make it seem like there's nothing you can do to change things for the better. And the low energy that is part of depression can make every problem (even small ones) seem like too much to handle.

When major depression lifts because a person gets the proper therapy or treatment, this distorted thinking is cleared and they can find pleasure, energy, and hope again. But while someone is seriously depressed, suicidal thinking is a real concern. When teens are depressed, they often don't realize that the hopelessness they feel can be relieved and that hurt and despair can be healed.

What Else Puts Teens At Risk For Suicide?

In addition to depression, there are other emotional conditions that can put teens at greater risk for suicide—for example, girls and guys with conduct disorder are at higher risk. This may be partly because teens with conduct disorder have problems with aggression and may be more likely than other teens to act in aggressive or impulsive ways to hurt themselves when they are depressed or under great stress. The fact that many teens with conduct disorder also have depression may partly explain this, too. Having both serious depression and conduct disorder increases a teen's risk for suicide.

Substance abuse problems also put teens at risk for suicidal thinking and behavior. Alcohol and some drugs have depressive effects on the brain. Misuse of these substances can bring on serious depression, especially in teens prone to depression because of their biology, family history, or other life stressors.

Besides depressive effects, alcohol and drugs alter a person's judgement. They interfere with the ability to assess risk, make good choices, and think of solutions to problems. Many suicide attempts occur when a teen is under the influence of alcohol or drugs. Teens with substance abuse problems often have serious depression or intense life stresses, too, further increasing their risk.

Life Stress And Suicidal Behavior

Let's face it—being a teen is not easy for anyone. There are many new social, academic, and personal pressures. And for teens who have additional problems to deal with, life can feel even more difficult. Some teens have been physically or sexually abused, have witnessed one parent abusing another at home, or live with lots of arguing and conflict at home. Others witness violence in their neighborhoods. Many teens have parents who divorce, and others may have a parent with a drug or alcohol addiction.

Some teens are struggling with concerns about sexuality and relationships, wondering if their feelings and attractions are normal, if they will be loved and accepted, or if their changing bodies are developing normally. Others struggle with body image and eating problems, finding it impossible to reach a perfect ideal, and therefore having trouble feeling good about themselves. Some teens have learning problems or attention problems that make it hard for them to succeed in school. They may feel disappointed in themselves or feel they are a disappointment to others.

All these things can affect mood and cause some people to feel depressed or to turn to alcohol or drugs for a false sense of soothing. Without the necessary coping skills or support, these social stresses can increase the risk of serious depression and, therefore, of suicidal ideas and behavior. Teens who have had a recent loss or crisis or who had a family member who committed suicide may be especially vulnerable to suicidal thinking and behavior themselves.

Guns And Suicide Risk

Finally, having access to guns is extremely risky for any teen who has any of the other risk factors. Depression, anger, impulsivity, life stress, substance abuse, feelings of alienation or loneliness—all these factors can place a teen at major risk for suicidal thoughts and behavior. Availability of guns along with one or more of these risk factors is a deadly equation. Many teen lives could be saved by making sure those who are at risk don't have access to guns.

Different Types Of Suicidal Behaviors

Teen girls attempt suicide far more often (about nine times more often) than teen guys, but guys are about four times more likely to succeed when they try to kill themselves. This is because teen guys tend to use more deadly methods, like guns or hanging. Girls who try to hurt or kill themselves tend to use overdoses of medications or cutting. More than 60% of teen suicide deaths happen with a gun. But suicide deaths can and do occur with pills and other harmful substances and methods.

Sometimes a depressed person plans a suicide in advance. Many times, though, suicide attempts are not planned in advance, but happen impulsively, in a moment of feeling desperately upset. Sometimes a situation like a breakup, a big fight with a parent, an unintended pregnancy, being harmed by abuse or rape, being outed by someone else, or being victimized in any way can cause a teen to feel desperately upset. In situations such as these, teens may fear humiliation, rejection, social isolation, or some terrible consequence they think they can't handle. If a terrible situation feels too overwhelming, a teen may feel that there is no way out of the bad feeling or the consequences of the situation. Suicide attempts can occur under conditions like this because, in desperation, some teens—at least for the moment—see no other way out and they impulsively act against themselves.

Sometimes teens who feel or act suicidal mean to die and sometimes they don't. Sometimes a suicide attempt is a way to express the deep emotional pain they're feeling in hopes that someone will get the message they are trying to communicate.

Even though a teen who makes a suicide attempt may not actually want or intend to die, it is impossible to know whether an overdose or other harmful action they may take will actually result in death or cause a serious and lasting illness that was never intended. Using a suicide attempt to get someone's attention or love or to punish someone for hurt they've caused is never a good idea. People usually don't really get the message, and it often backfires on the teen. It's better to learn other ways to get what you need and deserve from people. There are always people who will value, respect, and love you—sure, sometimes it takes time to find them—but it is important to value, respect, and love yourself, too.

♣ It's A Fact!!
What You Can Do If You Are Worried About A Friend

Ask directly if he or she is considering suicide. Ask whether he or she has made a specific plan and has done anything to carry it out. Listen openly to your friend, tell your friend that you care deeply, and that no matter how overwhelming his or her problems seem, help is available.

Then, help your friend to find someone trained to help, such as a doctor, community health center, counselor, psychologist, social worker, youth worker, or minister. Numbers for suicide hotlines and crisis centers should be available in your local phone book or call 1-800-SUICIDE.

If your friend has a detailed plan or appears acutely suicidal and will not talk, he or she could be in immediate danger and it is important to get help right away. Do not leave your friend alone, and seek help immediately, taking your friend to a hospital emergency room if necessary.

Even if it will anger your friend, talk with an adult you trust about your friend's situation so that you aren't carrying the burden by yourself. Do not try to "rescue" your friend or be a hero and try to handle the situation on your own. You can be the most help by referring your friend to someone with the professional skills to provide the help that he or she needs, while you continue to offer support.

Source: Excerpted from "Teen Suicide," National Youth Violence Prevention Resource Center (www.safeyouth.org), 2002.

Unfortunately, teens who attempt suicide as an answer to problems tend to try it more than once. Though some depressed teens may first attempt suicide around age 13 or 14, suicide attempts are highest during middle adolescence. Then by about age 17 or 18, the rate of teen suicide attempts lowers dramatically. This may be because with maturity, teens have learned to tolerate sad or upset moods, have learned how to get support they need and deserve, and have developed better coping skills to deal with disappointment or other difficulties.

Warning Signs—What To Look For

Many times, there are warning signs that someone is seriously depressed and may be thinking about or planning a suicide attempt. Here are some of them:

- pulling away from friends or family and losing desire to go out

- trouble concentrating or thinking clearly

- changes in eating or sleeping habits

- major changes in appearance (for example, if a normally neat person looks very sloppy—as if they're not taking the usual care of themselves)

- talk about feeling hopeless or feeling guilty

- talk about suicide

- talk about death

- talk about "going away"

- self-destructive behavior (drinking alcohol, taking drugs, or driving too fast, for example)

- no desire to take part in favorite things or activities

- the giving away of favorite possessions (like offering to give away a favorite piece of jewelry, for example)

- suddenly very happy and cheerful moods after being depressed or sad for a long time (this may mean that a person has decided to attempt suicide and feels relieved to have found a "solution")

Paying attention to and responding to these clues can sometimes save a life and prevent a tragedy. Most of the time, teens who are considering suicide are willing to discuss it if someone asks them out of concern and care. Some people (teens and adults) are reluctant to ask teens if they have been thinking about suicide or hurting themselves for fear that, by asking, they may plant the idea of suicide. This is a myth. It is always a good thing to ask and to initiate the conversation with someone you think may be considering suicide.

First, it allows you to get help for the person. Second, just talking about it may help the person to feel less alone, less isolated, more cared about and understood—the opposite of many feelings that may have led to suicidal thinking to begin with. Third, it may give the person an opportunity to consider that there may be another solution.

Sometimes, a specific event, stress, or crisis can trigger suicidal behavior in someone who's at risk. Common triggers are a parent's divorce, a breakup with a boyfriend or girlfriend, or the death of a friend or relative, for example. It's always good to ask a friend who's going through a crisis how they're doing, if they're getting any support, how they're coping, and if they need some more support. There are plenty of adults who can help you or a friend find the support you need. Everyone deserves that support.

Sometimes, teens who make a suicide attempt—or who die as a result of suicide—seem to give no clue beforehand. This can leave loved ones feeling not only grief stricken but guilty and wondering if they missed something. It is important for family members and friends of those who die by suicide to know that sometimes there is no warning and they should not blame themselves.

Getting Help

If you have been thinking about suicide, get help right away, rather than simply hoping your mood might improve. When a person has been feeling down for so long, it's hard for him to understand that suicide isn't the answer—it's a permanent solution to a temporary problem. Talk to anyone you know as soon as you can—a friend, a coach, a relative, a school counselor, a religious leader, a teacher, or any trusted adult. Call your local emergency number or check in the front pages of your phone book for the number of a local suicide crisis line. These toll-free lines are staffed 24 hours a day, 7 days a week by trained professionals who can help you without ever knowing your name or seeing your face. All calls are confidential—nothing is written down and no one you know will ever find out that you've called. There is also a National Suicide Helpline: 1-800-SUICIDE.

If you have a friend or classmate who you think is considering suicide, get help right away rather than waiting to see if he will feel better. Even if your friend or classmate swears you to secrecy, you must get help as soon as possible—your friend's life could depend on it. A person who is seriously thinking about suicide is depressed—and isn't able to see that suicide is never the answer to his problems.

Although it is never your job to single-handedly prevent your friend from attempting suicide, you can help by first reassuring your friend, then going to a trusted adult as soon as possible. If necessary, you can call your local emergency number or the toll-free number of the National Suicide Helpline: 1-800-SUICIDE. However you go about finding assistance for your friend, you must involve an adult—even if you think you can handle your friend on your own, this may not be the case.

After Suicide

Sometimes even if you get help and adults intervene, a friend or class-mate may attempt or commit suicide. When this happens, it's common to have many different emotions. Some teens say they feel guilty—especially if they felt they could have interpreted their friend's actions and words better. Others say they feel angry with the person who committed or attempted suicide for doing something so selfish. Still others say they feel nothing at all—they are too filled with grief. When someone attempts suicide, the people around him may feel afraid or uncomfortable about talking with him about it. Try to resist this urge; this is a time when a person absolutely needs to feel connected to others.

When someone commits suicide, the people around him may become very depressed and even think about suicide themselves. It's important to know that you should never blame yourself for someone's death—you could question yourself forever, which will only make you unhappy and won't bring your friend back. It's also good to know that any emotion you feel is appropriate; there is no right or wrong way to feel. Many schools will address the problem of a student's suicide head-on and call in special counselors to talk with students and help them deal with their feelings. If you are having difficulty dealing with a friend or classmate's suicide, it's best to make use of these resources or talk to an adult you trust. Feeling grief after a friend commits suicide is normal; it's when it begins to interfere with your everyday life that you may need to speak with someone about your feelings.

Part Six

If You Need More Information

Chapter 47

Helplines, Hotlines, And Internet Resources For Mental Health Concerns

Helplines And Hotlines

Alateen Hotline
800-344-2666
For relatives and friends of someone with a drinking problem

Alcohol and Drug Helpline
Toll-Free: 800-821-4357

ARK Crisis Line
800-873-TEEN (8336)
Emergency and crisis intervention center for youth and their families

Center for Substance Abuse Treatment
800-662-HELP (4357)
TDD: 800-487-4889
Spanish: 877-767-8432

The hotlines and helplines listed in this chapter were compiled from multiple sources deemed accurate. All phone numbers were verified in March 2006.

Covenant House Nine-Line
800-999-9999
A 24-hour crisis hotline

Eating Disorders Information and Referral Helpline
800-931-2237

Girls and Boys Town National Hotline
800-448-3000
A 24-hour crisis, resource, and referral line

NAMI (Nation's Voice on Mental Illness) Information Helpline
800-950-NAMI (6264)
Support, information, and referrals

National Center for Victims of Crime
800-FYI-CALL (800-394-2255)
Victim assistance and resources

National Child Abuse Hotline
Toll-Free: 800-4-A-CHILD (800-422-4453)
Childhelp USA; serves abused and neglected children

National Domestic Violence Hotline
800-799-SAFE (7233)
A 24-hour service providing crisis intervention, safety planning, information, and referrals

National Drug and Alcohol Treatment Hotline
800-662-HELP (4357)
Provides referrals

National Mental Health Association Resource Center
800-969-NMHA (6642)
Referrals for mental health services or support programs

National Organization for Victim Assistance

800-TRY-NOVA (800-879-6682)

Information and referrals for victims of crime and disaster

National Runaway Switchboard

800-621-4000

TDD: 800-621-0394

A confidential crisis intervention hotline for America's runaway and at-risk youth

National Sexual Assault Hotline

800-656-4673

National Suicide Prevention Hotline

800-SUICIDE (784-2433)

Panic Disorder Information Hotline

800-64-PANIC (800-64-72648)

Self-Abuse Information Line

800-DONT-CUT (800-366-8288)

Trevor Helpline

800-850-8078

A suicide prevention hotline for gay and questioning teens

Internet Resources

4 Girls Health

http://www.4girls.gov

Includes information about the mind, emotions, relationships, bullying, and more

APA Help Center

http://www.apahelpcenter.org

Online articles from the American Psychological Association

Break the Cycle
http://www.breakthecycle.org
Provides young people with information about domestic violence

Facts for Families
http://www.aacap.org/publications/factsfam
A series of fact sheets from the American Academy of Child and
Adolescent Psychiatry

Girl Power!
http://www.girlpower.gov
Click on "BodyWise" for information about self-esteem and eating
disorders

Helpguide
http://www.helpguide.org
Offers articles on a wide variety of mental health issues

If You Are Feeling Suicidal
www.tcrs211.org/suicide/suicidal.htm
A fact sheet provided by 2-1-1 Big Bend, Inc. in Florida.

LD OnLine
http://www.ldonline.org
For information about learning disabilities

Love Doesn't Have to Hurt
http://www.apa.org/pi/pii/teen
Information about teen dating violence from the American Psychological
Association

Love Is Not Abuse
http://www.loveisnotabuse.com
Facts about teens dating violence

Making Waves
www.mwaves.org
A Canadian resource for dating violence prevention

Mental Health and Behavior
http://familydoctor.org/x5411.xml
A series of fact sheets from the American Academy of Family Physicians

Mental Health and Growing Up
http://www.rcpsych.ac.uk/info/mhgu
A series of fact sheets by the Royal College of Psychiatrists (UK)

PMS and PMDD: Information For Teens
http://womensmentalhealth.org/topics/pms_teensite.html
Information about premenstrual syndrome and premenstrual dysphoric disorder from the Massachusetts General Hospital, Center for Women's Mental Health

Stop A Suicide, Today
www.StopaSuicide.org
Information for friends and family members of people who may be depressed or suicidal

Stop Bullying Now!
http://stopbullyingnow.hrsa.gov

Suicide Crisis Center
http://www.suicidecrisiscenter.com

TalkListen.org
http://www.talklisten.org
Information to support mental wellness, produced by the Boston Public Health Commission.

Teen Relationships Website
www.teenrelationships.org
Talks about healthy relationships and signs of abuse

Teen Victim Project
www.ncvc.org/tvp
A for teens dealing with dating violence, sexual assault, and stalking

TeensHealth.org

http://www.teenshealth.org
Click on "Your Mind" for information about mental health concerns

When Love Hurts

http://www.dvirc.org.au/whenlove/
An Australian resource for dating violence prevention

Young Men's Health Site

http://www.ohsu.edu/library/teenhealth/youngmen/mental.shtml
Links to mental health information for males, from Oregon Health and
Science University

Chapter 48

A Directory Of Mental Health Organizations

The resources in this chapter provide information about mental health and conditions than can impact mental health. To make information easier to access, organizations listed in this chapter are arranged in four categories:

- General Information, Counseling, And Support
- Mood Disorders And Information About Suicide
- Anxiety, Personality, Psychotic, And Behavioral Disorders
- Resources For Issues Related To Mental Health

When an organization's area of expertise is not discernible from its name, a clarifying notation has been added in parentheses.

General Information, Counseling, And Support

American Academy of Child and Adolescent Psychiatry

3615 Wisconsin Ave., NW
Washington, DC 20016-3007
Phone: 202-966-7300
Fax: 202-966-2891
Website: http://www.aacap.org

American Association for Marriage and Family Therapy

112 South Alfred Street
Alexandria, VA 22314-3061
Phone: 703-838-9808
Fax: 703-838-9805
Website: http://www.aamft.org

American Association of Pastoral Counselors

9504-A Lee Highway
Fairfax, VA 22031-2303
Phone: 703-385-6967
Fax: 703-352-7725
Website: http://www.aapc.org
E-mail: info@aapc.org

American Counseling Association

5999 Stevenson Ave.
Alexandria, VA 22304
Toll-Free: 800-347-6647
Fax: 800-473-2329
TDD: 703-823-6862
Website: http://www.counseling.org

American Group Psychotherapy Association

25 East 21st Street, Sixth Floor
New York, NY 10010
Toll-Free: 877-668-2472
Phone: 212-477-2677
Fax: 212-979-6627
Website: http://www.agpa.org
E-mail: info@agpa.org

American Mental Health Counselors Association

801 N. Fairfax Street, Suite 304
Alexandria, VA 22314
Toll-Free: 800-326-2642
Phone: 703-548-6002
Fax: 703-548-4775
Website: http://www.amhca.org

American Psychiatric Association

1000 Wilson Blvd., Suite 1825
Arlington, VA 22209-3901
Toll-Free: 888-357-7924
Phone: 703-907-7300
Fax: 703-907-1085
Website: http://www.psych.org
E-mail: apa@psych.org

American Psychological Association

750 First Street, NE
Washington, DC 20002-4242
Toll-Free: 800-374-2721
Phone: 202-336-5500
TDD/TTY: 202-336-6123
Website: http://www.apa.org

Association for Behavioral and Cognitive Therapies

(formerly known as Association for Advancement of Behavior Therapy)
305 7th Avenue, 16th Floor
New York, NY 10001-60008
Phone: 212-647-1890
Fax: 212-647-1865
Website: http://www.aabt.org

Bazelon (Judge David L.) Center for Mental Health Law

1101 15th Street, NW
Suite 1212
Washington, DC 20005-5002
Phone: 202-467-5730
Fax: 202-223-0409
Website: http://www.bazelon.org
E-mail: info@bazelon.org

Center for the Advancement of Children's Mental Health

Columbia University
Website: http://
www.kidsmentalhealth.org

Center for Women's Mental Health

Massachusetts General Hospital
185 Cambridge Street,
CPZN 2256
Boston, MA 02114
Website: http://
www.womensmentalhealth.org

Emotions Anonymous

P.O. Box 4245
St. Paul, MN 55104-0245
Phone: 651-647-9712
Fax: 651-647-1593
Website: http://
www.emotionsanonymous.org
E-mail:
info@emotionsanonymous.org

Families Anonymous

P.O. Box 3475
Culver City, CA 90231-3475
Toll-Free: 800-736-9805
Fax: 310-815-9682
Website: http://
www.FamiliesAnonymous.org
E-mail:
famanon@FamiliesAnonymous.org

Federation of Families for Children's Mental Health

9605 Medical Center Drive,
Suite 280
Rockville, MD 20850
Phone: 240-403-1901
Fax: 240-403-1909
Website: http://www.ffcmh.org
E-mail: ffcmh@ffcmh.org

Kids Help (Canadian Counseling and Referral Service)

439 University Avenue
Suite 300
Toronto, ON M5G 1Y8
Canada
Toll Free:
800-668-6868 (in Canada)
Phone: 416-586-5437
Fax: 416-586-0651
Website: http://
www.kidshelpphone.ca

NAMI: The Nation's Voice on Mental Illness

Colonial Place Three
2107 Wilson Blvd.
Suite 300
Arlington, VA 22201
Toll-Free: 800-950-6264
Phone: 703-524-7600
TDD: 703-516-7227
Fax: 703-524-9094
Website: http://www.nami.org

NARSAD Mental Health Research Association

60 Cutter Mill Road
Suite 404
Great Neck, NY 11021
Toll-Free: 800-829-8289
Phone: 516-829-0091
Fax: 516-487-6930
Website: http://www.narsad.org
E-mail: info@narsad.org

National Association for Rural Mental Health

300 33rd Ave. S.
Suite 101
Waite Park, MN 56387
Phone: 320-202-1820
Fax: 320-202-1833
Website: http://www.narmh.org
E-mail: narmh@facts.ksu.edu

National Association of Social Workers

750 1st Street NE, Suite 700
Washington, DC 20002-4241
Toll-Free: 800-742-4089
Phone: 202-408-8600
Fax: 202-336-8331
Website: http://www.socialworkers.org

National Empowerment Center (Recovery from Mental Illness)

599 Canal Street, 5th Floor East
Lawrence, MA 01840
Toll-Free: 800-POWER-2-U
(800-769-3728)
Phone: 978-685-1494
Fax: 978-681-6426
Website: http://www.power2u.org
E-mail: info4@power2u.org

National Institute of Mental Health

Public Information and
Communications Branch
6001 Executive Boulevard
Room 8184, MSC 9663
Bethesda, MD 20892-9663
Toll-Free: 866-615-6464
Phone: 301-443-4513
TTY: 866-415-8051
Fax: 301-443-4279
Website: http://www.nimh.nih.gov
E-mail: nimhinfo@nih.gov

National Mental Health Association

2001 N. Beauregard St., 12th Floor
Alexandria, VA 22311
Toll-Free: 800-969-NMHA (6642)
Phone: 703-684-7722
TTY: 800-433-5959
Fax: 703-684-5968
Website: http://www.nmha.org

National Mental Health Consumers' Self-Help Clearinghouse

1211 Chestnut Street, Suite 1207
Philadelphia, PA 19107
Toll-Free: 800-553-4539
Phone: 215-751-1810
Fax: 215-636-6312
Website: http://
www.mhselfhelp.org
E-mail: info@mhselfhelp.org

National Mental Health Information Center

Substance Abuse and Mental
Health Services Administration
P.O. Box 42557
Washington, DC 20015
Toll-Free: 800-789-2647
Phone: 240-747-5484
Fax: 240-747-5470
TDD: 866-889-2647
Website: http://
www.mentalhealth.org
E-mail: info@mentalhealth.org

NYU Child Study Center (Mental Health Research and Services)

New York University School of
Medicine
577 First Avenue
New York, NY 10016
Phone: 212-263-6622
Website: http://
www.aboutourkids.org

Psychology Today

115 E. 23rd St., 9th Floor
New York, NY 10010
Phone: 212-260-7210
Website: http://
www.psychologytoday.com

Recovery, Inc.

802 North Dearborn Street
Chicago, IL 60610
Phone: 312-337-5661
Fax: 312-337-5756
Website: http://
www.recovery-inc.com
E-mail: inquiries@recovery-inc.org

Royal College of Psychiatrists

17 Belgrave Square
London SW1X 8PG
England
Phone: 011 44 020-7235-2351
Fax: 011 44 020-7245-1231
Website: http://www.rcpsych.ac.uk
E-mail: rcpsych@rcpsych.ac.uk

Teen Health Centre (Emotional Health)
1585 Ouellette Avenue
Windsor, ON N8X 1K5
Canada
Phone: 519-253-8481
Website: http://
www.teenhealthcentre.com

Treatment Advocacy Center
3300 N. Fairfax Drive
Suite 220
Arlington, VA 22201
Phone: 703-294-6001
Fax: 703-294-6010
Website: http://www.psychlaws.org
E-mail: info@psychlaws.org

Mood Disorders And Information About Suicide

American Association of Suicidology
5221 Wisconsin Avenue, NW
Washington, DC 20015
Phone: 202-237-2280
Fax: 202-237-2282
Website: www.suicidology.org
E-mail: info@suicidology.org

Child and Adolescent Bipolar Foundation
1000 Skokie Blvd., Suite 425
Willmette, IL 60091
Phone: 847-256-8525
Fax: 847-920-9498
Website: http://www.bpkids.org
E-mail: cabf@bpkids.org

American Foundation for Suicide Prevention
120 Wall Street
22nd Floor
New York, NY 10005
Toll-Free: 888-333-AFSP
Phone: 212-363-3500
Fax: 212-363-6237
Website: http://www.afsp.org
E-mail: inquiry@afsp.org

CrisisLink
5275 Lee Hwy., Suite 301
Arlington, VA 22207
24-hour hot lines: 800-273-TALK
or 800-SUICIDE, or 703-527-4077
TTY: 703-752-5254
Phone: 703-527-6603 (business)
Fax: 703-516-6767
Website: http://www.crisislink.org
E-mail: development@crisislink.org

Depression Alliance

212 Spitfire Studios
63 – 71 Collier Street
London N1 9BE
England
Phone: 011 44 0845 123 23 20
Fax: 011 44 0207-633-0559
Website: http://
www.depressionalliance.org
E-mail:
feedback@depressionalliance.org

Depression and Bipolar Support Alliance

730 N. Franklin Street
Suite 501
Chicago, IL 60601-7224
Toll-Free: 800-826-3632
Phone: 312-642-0049
Fax: 312-642-7243
Website: http://
www.dbsalliance.org
E-mail: questions@dbsalliance.org

Depression and Related Affective Disorders Association

8201 Greensboro Drive
Suite 300
McLean, VA 22102
Toll Free: 888-288-1104
Phone: 703-610-9026
Website: http://www.drada.org
E-mail: Info@drada.org

Families for Depression Awareness

395 Totten Pond Road
Suite 404
Waltham, MA 02472-4808
Phone: 781-890-0220
Fax: 781-890-2411
Website: http://
www.familyaware.org
E-mail: info@familyaware.org

Feeling Blue Suicide Prevention Committee

P.O. Box 7193
St. Davids, PA 19087
Phone: 610-715-0076
Website: http://
www.feelingblue.org
E-mail: feelingbluespc@aol.com

Jason Foundation (Suicide Prevention)

181 East Main Street
Jefferson Bldg.
Suite 5
Henderson, TN 37075
Toll-Free: 888-881-2323
Phone: 615-264-2323
Fax: 615-264-0188
Website: http://
www.jasonfoundation.com
E-mail: info@
jasonfoundation.com

Jed Foundation (Suicide Prevention)

583 Broadway, Suite 8B
New York, NY 10012
Phone: 212-647-7544
Fax: 320-210-6089
Website: http://www.jedfoundation.org
E-mail: emailus@jedfoundation.org

Mood Disorders Society of Canada

3-304 Stone Road West, Suite 736
Guelph, ON N1G 4W4
Phone: 519-824-5565
Fax: 519-824-9569
Website: http://www.mooddisorderscanada.ca

Mood Disorders Support Group

P.O. Box 30377
New York, NY 10011
Phone: 212-533-6374
Fax: 212-675-0218
24 Hr Suicide Hotline: 212-673-3000
Website: http://www.mdsg.org
E-mail: info@mdsg.org

National Organization for People of Color Against Suicide

4715 Sargent Rd. N.E.
Washington, DC 20017
Toll-Free: 866-899-5317
Website: http://www.nopcas.com
E-mail: info@nopcas.org

National Organization for Seasonal Affective Disorders

Website: http://www.nosad.org

SAVE—Suicide Awareness Voices of Education

9001 E. Bloomington Fwy., Suite 150
Bloomington, MN 55420
Phone: 952-946-7998
Fax: 952-829-0841
Website: http://www.save.org
E-mail: save@save.org

Society for Light Treatment and Biological Rhythms

4648 Main Street
Chincoteague, VA 23336
Fax: 757-336-5777
Website: http://www.sltbr.org

Suicide Prevention Advocacy Network

1025 Vermont Ave., NW, Suite 1066
Washington, DC 20005
Phone: 202-449-3600
Fax: 202-449-3601
Website: http://www.spanusa.org
E-mail: info@spanusa.org

Suicide Prevention Resource Center

55 Chapel Street
Newton, MA 02458-1060
Toll-Free: 877-438-7772
TTY: 617-964-5448
Website: http://www.sprc.org
E-mail: info@sprc.org

**Yellow Ribbon Suicide
Prevention Program**
P.O. Box 644
Westminster, CO 80030-0644
Phone: 303-429-3530
Fax: 303-426-4496
Website: http://
www.yellowribbon.org
E-mail: ask4help@yellowribbon.org

Anxiety, Personality, Psychotic, And Behavioral Disorders

**Anxiety Disorders
Association of America**
8730 Georgia Ave., Suite 600
Silver Spring, MD 20910
Phone: 240-485-1001
Fax: 240-485-1035
Website: http://www.adaa.org
E-mail: anxdis@adaa.org

**Borderline Personality
Disorder Resource Center**
New York-Presbyterian Hospital-
Westchester Division
21 Bloomingdale Rd., Room 103
White Plains, NY 10605
Phone: 888-694-2273
Website: http://
www.bpdresourcecenter.org

Freedom from Fear
308 Seaview Ave.
Staten Island, NY 10305
Phone: 718-351-1717
Fax: 718-980-5022
Website: http://
www.freedomfromfear.org
E-mail: help@
freedomfromfear.org

**National Anxiety
Foundation**
3135 Custer Drive
Lexington, KY 40517
Website: http://
www.lexington-on-line.com/
naf.html

National Association of Anorexia Nervosa and Associated Disorders

P.O. Box 7
Highland Park, IL 60035
Phone: 847-831-3438
Fax: 847-433-4632
Website: http://www.anad.org

National Center for Post Traumatic Stress Disorder

VA Medical Center (116D)
215 N. Main Street
White River Junction, VT 05009
Phone: 802-296-6300
Phone: 802-296-5132
Fax: 802-296-5135
Website: http://www.ncptsd.org
E-mail: ncptsd@ncptsd.org

National Eating Disorders Association

603 Stewart St.
Suite 803
Seattle, WA 98101
Toll Free: 800-931-2237
Phone: 206-382-3587
Website: http://
www.nationaleatingdisorders.org
E-mail: info@NationalEating
Disorders.org

Obsessive Compulsive Foundation

676 State Street
New Haven, CT 06511
Phone: 203-401-2070
Fax: 203-401-2076
Website: http://
www.ocfoundation.org
E-mail: info@ocfoundation.org

SAFE (Self-Abuse Finally Ends) Alternatives

800-DONT-CUT (800-366-8288)
Website: http://www.selfinjury.com

Schizophrenia Home Page

Website: http://
www.schizophrenia.com

Sidran Institute (Dissociative Disorders)

200 E. Joppa Road, Suite 207
Towson, MD 21286
Phone: 410-825-8888
Fax: 410-337-0747
Website: http://www.sidran.org
E-mail: help@sidran.org

Social Phobia/Social Anxiety Association

Website: http://
www.socialphobia.org

Trichotillomania Learning Center

303 Potrero, Suite 51
Santa Cruz, CA 95060
Phone: 831-457-1004
Fax: 831-426-4383
Website: http://www.trich.org
E-mail: info@trich.org

World Fellowship for Schizophrenia and Allied Disorders

124 Merton Street, Suite 507
Toronto, Ontario, M4S 2Z2
Canada
Phone: 416-961-2855
Fax: 416-961-1948
Website: http://
www.world-schizophrenia.org
E-mail: info@
world-schizophrenia.org

Resources For Issues Related To Mental Health

American Institute of Stress

124 Park Avenue
Yonkers, New York 10703
Phone 914-963-1200
Fax 914-965-6267
Website: http://
www.stress.org

Centre for Addiction and Mental Health

33 Russell Street
Toronto, ON M5S 2S1
Canada
Toll Free: 800-463-6273
Phone: 416-535-8501
Website: http://
www.camh.net

Childhelp USA (Child Abuse)

15757 N. 78th Street, Suite B
Scottsdale, AZ 85260
Hotline: 800-4-A-CHILD
Phone: 480-922-8212
Fax: 480-922-7061
Website: http://
www.childhelpusa.org

Children and Adults with Attention-Deficit/ Hyperactivity Disorder

8181 Professional Place, Suite 150
Landover, MD 20785
Toll-Free: 800-233-4050
Phone: 301-306-7070
Fax: 301-306-7090
Website: http://www.chadd.org
Website: http://www.help4adhd.org

Children of Alcoholics Foundation
164 W. 74th Street
New York, NY 10023
Toll Free: 800-488-DRUG (3784)
Phone: 201-595-2553
Website: http://www.coaf.org
E-mail: coaf@phoenixhouse.org

Compassionate Friends (Grief Support)
P.O. Box 3696
Oak Brook, IL 60522-3696
Toll-Free 877-969-0010
Phone: 630-990-0010
Fax: 630-990-0246
Website: http://
compassionatefriends.org
E-mail: nationaloffice@
compassionatefriends.org

Covenant House New York (Crisis Support)
460 W. 41st Street
New York, NY 10036
Toll-Free Nineline:
800-999-9999
Phone: 212-613-0300
Fax: 212-629-3756
Website: http://
www.covenanthouseny.org
E-mail: chny@covenanthouse.org

Do It Now Foundation (Drug Information)
P.O. Box 27568
Tempe, AZ 85285-7568
Phone: 480-736-0599
Fax: 480-736-0771
Website: http://
www.doitnow.org
E-mail: email@doitnow.org

Dual Recovery Anonymous (Chemical Dependency)
P.O. Box 8107
Prairie Village, KS 66208
Toll-Free: 877-883-2332
Fax: 615-297-9346
Website: http://draonline.org
E-mail: draws@draonline.org

Girls and Boys Town USA (Crisis Information)
14100 Crawford St.
Boys Town, NE 68010
Toll Free Crisis Hotline:
800-448-3000
TTY: 800-448-1833
Phone: 402-498-1300
Fax: 402-498-1348
Website: http://
www.girlsandboystown.org
E-mail:
hotline@girlsandboystown.org

International Dyslexia Association

Chester Building
8600 La Salle Road
Suite 382
Baltimore, MD 21286
Toll Free: 800-ABC-D123
Phone: 410-296-0232
Fax: 410-321-5069
Website: http://
www.interdys.org

Learning Disabilities Association of America

4156 Library Road
Pittsburgh, PA 15234
Toll Free: 888-300-6710
Phone: 412-341-1515
Fax: 412-244-0224
Website: http://
www.ldaamerica.org

Learning Disabilities Association of Canada

250 City Centre Ave.
Suite 616
Ottawa, Ontario K1R 6K7
Canada
Phone: 613-238-5721
Fax: 613-235-5391
Website: http://www.ldac-taac.ca
E-mail: information@ldac-taac.ca

National Association for Children of Alcoholics

11426 Rockville Pike
Suite 301
Rockville, MD 20852
Toll-Free: 888-55-4COAS (2627)
Phone: 301-468-0985
Fax: 301-468-0987
Website: http://
www.childrenofalcoholics.org
E-mail: nacoa@nacoa.org

National Attention Deficit Disorder Association

P.O. Box 543
Pottstown, PA 19464
Phone: 484-945-2101
Fax: 610-970-7520
Website: http://www.add.org
E-mail: mail@add.org

National Center for Learning Disabilities

381 Park Avenue South
Suite 1401
New York, NY 10016
Toll Free: 888-575-7373
Phone: 212-545-7510
Fax: 212-545-9665
Website: http://www.ncld.org

National Center for Victims of Crime
2000 M Street NW
Suite 480
Washington DC 20036
Toll Free: 800-394-2255
Phone: 202-467-8700
Fax: 202-467-8701
Website: http://www.ncvc.org
E-mail: gethelp@ncvc.org

National Center on Addiction and Substance Abuse at Columbia University
633 Third Ave.
19th Floor
New York, NY 10017-6706
Phone: 212-841-5200
Website: http://www.casacolumbia.org

National Clearinghouse for Alcohol and Drug Information
P.O. Box 2345
Rockville, MD 20847-2345
Toll Free: 800-729-6686
Linea gratis en Español:
877-767-8432
Phone: 301-468-2600
TDD: 800-487-4889
Fax: 301-468-6433
Website: www.health.org
E-mail: info@health.org

National Clearinghouse on Child Abuse and Neglect Information
1250 Maryland Avenue, SW
8th Floor
Washington, DC 20024
Toll-Free: 800-394-3366
Phone: 703-385-7565
Fax: 703-385-3206
Website: http://nccanch.acf.hhs.gov
E-mail: nccanch@icfcaliber.com

National Coalition Against Domestic Violence
1120 Lincoln Street
Suite 1603
Denver, CO 80203
Phone: 303-839-1852
Fax: 303-831-9251
TTY: 303-839-1681
Website: http://www.ncadv.org

National Council on Alcoholism and Drug Dependence, Inc.
22 Cortlandt Street
Suite 801
New York, NY 10007-3128
Toll-Free: 800-622-2255 or
800-475-4673
Phone: 212-269-7797
Fax: 212-269-7510
Website: http://www.ncadd.org
E-mail: national@ncadd.org

National Institute on Alcohol Abuse and Alcoholism

5635 Fishers Lane, MSC 9304
Bethesda, MD 20892-9304
Website: http://www.niaaa.nih.gov
E-mail: niaaweb-r@exchange.nih.gov

National Institute on Drug Abuse

6001 Executive Boulevard
Room 5213
Bethesda, MD 20892-9561
Phone: 301-443-1124
Website: http://www.drugabuse.gov
Website: http://teens.drugabuse.gov

National Organization for Victim Assistance

510 King Street, Suite 424
Alexandria, VA 22314
Toll-Free: 800-879-6682
Phone: 703-535-6682
Fax: 703-535-5500
Website: http://www.try-nova.org
E-mail: nova@try-nova.org

National Youth Violence Prevention Resource Center

P.O. BOX 10809
Rockville, MD 20849-0809
Toll-Free: 1-866-723-3968
TTY: 888-503-3952
Website: http://www.safeyouth.org
E-mail: NYVPRC@safeyouth.org

Safe and Drug-Free Schools

400 Maryland Avenue, SW
Washington, DC 20202
Toll-Free: 800-872-5327
Phone: 202-260-3954
TTY: 800-437-0833
Fax: 202-401-0689
Website: http://www.ed.gov/offices/OESE/SDFS
E-mail: safeschl@ed.gov

Samaritans (Crisis Support)

The Upper Mill
Kingston Road
Ewell Surrey KT17 2AF
Phone: 011-44-020-8394-8300
Fax: 011-44-020-8394-8301
Website: http://www.Samaritans.org.uk
E-mail: admin@Samaritans.org

Substance Abuse and Mental Health Services Administration

1 Choke Cherry Road
Rockville, MD 20857
Phone: 240-276-2130
Website: http://www.samhsa.gov

Tourette Syndrome Association, Inc.

42-40 Bell Boulevard
Bayside, NY 11361-2820
Phone: 718-224-2999
Fax: 718-279-9596
Website: http://www.tsa-usa.org
E-mail: ts@tsa-usa.org

Chapter 49

Additional Reading About Mental Wellness And Mental Illness

Books listed in this chapter present information on many different aspects of mental illness, mental wellness, and issues related to mental wellness in teens. To make topics easier to identify, books are listed alphabetically by title. Book titles are followed by author (or editor) name, publisher, year of publication, and ISBN. Entries marked with an asterisk (*) indicate that the text was written especially for teens.

Alcohol 101: An Overview for Teens, by Margaret O. Hyde and John F. Setaro, Lerner Publishing, 1999; ISBN: 0761312749*

Antidepressants, by Judy Monroe, Enslow Publishers, 2001; ISBN: 0766019179*

Bipolar Child: The Definitive and Reassuring Guide to Childhood's Most Misunderstood Disorder, Revised Edition, by Demitri F. Papolos, M.D. and Janice Papolos, Broadway Books, 2002; ISBN: 0767912853

Bipolar Disorder: A Guide for Patients and Families, Second Edition by Francis Mondimore, M.D., Johns Hopkins University Press, 2006; ISBN: 0801883148

Bipolar Disorder, Depression, and Other Mood Disorders, by Helen A. Demetriades, Enslow Publishers, 2002; ISBN: 0766018989*

A Bird's-Eye View of Life with ADD and ADHD: Advice from Young Survivors, by Chris A. Zeigler Dendy and Alex Zeigler, Cherish the Children, 2003; ISBN: 0967991137

Body Blues: Weight and Depression, by Laura Weeldreyer, Rosen Publishing Group, 1998; ISBN: 082392761X*

The Boy Who Couldn't Stop Washing: The Experience and Treatment of Obsessive Compulsive Disorder, by Judith L. Rapoport, Signet Books, 1997; ISBN: 0451172027

Brave New Brain: Conquering Mental Illness in the Era of the Genome, by Nancy C. Andreasen, Oxford University Press, 2004; ISBN: 0195167287

Bullying: How to Deal with Taunting, Teasing, and Tormenting, by Kathleen Winkler, Enslow Publishers, 2005; ISBN: 0766023559*

Cliques, Phonies, and Other Baloney, by Trevor Romain, Free Spirit Publishing, 1998; ISBN: 1575420457*

Cool It! How Teenagers Can Keep Hot Tempers from Boiling Over, by Michael Hershorn, New Horizon Press, 2003; ISBN 0882822306*

Coping with Self-Mutilation: A Helping Book for Teens Who Hurt Themselves, by Alicia Clarke and Carolyn Simpson, Rosen Publishing Group, 1997; ISBN: 0823925595*

Delivered from Distraction: Getting the Most out of Life with Attention Deficit Disorder, by Edward M. Hallowell and John J. Ratey, Random House, 2005; ISBN: 034544230X

Depression Sourcebook: Basic Consumer Health Information about Unipolar Depression, Bipolar Disorder, Postpartum Depression, Seasonal Affective Disorder, and Other Types of Depression in Children, Adolescents, Women, Men, the Elderly, and Other Selected Populations; Along with Facts about Causes, Risk Factors, Diagnostic Criteria, Treatment Options, Coping Strategies, Suicide Prevention, a Glossary, and a Directory of Sources for Additional Help and Information, edited by Karen Bellenir, Omnigraphics, 2002; 0780806115

Depression: What It Is, How to Beat It, by Linda Wasmer Smith, Enslow Publishers, 2000. ISBN: 076601357X*

Depression: What You Need to Know, by Margaret O. Hyde and Elizabeth H. Forsyth, Scholastic Library, 2002; 0531118924*

Diagnosis: Schizophrenia: A Comprehensive Resource for Patients, Families, and Helping Professionals, by Rachel Miller and Susan E. Mason, Columbia University Press, 2002; ISBN: 0231126255

Diagonally Parked in a Parallel Universe: Working through Social Anxiety, by Signe A. Dayhoff, Effectiveness-Plus, 2000; ISBN: 0967126509

Drugs 101, by Margaret O. Hyde and John F. Setaro, Lerner Publishing, 2003; ISBN: 0761326081*

Eating Disorders Information For Teens: Health Tips about Anorexia, Bulimia, Binge Eating, and Other Eating Disorders, edited by Sandra Augustyn Lawton, Omnigraphics, 2005; ISBN: 0780807839*

Everything You Need to Know about Anxiety and Panic Attacks, by John Giacobello, Rosen Publishing, 2000; ISBN: 0823932192*

The Feelings Book: The Care and Keeping of Your Emotions, by Lynda Madison, Pleasant Company Publications, 2002; ISBN: 1584855282*

Get Me Out of Here: My Recovery from Borderline Personality Disorder, by Rachel Reiland, Hazelden, 2004; ISBN: 1592850995

Healing Your Grieving Heart for Teens: 100 Practical Ideas, by Alan D. Wolfelt, Companion Press, 2001; ISBN: 1879651238*

Help Me, I'm Sad: Recognizing, Treating and Preventing Childhood and Adolescent Depression, by David G. Fassler and Lynne S. Dumas, Penguin Books, 1998; ISBN: 0140267638

Learning Disabilities Information For Teens: Health Tips about Academic Skills Disorders and Other Disabilities That Affect Learning, edited by Sandra Augustyn Lawton, Omnigraphics, 2005; ISBN: 0780807960*

Learning Disabilities: The Ultimate Teen Guide, by Penny Hutchins Paquette, Rowman and Littlefield, 2006; ISBN: 0810856433*

Mental Health Disorders Sourcebook: Basic Consumer Health Information about Mental and Emotional Health and Mental Illness, Including Facts about Depression, Bipolar Disorder, and Other Mood Disorders, Phobias, Post-Traumatic Stress Disorder (PTSD), Obsessive-Compulsive Disorder, and Other Anxiety Disorders, Impulse Control Disorders, Eating Disorders, Personality Disorders, and Psychotic Disorders, Including Schizophrenia and Dissociative Disorders; Along with Statistical Information, a Special Section Concerning Mental Health Issues in Children and Adolescents, a Glossary, and Directories of Resources for Additional Help and Information, Third Edition, edited by Karen Bellenir, Omnigraphics, 2005; ISBN: 0-7808-0747-2

Mind, Stress, and Emotions: The New Science of Mood, by Gene Wallenstein, Ph.D., Commonwealth Press, 2002; ISBN: 0972060731

Misdiagnosis and Dual Diagnoses of Gifted Children and Adults: ADHD, Bipolar, OCD, Asperger's, Depression, and Other Disorders, by James T. Webb and others, Great Potential Press, 2005; ISBN: 0910707642

Mood Genes: Hunting for Origins of Mania and Depression, by Samuel W. Barondes, M.D., Oxford University Press, 1999, ISBN: 0195131061

Night Falls Fast: Understanding Suicide, by Kay Redfield Jamison, Vintage Books, 2000; ISBN: 0375701478

No Body's Perfect, by Kimberly Kirberger, Scholastic, Inc., 2003; ISBN: 0439426383*

Noonday Demon: An Atlas of Depression, by Andrew Solomon, Scribner, 2002; ISBN: 0684854678

Odd Girl Out: The Hidden Culture of Aggression in Girls, by Rachel Simmons, Harcourt, 2003; ISBN: 0156027348*

Overcoming Panic Disorder, by Lorna Weinstock and Eleanor Gilman, NTC Publishing Group, 1998; ISBN: 0809231026

Phobias, by Gail B. Stewart, Thomson Gale, 2000; ISBN: 1560067268*

Stepliving for Teens: Getting along with Stepparents and Siblings, by Joel D. Block and Susan S. Bartell, Penguin Young Readers, 2001; ISBN: 0843175680*

Stick up for Yourself! Every Kid's Guide to Personal Power and Positive Self-Esteem, Revised Edition, by Gershen Kaufman, Pamela Espeland, and Lev Raphael, Free Spirit Publishing, 1999; ISBN: 1575420686*

Suicide Information For Teens: Health Tips about Suicide Causes and Prevention, edited by Joyce Brennfleck Shannon, Omnigraphics, 2005; ISBN: 0780807375*

The Survival Guide for Kids with LD, by Gary L. Fisher, Rhoda Cummings, and Jackie Urbanovic, Free Spirit Publishing, 2002; 1575421194*

Surviving Manic Depression: A Manual on Bipolar Disorder for Patients, Families and Providers, by E. Fuller Torrey and Michael B. Knable, Basic Books, 2005; ISBN 0465086640

Surviving Schizophrenia: A Manual for Families, Consumers, and Providers, Fourth Edition, by E. Fuller Torrey, Perennial Currents, 2001; ISBN: 0060959193

Teens, Depression and the Blues, by Kathleen Winkler, Enslow Publishers, 2000; ISBN: 0766013693*

Too Old for This, Too Young for That! Your Survival Guide for the Middle-School Years, by Harriet S. Mosatche, Karen Unger, and Elizabeth Verdick, Free Spirit Publishing, 2000; ISBN: 1575420678*

Triumph Over Fear: A Book of Help and Hope for People with Anxiety, Panic Attacks, and Phobias, by Jerilyn Ross and Rosalynn Carter, Bantam Doubleday, 1995; ISBN: 0553374443

Unquiet Mind: A Memoir of Moods and Madness, by Kay Redfield Jamison, Random House, 1996; ISBN: 0679763309

What to Do When You're Scared and Worried: A Guide for Kids, by James J. Crist, Free Spirit Publishing, 2004; ISBN: 1575421534*

When Nothing Matters Anymore: A Survival Guide for Depressed Teens, by Bev Cobain, Free Spirit Publishing, 1998; ISBN: 1575420368*

When Your Parent Drinks Too Much: A Book for Teenagers, by Eric Ryerson, Facts on File, 1985; ISBN: 0816012598*

The Worried Child: Recognizing Anxiety in Children and Helping Them Heal, by Paul Foxman, Hunter House, 2004; ISBN: 0897934202

Index

Index

Page numbers that appear in *Italics* refer to illustrations. Page numbers that have a small 'n' after the page number refer to information shown as Notes at the beginning of each chapter. Page numbers that appear in **Bold** refer to information contained in boxes on that page (except Notes information at the beginning of each chapter).

Index